Seabrook and the
Nuclear Regulatory Commission

Seabrook and the Nuclear Regulatory Commission

The Licensing of a
Nuclear Power Plant

Donald W. Stever, Jr.

University Press of New England
Hanover, New Hampshire and London, England
1980

Copyright © 1980 by Trustees of Dartmouth College
Library of Congress Catalogue Card Number: 79-56160
International Standard Book Number: 0-87451-181-X
Printed in the United States of America

Library of Congress Cataloging in Publication Data

Stever, Donald W   1944-
    Seabrook and the Nuclear Regulatory Commission.

    Includes bibliographical references and index.
    1. Atomic power-plants—Licenses—United States.
2. United States. Nuclear Regulatory Commission.
3. Atomic power-plants—Location—Law and legislation—
United States. 4. Seabrook Nuclear Power Plant, N.H.
5. Atomic power-plants—New Hampshire. I. Title.
KF2138.S73   343.73'0925   79-56160
ISBN 0-87451-181-X

The University Press
of New England

Sponsoring Institutions
Brandeis University
Clark University
Dartmouth College
University of New Hampshire
University of Rhode Island
Tufts University
University of Vermont

For Margo and Heather

Contents

A Table of Organization of the NRC appears on page 6.

Preface

Except for updating prior to publication, this book was written between September 1977 and August 1978. Subsequent to that time and before printing, a significant event occurred that affects much of what is discussed in the text—on March 28, 1979, a nuclear power plant located near Middletown, Pennsylvania, called Three Mile Island, experienced a serious accident, one of greater magnitude than the NRC had previously stated was likely to occur. That accident, which involved serious core degradation and the release of large amounts of radiation, caught the NRC and the public unaware. It will, no doubt, have a profound effect on the future of nuclear power.

This book is not about Three Mile Island. It is about a nuclear power plant called Seabrook, which is now under construction in a town of the same name on the New Hampshire seacoast. There are differences between these two plants—Seabrook is a Westinghouse design reactor, TMI is a Babcock-Wilcox reactor. Seabrook is much larger. TMI was licensed and constructed with little opposition, but Seabrook made national headlines, both because there was a bitterly contested licensing battle before the NRC, and because at Seabrook occurred the largest site-specific, antinuclear, disobedience rally in the history of the United States. There is also an important similarity. Both plants were licensed by the Nuclear Regulatory Commission.

I chose to write about Seabrook in 1977 as a logical outgrowth of my involvement in the proceeding while an assistant attorney general in New Hampshire. I suspected that several of the issues surrounding Seabrook, never explained well to the public, were of critical importance to the future role of nuclear energy in our society, and were profoundly related to fundamental questions of public safety. The TMI accident dramatically confirmed my suspicions, and emphatically underscores much of what is said in this book.

The president of the United States commissioned a blue-ribbon panel to review the TMI accident. Several of the conclusions and recommendations of the President's Commision on the Accident at Three Mile Island corroborate suggestions made in this book. Although the Commission approached the subject from the perspective of the TMI accident, its focus, like the focus of this book, was on the NRC. The Commission, at page 51 of its Report, concludes: "We find that the NRC is so preoccupied with the licensing of plants that it has not given primary consideration to overall safety issues." Later, on the same page, it states: "The NRC commissioners have largely isolated themselves from the licensing process . . . they have also delegated most of their adjudicative duties to the Atomic Safety and Licensing Appeal Board . . ."

The Commission found "serious inadequacies" in the NRC licensing process (Report, page 52). Its examination of that process is, however, brief, and limited by constraints of its principal charge—to investigate the TMI accident. My primary purpose in this book is to examine the NRC's licensing process, to look at how the NRC, its Appeal Board, and its Licensing Board dispense regulatory judgments concerning a nuclear power plant. Although the President's Commission focused principally on the NRC's inattention to generic safety issues, several chapters of this book look closely at the day-to-day conducting of the business of licensing a nuclear plant. I hope that the reader will gain a sense of how and why, in the ordinary course of its daily business, the NRC could license a plant as potentially dangerous as TMI—or one resting on as thin a financial, safety, and environmental premise as Seabrook.

One of the strongest recommendations of the President's Commission involves a subject to which I devote considerable space—remote siting of nuclear plants. The Commission recommended:

> In order to provide an added contribution to safety, the NRC should be required to the maximum feasible extent to site new power plants in locations remote from concentrations of population. Siting determinations should be based on technical assessments of various classes of accidents which can take place, including those involving releases of low dosages of radiation. (*Supplemental Views By Members of the President's Commission on the Accident at Three Mile Island*, October 31, 1979, p. 1.)

What the Commission does not discuss is the fascinating history of the AEC/NRC's site-suitability criteria, which were designed initially to embody just such a concept. One chapter in this book traces that history, and the AEC/NRC's inexorable move away from remote siting. It also explains how the current regulations were used in the Seabrook case to legitimize a site that should have been avoided for safety reasons.

It is my hope that the following pages will contribute to an enhanced appreciation of the difficulty of the nuclear regulatory task, and to a fuller understanding of the structural mechanisms through which nuclear power has been regulated in the United States. It is not my intent so much to indict the NRC as to understand it.

I wish to thank the following people who contributed in one way or another to this project: Gordon J. MacDonald, who invited me to Dartmouth College and hence gave me time to write this book; the students of my course at Dartmouth who read and criticized parts of the manuscript; Anita Kirouac, Administrative Assistant to the Environmental Studies Program, who typed and organized the early versions of the book; Joe Lux, who did research; Ellen Weiss, who gave me feedback; the people at the University Press, who bore with me during revisions; and Margo Stever, without whom this book would never have been written.

D.W.S., Jr.

Washington, D.C.
November 1979

Glossary of Acronyms and Abbreviations

ACRS	Advisory Committee on Reactor Safeguards, a quasi-independent committee that advises the NRC on nuclear safety issues
AEC*	Atomic Energy Commission
AFDC	Allowance for Funds Used During Construction, an accounting device that permits certain industries to treat negative cash flows as income during capital-intensive construction projects
ALAB	Atomic Safety and Licensing Appeal Board
ALJ	Administrative Law Judge
APA	Administrative Procedures Act
ASLB	Atomic Safety and Licensing Board
BWR	Boiling Water Reactor
CFR	Code of Federal Regulations
CVPSC	Central Vermont Public Service Company
CWIP	Construction Work in Progress, a utility rate regulation concept that permits utilities to bill current rate-payers for the cost of constructing new facilities, which will also serve future rate-payers
DES	Draft Environmental Statement
DOE	Department of Energy
EIS	Environmental Impact Statement
EPA	Environmental Protection Agency
ER	Environmental Report, required to be produced by a license applicant; it forms the basis of the NRC's EIS
ERDA	Energy Research and Development Administration, a subdivision of the U.S. Department of Energy
FPC	Federal Power Commission, a federal agency now called the Federal Energy Regulatory Commission
FWPCA	Federal Water Pollution Control Act of 1972, sometimes called the Clean Water Act

GESMO	Generic Environmental Statement on Mixed Oxide Fuel
gpm	gallons per minute
JCEAC	Joint Committee on Atomic Energy, a committee of the Congress, which had jurisdiction over atomic energy matters until 1975
LMFBR	liquid metal fast breeder reactor
LPZ	Low Population Zone, a term used in 10 CFR Part 100
mw(e)	megawatts (electrical), a measure of electrical energy output
mw(th)	megawatts (thermal), a measure of total energy output
NECNP	New England Coalition on Nuclear Pollution
NEPA	National Environmental Policy Act of 1969
NEPCO	New England Power Company, a Massachusetts utility
N.H.R.S.A.	New Hampshire Revised Statutes Annotated
NPDES	National Pollutant Discharge Elimination System, a permit program under FWPCA
NRC*	Nuclear Regulatory Commission
NRDC	Natural Resources Defense Council
NU	Northeast Utilities Company
PCD	Population Center Distance (a term used in 10 CFR Part 100)
PSAR	Preliminary Safety Analysis Report, the basic documentation required by the NRC to support a construction license application
PSCO or *PSNH*	Public Service Company of New Hampshire
PUC	Public Utilities Commission, a state regulatory body with jurisdiction over utility services and rates
PWR	Pressurized Water Reactor
rem	roentgen equivalent man, a measure of human radiation exposure
RA	Regional Administrator of the U.S. Environmental Protection Agency
RSS	The NRC's 1975 Reactor Safety Study, also termed the Rasmussen Report
SAPL	Seacoast Anti-Pollution League

SER	Safety Evaluation Report, an NRC staff document evaluating a construction license application
SPNHF	Society for the Protection of New Hampshire Forests
TMI	Three Mile Island Nuclear Power Plant
UI	United Illuminating Company, a Connecticut utility

*The term NRC is used, unless otherwise noted, to refer to both the Atomic Energy Commission and the Nuclear Regulatory Commission.

Introduction

Site-related opposition to nuclear power plants is now a world-wide phenomenon.[1] This opposition falls into two general categories—that which is concerned with the environmental or economic, social, and land use impacts of a particular facility, and that which is related to safety, in the sense of concern over radiation generated as a consequence of the nuclear fuel cycle. Primarily because of the way in which United States nuclear licensing laws are constructed, organized legal opposition to nuclear power plants in this country (as opposed to such extralegal opposition as civil disobedience) developed around environmental rather than safety issues. Extralegal opposition, until recently more prevalent in Europe than here, has sometimes coalesced around environmental issues.[2] More often, though, public demonstrations in opposition to nuclear plants, and much of the antinuclear rhetoric, have as their premise safety, and the threat of long-term harm in one form or another from the radioactive by-products of nuclear power production.

Anti-nuclear demonstrations have involved[3] 30,000 demonstrators at Brokdorf (Germany, 1976), 20,000 at Itzehoe (Germany, 1976), 1,500 at Lirgen (Germany, 1976), up to 30,000 at Marckolsheim, Whyl, and Kaiseraugust (France, Germany, Switzerland, 1975),[4] 15,000 at Gorleben (Germany, 1976), 15,000 at Malville (France, 1976), 2,500 at Seabrook (New Hampshire, 1977), 50,000 at Malville (France, 1977), 10,000 at Seabrook (New Hampshire, 1978), and 60,000 to 100,000 at Washington, D.C. (May 6, 1979). In each case the primary issue was public safety, with many demonstrators apparently motivated by fear of nuclear technology. In 1976 a three-judge local court enjoined a construction permit at Freiburg, Germany, stating that the "unquantifiable risk [of public harm due to technical failures], no matter how small, is unjustified when the enormous consequences of the accident are considered."[5]

Other West German courts have made similar findings, premising

1

injunctions on the lack of a permanent solution of the problem of where to store radioactive waste, and on May 8, 1979, the German government, under immense public pressure, curtailed the reactor program. In the first week of November 1978, moreover, the Austrian voters in a close referendum, refused to allow an already constructed nuclear facility to operate, the issue being "potential dangers of nuclear power."[6]

Opponents to nuclear plants are people of "diverse interests and opinions."[7] They range from farmers fearful of the impact of the facility on their crops to social altruists to environmentalists, and their opposition stems both from mistrust of the technology to "mistrust of bureaucratic decision-making, especially where it takes place behind closed doors."[8] While the comparatively open regulatory process in the United States may account in part for the relatively minor amount of civil disobedience in this country in the past, there are signs that increasing numbers of people are abandoning the licensing arena for civil disobedience. It is not clear that the recent increase in civil disobedience in the United States is directly linked to distrust of the government's regulation of nuclear energy, but any dissatisfaction will increase if the processes by which critical decisions are made are shown to be less than fully competent, and if the level of risk to the public is perceived by it as too high.

Reactor-siting decisions in this country were, until the passage of the National Environmental Policy Act of 1969, technical exercises. The Atomic Energy Act limited the Atomic Energy Commission (AEC) to "public safety" concerns, and the AEC's method of implementation of the Act's mandate was to construct standards against which to measure plant design. Perhaps because the early licensed reactors were small, or because of a lack of sufficient knowledge with which to mount effective opposition, early attempts to block nuclear plants through intervention in the licensing process were few, and their level of sophistication and effectiveness was low.[9] In fact, the earliest interventions were not by antinuclear activists or environmentalists, but by labor unions and competitors of the license applicant.[10]

The enormous implications of reactor-siting decisions, though much debated in the atomic energy community of scientists and engineers, were not explored in early individual licensing cases. Indeed, a kind of complacency dominated the public positions taken by the nuclear regulators. Thus in a 1976 paper, L. Manning Muntzing, formerly director of regulation at the AEC, stated that "nuclear sites . . . should be (1) close to load centers for reasons of economy, (2) remote from high density populations for reasons of maximizing safety . . ."[11] The apparent inconsistency of these two criteria was typical of the AEC's rhetoric and did little to engender confidence in the government's regulatory policies once opposition to nuclear power grew so strong that it had to be reckoned with.

The National Environmental Policy Act of 1969 (NEPA) required the AEC to consider the environmental impacts associated with nuclear power generation. It coincided with the rapid rise in environmental activism in all types of government regulation of industrial activity. Environmental groups, which in the 1970's became willing to expend resources on lawyers and experts, spearheaded the movement toward full-scale, sophisticated intervention in AEC licensing proceedings. Their efforts at times were indistinguishable from the interests of the more fundamentally antinuclear segments of the society, though the goals and measures of each have not always been the same. As the Seabrook experience suggests, the divergence has at times become wide; they both perceive the nuclear industry and its government regulator as a common enemy, but their ideas about how to wage the war are very different.

Some environmental groups have, of course, been concerned with radiation hazards, particularly long-term hazards. However, their opposition to individual plants is often, as the Seabrook case illustrates, focused on particular environmental impacts not necessarily associated with a nuclear plant. Thermal pollution and impacts of transmission lines, for example, are issues that would also arise in relation to a fossil-fueled facility. The environmental groups have generally been less polarized in their opposition, and their concerns are more easily dealt with in the licensing process (at least as a theoretical matter), than are those groups whose position is simply that there should be no nuclear plants at all. This difference has produced confusion in the minds of not only the industry, but the press and public as well, further complicating the already murky nuclear power issue.

Most of the history of nuclear power involves the Atomic Energy Commission, which no longer exists.[12] Originally charged with regulating, promoting, and undertaking research on nuclear energy, the AEC was abolished by Congress in 1975. Its promotional and research roles have now been assumed by the Department of Energy, nuclear regulation being left to a reconstituted AEC now called the Nuclear Regulatory Commission. The NRC, though technically a new agency, inherited all of the regulations, policies, past decision-making history, and regulatory personnel of the AEC. Thus any examination of its current practice must begin with and take account of the prior practices of the AEC.

In this book, the NRC is examined in the context of its handling of a specific licensing case—involving the Seabrook Nuclear Power Station proposed for construction in coastal New Hampshire. The Seabrook project is appropriate to study because it has generated significant opposition, both from citizen groups participating in licensing proceedings before the NRC and from demonstrators who have attracted national attention by staging acts of civil disobedience at the plant site in 1977 and 1978. The Seabrook licensing dilemma stretched the NRC to or beyond its bureaucratic limits and exposed its processes and personnel to public scrutiny the likes of which it had never before experienced.

The Seabrook controversy may turn out to be a watershed. It could lead to a more responsible regulatory program. It could also mark the beginning of an era of antinuclear civil disobedience in the United States similar to Europe's experience over the last several years, sparked by a growing disenchantment with regulatory policies perceived to be unfair and biased on the side of the nuclear establishment. Which of these will occur cannot presently be predicted. The nuclear issue has become so large a social issue, however, that further analysis of the way the technology is regulated seems imperative.

This book focuses on the NRC as the primary agency charged with regulating nuclear technology and, incidentally, on the states and on the Environmental Protection Agency (EPA). The NRC is one of the most powerful regulatory agencies ever created by the Congress.[13] It has authority to control every aspect of the nuclear fuel cycle, from mining uranium to the ultimate storage of wastes produced by the power plants. It has plenary authority over power-plant design, construction, and operation and can shut down existing plants without seeking recourse to the courts. It decides where and how nuclear plants are constructed. How an agency with such power carries out its responsibility to the public is a matter that has received, unfortunately, little critical attention outside of the polarized polemics of the nuclear power debate.

The states, too, have a role in the nuclear power game, and that role is at present poorly defined and under congressional scrutiny. By and large, the states are seeking more control over nuclear site decisions. Hence, it becomes relevant to consider how well they have done in the past in exercising the authority they now have. Accordingly, a portion of the book is devoted to that issue, again using Seabrook as a case study. Political considerations, sometimes of importance in state decision-making, are given special treatment.

Finally, the Seabrook proceedings laid bare some glaring governmental inefficiencies in the interaction between two federal regulatory agencies. Far from unique, the problem of overlapping and confused jurisdiction is not uncommon in the federal government bureaucracy. One chapter of the book explores this problem.

NUCLEAR REGULATORY COMMISSION

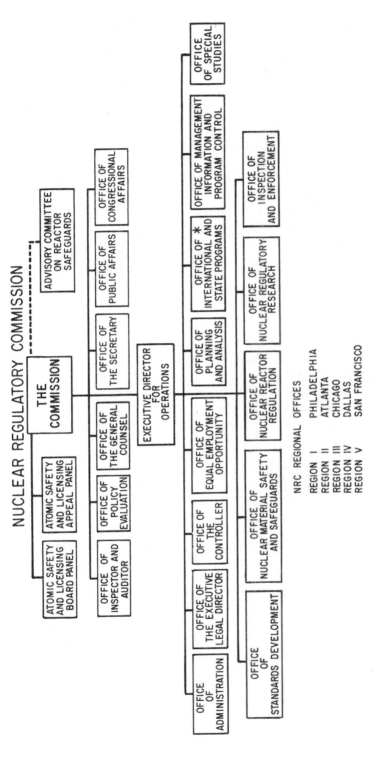

THE COMMISSION

ADVISORY COMMITTEE ON REACTOR SAFEGUARDS

ATOMIC SAFETY AND LICENSING BOARD PANEL

ATOMIC SAFETY AND LICENSING APPEAL PANEL

OFFICE OF INSPECTOR AND AUDITOR

OFFICE OF POLICY EVALUATION

OFFICE OF THE GENERAL COUNSEL

OFFICE OF THE SECRETARY

OFFICE OF PUBLIC AFFAIRS

OFFICE OF CONGRESSIONAL AFFAIRS

EXECUTIVE DIRECTOR FOR OPERATIONS

OFFICE OF THE EXECUTIVE LEGAL DIRECTOR

OFFICE OF THE CONTROLLER

OFFICE OF EQUAL EMPLOYMENT OPPORTUNITY

OFFICE OF PLANNING AND ANALYSIS

OFFICE OF INTERNATIONAL AND STATE PROGRAMS *

OFFICE OF MANAGEMENT INFORMATION AND PROGRAM CONTROL

OFFICE OF SPECIAL STUDIES

OFFICE OF STANDARDS DEVELOPMENT

OFFICE OF ADMINISTRATION

OFFICE OF NUCLEAR MATERIAL SAFETY AND SAFEGUARDS

OFFICE OF NUCLEAR REACTOR REGULATION

OFFICE OF NUCLEAR REGULATORY RESEARCH

OFFICE OF INSPECTION AND ENFORCEMENT

NRC REGIONAL OFFICES

REGION I	PHILADELPHIA
REGION II	ATLANTA
REGION III	CHICAGO
REGION IV	DALLAS
REGION V	SAN FRANCISCO

*At year end, NRC was in the process of establishing separate offices for International Programs and State Programs.

1

The Beginnings

On a summer day a few years ago, if you stood on the point of land at the end of Rocks Road in the Town of Seabrook, New Hampshire, you could hear only the sound of the wind rippling through the reedlike marsh grass to the east. Across the large salt marsh you would see the back end of a long barrier beach, and the houses clustered on it that form the community called Hampton Beach, and the bridge that carries Route 1-A over the Hampton Harbor inlet. The wide, flat salt marsh, though, would dominate the landscape. There are few hills, only a broad seacoast plain behind, reaching inland for miles. If it were a warm summer day, you would see, across the marsh, some of the tens of thousands of vacationers lying on Hampton Beach, temporary residents of one of New Hampshire's most successful state parks.

A hundred years ago this place had been a farm, perhaps the very point at which the farmer and his oxen, shod with wide boards, stepped down into the marshes to cut the grass, fed to upland cattle as salt hay. It takes a long time for wood to rot in the peat that lies under the marsh grass, and you can see the remnants of the wooden racks used by those farmers in their work.

A thousand years ago a village stood here. It housed native fishermen who came to the shore in the fall to catch their food for the long northern winter. And a few thousand years before them, there were others. It is now the site of the reactor and turbine buildings for Seabrook Station, Unit 1, part of the largest private industrial project ever undertaken in New England.

Seabrook Station was conceived in 1971 by several utility companies, the major partners being the Public Service Company of New Hampshire, owning 50 percent; the United Illuminating Company of New Haven, Connecticut, 20 percent; and the Northeast Utilities (a Connecticut-based utility holding company), 10 percent. As designed it would ultimately consist of two 1100 megawatt (a megawatt is a thousand kilowatts, and a kilowatt is a thousand watts) nuclear generating units of the pressurized water variety. In 1972 it was projected to cost about 900 million dollars.

Because of its size and the fact that its owners chose to design it for "once through" condenser cooling,[1] the Seabrook power plant will require a large amount of water—on the order of 800,000 gallons per minute—which will constantly flow through the plant's condensers and will be heated about 37 degrees above its ambient temperature. Since the chosen site is over a mile and a half from the ocean—the only feasible source of so much water— getting the ocean water to and from the plant became a difficult issue.

The original scheme of the Public Service Company of New Hampshire (PSCO) for getting water to the plant involved digging a large, deep ditch through the salt marsh and laying pipes in it. The scheme was abandoned before PSCO filed its application for a construction license with the AEC, when it became apparent that the state would not accept such an intrusion on the marsh, protected by law and the subject of a strong legislatively mandated policy of preservation. Instead, PSCO decided to drill tunnels in the bedrock to the sea—two of them, eighteen feet in diameter and nearly three miles long.

The two units of the plant were intended to come on line in 1979 and 1981 respectively, to satisfy part of New England's demand for electricity, which had been growing at a rate of about 11 percent each year. Half of the energy was destined for New Hampshire. PSCO, the "owner" of the equivalent of one unit (1100 mw), had, at the time the plant was conceived, a total generating capacity of about 600 mw and served around 80 percent of the total New Hampshire demand. It is, compared to other owners of nuclear units of equivalent size, a small company. It had no experience with nuclear technology.

As industrial facilities, the Seabrook units are of an awesome size. As designed, the twin reactor containments will be clearly visible from the seacoast recreation centers in the Hampton area. If, as a result of environmental restrictions,[2] it became necessary for cooling towers to be constructed, Seabrook Station would dominate the coastal landscape. Even without cooling towers, the plant would be the largest feature in the area.

Early History

PSCO first proposed a nuclear plant at the Seabrook site in the late sixties, but on a more modest scale. With its partner, United Illuminating (UI), the company began preliminary regulatory talks with the AEC for an 860 mw single-unit station. Those talks ended abruptly when UI withdrew from the project, and PSCO's management concluded that the company could not afford to finance the project on its own.

Rumors that the Seabrook project was being reactivated surfaced in the New Hampshire State House early in 1970, and a semi-official working group of state officials, environmental organizations, and power company representatives was formed to study and develop a state power plant siting law. Such a law was soon enacted, patterned after federal legislation which was then being promoted by the Council on Environmental Quality (and which was never adopted by the Congress). It established a "bulk power site evaluation committee," which was composed of the heads of various state agencies whose job it was to hold hearings and decide whether a proposed generating facility would have an "unreasonable" environmental impact and whether it would have an "undue" influence on local economic and growth patterns.[3] The law also required that the state Public Utilities Commission (PUC) determine the need for the facility and its reliability, and combined all other state regulatory permits under a single hearing umbrella and time frame. It was a "permit coordinating" type of law rather than a "one stop" law.[4]

The membership of the committee was established by compromise among the various interests involved in drafting the legislation. The utilities sought to retain site-permitting authority in the PUC, which, they argued, was already familiar with the issues. The environmentalists, fearful that the relationship between the PUC and the utilities was too close, and distrustful of the attitudes of PUC members and staff toward environmental issues, insisted that a totally new entity be the decision-maker. The compromise produced the above-described bifurcated decision-making process and a committee of uncommonly large size, which has as its members all three PUC commissioners as well as at least one representative (and in some instances two) from each state resource and environmental regulatory agency. The committee ended with fifteen members and no staff.

The bill that became the siting law slid through the state legislature essentially without opposition, and emerged scarcely amended. Its selling point was that if the state did not act, the federal government would soon be in the siting business.

The power plant siting law brought to New Hampshire a dimension of environmental decision-making heretofore unknown—the adjudicatory (formal trial-type) hearing. The state's bureaucracy had been structured, and accustomed, to make decisions either without any public involvement (environmental permits were often negotiated, without public hearings) or, at most, to hold only legislative hearings, in which the agency involved would sit back, listen to a series of speakers with entreaties and complaints about the matter at hand, and then go about its business in much the same manner that a legislative committee does. Lawyers, witnesses, evidence, cross-examination, and the like were unknown quantities to the state's environmental agencies.

The PUC had traditionally held adjudicatory hearings of a sort as a part of its rate-regulation proceedings. Consumer groups had, however, begun to raise public questions about the fairness of its procedures, which did not permit full cross-examination on all issues by every party.

By requiring adjudicatory hearings, the framers of the power plant siting law sought to assure that a broader public voice would be heard in the decision-making process. The law also required that a public lawyer ("counsel for the public")[5] be appointed to represent the environmental and consumer interests,[6] in order to assure at least institutional opposition.

Unfortunately, the law provided no staff for the new committee, which immediately found itself at sea trying to sort out its rule-making and adjudicatory roles.[7] Moreover, since the state at that time had no statute regulating adminsitrative procedure and no body of judge-made administrative law of sufficient depth to provide a functional replacement for such a law, the new committee had no guidance whatever in conducting its affairs. It was also without substantive expertise and had no funds with which to engage a consultant to help it develop rules setting out, for example, the kinds of minimum information required in an application for a siting permit.[8]

The Committee had conducted only one proceeding prior to Seabrook, involving a proposal by PSCO for a transmission line. Its hearing lasted one day, and there was no organized opposition to the proposal. PSCO filed its application for a permit for Seabrook Station, under the state siting law, in February 1971. The application contained a meager amount of information—little more than a physical description of the plant as proposed. Hearings were scheduled to begin in June of that year. Those hearings proved to be a baptism by fire into adjudicatory practice for the state and were the beginning of a bitter, often emotional, battle that divided the state and sapped PSCO's resources and its credibility, as well as the limited resources of the citizen groups and environmental organizations that opposed the project.

Participants

The actors in the Seabrook drama at the state level all remained in the case to the bitter end, when the forum moved to the AEC and later to the courts.

Public Service Company of New Hampshire, applicant. PSCO was represented by its long-time New Hampshire counsel which ordinarily appeared on behalf of the company before the state PUC in its rate cases.[9] There are indications in the record of the state proceedings that PSCO's lawyers anticipated a short hearing and little opposition. The company was clearly unprepared for what followed.

PSCO, by national standards a medium-sized electric utility, had less than 1000 megawatts of generating capacity at the time it filed its permit application for Seabrook. Its largest generating station was a recently constructed oil-fired unit of 476 megawatts. It had no nuclear experience. It was, nevertheless, New Hampshire's largest utility, having grown steadily, under various corporate cloaks, since the 1930's by absorbing small, local electric companies. By 1970 its licensed franchise territory included about 80 percent of the state.

PSCO was a familiar figure to the state's government agencies. Its coal and oil generating units were the subject of air and water pollution regulation, and the company was a substantial customer of the state's PUC. It was one of the few corporations in New Hampshire substantial enough to employ a full-time lobbyist. Although it would be an exaggeration to call PSCO a political force in New Hampshire in 1971, it was plainly not politically insignificant. The fact, for example, that the company had not actively opposed passage of the power-plant siting law was counted by some as an important reason for its easy trip through the legislature.

PSCO's share of the Seabrook units was 50 percent of the 2200 megawatt capacity. Its corporate position was that it would need the 1100 mw to meet its winter peak loads by 1981, and that nuclear power was the cheapest way to get the power. It is not clear that PSCO in 1971 was concerned about its oil or coal supply—its arguments were based on economics.

PSCO did not, finally, enjoy a close political alliance with the state's governor in 1971, Walter Peterson, whose position was one of neutrality with respect to the Seabrook proposal.

The Seacoast Anti-Pollution League (SAPL) was formed to oppose construction of the Seabrook plants. Made up primarily of seacoast area residents of New Hampshire and Northern Massachusetts, SAPL retained the Washington-based public interest law firm of Berlin, Roisman and Kessler to represent it.[10] Forever short of funds, SAPL nevertheless mounted a significant effort to stop the Seabrook project. It spent more than $20,000 in the state hearing alone, most of which was raised by means of small, individual donations from its members and supporters.

SAPL's personality seemed to vary over the course of the proceedings. It was never altogether clear whether its motivating force was antinuclear bias or environmental concern. Although individual members from time to time became involved in other coastal environmental issues, the group as a whole appeared to confine its energies to the Seabrook controversy. Nor was it without internal conflicts. By 1977 several previously active members abandoned the group to join the Clamshell Alliance, a new organization formed around the idea of nonviolent civil disobedience as a means of opposing nuclear power. The number of people who actually belonged to SAPL at any one time was not more than several hundred. Its core consisted of 15 to 20 active workers, with a nucleus of three or four. It had an ability, however, to draw financial support from a wider group of southern New Hampshire and northern Massachusetts coastal residents.

Portrayed as radical by the conservative *Manchester Union Leader*, SAPL in its early years hardly fit that label. Its active membership included retired teachers, local housewives, and professionals. A SAPL business meeting around 1971 resembled a church social more than a political activist gathering. In more recent times the guest list at a SAPL fund-raising event often reads like a Who's Who in local politics.

The New Hampshire Audubon Society, the local affiliate of the national organization, owned marshland near the power plant site. Its resources were very limited, yet it managed to share the cost of an attorney (Robert Backus,[11] of Manchester, New Hampshire) with another intervenor. Audubon's continuing presence in the Seabrook controversy was due in large measure to the efforts of one of its most influential members, Jane Grant. Widow of a prominent state court judge and for many years a mainstay of New Hampshire's environmental community, she was able to keep Audubon's normally low key and conservative board of trustees actively involved in the Seabrook litigation. She and her Dunbarton, New Hampshire, neighbor, J. Wilcox Brown, a trustee of the New England Coalition on Nuclear Pollution, were the most visible of the people behind the organization in the Seabrook conflict.

The Society for the Protection of New Hampshire Forests shared Backus' services with Audubon. A large, well financed conservation-oriented organization, SPNHF had been in existence since around 1900 and had been instrumental in the establishment of the White Mountain National Forest. It had a board of trustees composed of some of the most influential members of the state's professional and business establishment. Its decision to participate in the Seabrook proceedings was difficult; it caused substantial disagreement among members of its board. Its intervention, in fact, charted a new course in the Society's life, moving it from a cautious, conservative organization with a single purpose to a more aggressive defender of environmental values.

The Society played a much broader role in the state proceedings than it did in the later NRC hearings. Its public position on intervention before the state siting committee was that it wanted to make certain that the new law worked as it was intended to work, and on that premise the group later challenged the siting committee's decision by appealing to the state supreme court. It limited itself before the NRC to a single issue: the impact of the plant's transmission lines on a white cedar swamp it owned.

Of all the intervenors, the Society had the most to lose from a negative public reaction to its intervention. It was an old, established "conservation" organization, whose influence in state policies had been built up over the years by a delicate network of personal relationships between the organization and key members of the state's political and business establishment. It had become one of the state's largest landholders, amassing large amounts of ecologically valuable acreage by gift or purchase, and its credibility as a reasonable entity was undoubtedly important to it in order to maintain an active program of land acquisition. Finally, it maintained a large staff, and relied upon substantial public contributions to fund its operations.

Elizabeth ("Dolly") Weinhold, a Hampton, New Hampshire, housewife represented herself. Her sole interest was earthquakes; and though she had no technical or legal training, she doggedly pursued that issue to the point where it became one of the major issues in the case and subsequently sparked a revision in the NRC's seismic criteria.

New England Coalition on Nuclear Pollution (NECNP), a major intervenor in the Seabrook case before the NRC, was not involved in the state proceedings. NECNP was established in the mid-1960's by a group of Vermonters opposed to the Vermont Yankee facility, and has grown to be a New England-wide antinuclear organization with a board of trustees representative of every state in the region. Its membership is opposed to nuclear power plants per se, on public health and safety grounds, and it has been an intervenor in every New England nuclear licensing proceeding since *Vermont Yankee*, which received a construction permit in 1967. An indication of the group's tenacity is the fact that it was still involved in litigation over Vermont Yankee in 1978, seven years after the plant started operation.

NECNP, like the other Seabrook intervenors, financed its intervention largely from membership contributions and such local fundraising events as bake sales and car washes, though it was able to attract a modest foundation grant to support the later stages of its Seabrook intervention.

NECNP's philosophy rules out active participation in civil disobedience and other similar approaches to antinuclear protest, preferring to work within the system; it opposes individual nuclear license applications in New England and is a vocal critic of the NRC, disseminating literature promoting its point of view and supplying speakers who debate nuclear issues before civic clubs and at other gatherings of people around New England.

The Counsel for the Public, an intervenor created by the siting law, was a role filled by the author, then a state assistant attorney general.

The Hearings

Depending on one's point of view, the state siting hearings were either high political comedy or a regulatory disaster. They were held, ironically, in the same armory where, six years later, many hundreds of antinuclear demonstrators were incarcerated following the first act of civil disobedience in the history of this country's nuclear power program. The scene was almost surrealistic. In the front of the armory, lined up on an elevated platform beside a national guard troop carrier, sat the fifteen members of the siting committee. Below them were the counsel tables and then the public. During the early sessions the hall was packed with spectators—but by the end there were more empty chairs than people. The members of the committee, not happy to be away from their daily bureaucratic duties, started the hearings with restlessness or boredom and ended them with hostility or slumber. The committee chairman, an engineer totally unfamiliar with the legal process, ruled on motions and challenges to evidence or questions with agonizing ineptitude, almost always in favor of PSCO.

PSCO had the burden of proof under the state siting law, and its case consisted of a series of general and conclusory opinions by its employees. It retained consultants about various environmental impacts expected to result from the construction and operation of the power plant. The factual and analytical content of the state hearing record was surprisingly thin, in light of the thousands of pages of transcript produced. Indeed, PSCO had few facts in its possession. It had barely retained its biological consultant before the hearings began and had set for itself a data-gathering timetable geared to its construction license application to the AEC some two and a half years later. It had not gone beyond the barest of conceptual designs, and accordingly it was impossible to pin down any facts on which to predicate assumptions about environmental impacts. It was, in the words of one intervenor lawyer, "like shooting at a moving target."

Nevertheless, several important issues arose. The three that received greatest attention were (1) the need for the 1100 mw share PSCO claimed, (2) the environmental impact of the proposed ditches on the salt marsh, and (3) the impact of the withdrawal and discharge of the facility's cooling water.[12]

The need for power issue was not well tried. None of the intervenors' lawyers was well enough grounded in economics to cross-examine PSCO's self-serving predictions very effectively. The issue became bogged in a dispute between PSCO and three intervenor witnesses (well known economist Charles Chicetti; his associate, William Gillen; and University of New Hampshire Professor Richard Mills) over whether the demand for electricity was sensitive to changes in price (whether it was "price elastic" or "price inelastic"). PSCO said it was not sensitive. The intervenors said it was. The siting committee, apparently oblivious to the significance of the issue, ignored it. Ironically, two years later during the energy crisis, PSCO's demand fell drastically as the price it charged for electricity skyrocketed.

The salt marsh ditching dispute consumed much of the hearing time, and, looking back on it, several of the intervenors felt that it might have been a red herring. It became very clear that PSCO could not defend the ditching scheme and probably would be denied a permit under the state's wetlands law; yet PSCO persisted in an attempt to pursuade the siting committee that it could restore the ditched salt marsh (though no one had ever succeeded in doing so north of the Chesapeake Bay, where tides are much lower).

Two days before the mandatory closing of the hearing record, PSCO boldly announced that for "environmental reasons" it had decided to abandon the ditching idea and would, instead, drill bedrock tunnels to the ocean—which, it claimed, it would do despite high cost.[13] PSCO's timing and motivation for this switch are not clear. In one of his rare appearances at the state hearings, the lawyer retained by PSCO for its federal licensing battle, Thomas Dignan of Ropes and Gray, approached several of the intervenors privately and suggested that since the "principal environmental problem" had been "solved," there might be a basis to "settle the case." Clearly, after twelve months of bitter hearings, PSCO had little interest in a repetition before the AEC. Dignan's response from intervenor SAPL was a motion to reopen the record to permit it to explore the impacts of the tunnel construction and an appeal to the State Supreme Court of the siting committee's denial of that motion.

The state committee's handling of the ocean impacts issue is difficult to defend. PSCO did not make much of a case, relying essentially on the opinion of one witness who concluded, without any supporting data, that since the intake and discharge of cooling water was from the Gulf of Maine, a part of the Atlantic Ocean, it was impossible for them to do any significant harm, those bodies being so large.[14] SAPL, on the other hand, produced fishery expert John Clark who testified, on the basis of PSCO's own, limited hydrographic data, that the area off Hampton Beach was actually a nearly closed ecosystem, under the influence of the important salt marsh-estuarine complex, and that by withdrawing large amounts of water, the Seabrook plant would destroy a disproportionate number of organisms, doing potentially severe damage to some of the life systems within the estuary.[15] PSCO itself later abandoned its position, admitting before the U.S. Environmental Protection Agency the presence of a critical, biological area just off the coast, interference with which ought to be avoided. It did not, of course, adopt Clark's extreme position, which rested on no firmer factual basis than PSCO's initial claim.

The data base was paltry. PSCO hired a fledgling biological consulting firm, Normandeau Associates, Inc. (NAI), to study the offshore areas. By the end of the state hearings, NAI had produced only preliminary reports. Before the end of federal hearings in 1977, it would produce more than 45 separate reports, with some scientists contending that they contained insufficient data on which to predict the impact of the cooling water system. The siting committee never dealt with the conflict that arose between Clark and PSCO. When it came to the water quality issue in its decision, it simply deferred to the State Water Supply and Pollution Control Commission, making no independent evaluation of the record.[16]

Finally, PSCO admitted during the state hearings that a consultant's report to it in 1967 had ranked the Seabrook site low among a list of potential power plant sites studied, purely on economic grounds. PSCO's biological consultant also testified that the Seabrook site would not, on environmental grounds, be his first choice. Yet no meaningful exploration of alternatives was required by the state siting committee. By the time the state hearings had ended, PSCO was ready to file its license application with the AEC.

Politics, Fish, and Power

The governorship of New Hampshire changed in the midst of the State's Seabrook hearings. Walter Peterson, who was the incumbent at the time the siting law was enacted and during the early sessions of the hearings, took a laissez-faire attitude toward the state's regulators. He publicly stated that he would neither support nor oppose the project but would leave the task of determining its acceptability to the state's regulatory agencies. Peterson was defeated in the state Republican primary in 1972 by Meldrim Thomson, who became governor on a "no new taxes" platform after defeating a weak Democratic opponent in the general election. Thomson, an ultraconservative, was strongly supported by the like-minded William Loeb, whose *Manchester Union Leader* vociferously stood behind the Seabrook project. So, of course, did Thomson.

Thomson, whose dislike for environmentalists rivaled his avowed disdain for the state's bureaucracy, immediately set out to replace any state officials having "environmental leanings" with persons sharing his philosophy of economic development. The Manchester newspaper began editorializing against environmental opposition to the Seabrook project shortly after the state hearings began, and repeatedly alleged that the Seabrook intervenors were either socialists or communists, whose ultimate aim was to stop progress and, indeed, overthrow the capitalist system.[17] The new governor's rhetoric had a similar ring.

Two of Thomson's initial targets were Mary Louise Hancock, director of the Office of State Planning, and Bernard "Buck" Corson, director of the state Fish and Game Department, both then members of the state siting committee. Thomson had the power to remove Hancock, an outspoken environmentalist, since her position was part of the governor's staff. His attempt to remove Hancock prior to the end of the state hearings was thwarted, however, by lawyers in the state attorney general's office, who pursuaded Thomson's legal counsel that by refusing to allow Hancock to sit on the Seabrook case, Thomson might open the way for a due process challenge by one or more of the parties to the case. (Thomson later did remove Hancock, who subsequently was elected to the state senate. She remained a political thorn in the governor's side, ultimately helping to engineer his defeat in 1978.)

Both Hancock and Corson dissented to the committee's decision on the Seabrook matter. Corson relied greatly on a dedicated staff of biologists in the fisheries division of the Fish and Game Department, who were convinced that the "once through" cooling system would decimate the already stressed clam population in the Hampton-Seabrook estuary.

Since the state siting committee had essentially abandoned its responsibility to decide on water-quality impacts, the focus after the siting decision shifted to the State's Water Supply and Pollution Control Commission, charged under state law with the responsibility of issuing water-pollution discharge permits. Since the new Federal Water Pollution Control Act Amendments had barely become law,[18] the state WSPCC was still functioning primarily under the state water pollution statute, and the state law contained a provision that allowed the Fish and Game Department to establish thermal discharge standards. That placed Fish and Game Director Corson in a difficult position politically. N.H.R.S.A. Section 149:5(a) provided essentially that the Fish and Game Department, rather than the state water pollution agency, had the authority to establish standards for the discharge of heat into the state's waters. Thus, although the water pollution agency was responsible for issuing a permit to PSCO, what that permit contained was to be determined largely by Corson.

There were at that time four experienced fisheries biologists in the employ of the Fish and Game Department. Richard Seamans, head of the fisheries division and a seasoned veteran of past disputes with the state's water pollution engineers over the implementation of the water pollution program, relied for advice primarily on Arthur Newell, supervisor of fisheries research and somewhat of an expert on fish behavior and power plant intakes in river systems. Newell, in turn, consulted with Edward Spurr and Burdett "Bud" Barrett, both marine biologists, in formulating conclusions about the probable impacts of the Seabrook plants. All four were convinced that the Seabrook cooling water system would further stress the clam population and kill a large number of fish. Corson therefore wrote a letter to William Healy, director of the water pollution agency, stating that the appropriate thermal standard for the Seabrook plant was either that there be no discharge of heat except residual heat from cooling towers, or that the intake and discharge pipes be extended far out to sea, into biologically unproductive water.

The Department's conclusion does not appear to have been based on any sort of cost-benefit calculation, or even on hard data demonstrating convincingly how many organisms were likely to be killed. There simply were no such data at that time. The biologists took a cautious position. They reasoned that since there was evidence that the cooling water system would kill large numbers of organisms by entrainment and entrapment, even though the data were inadequate to determine the ecological significance of that mortality, the wise course was to prohibit the discharge, in view of the fact that alternative means of disposing of the heat were available, which had no environmental risk at all.

Corson's letter unleashed a storm of political fury from Governor Thomson, who by this time was having regular meetings with PSCO's management and public relations personnel and who rarely if ever solicited information from within the state government. Thomson had the authority to appoint new Fish and Game commissioners, as the terms of present members expired and the Fish and Game Commission controlled the Department's budget. He vowed to appoint a majority of the Commission from his supporters and to get rid of Corson. Since the Commission exerted some control over Corson and, Thomson thought, had the power to remove him from office, he embarked on a course deliberately intended to cripple the Department's inland and marine fisheries programs.[19]

The water permit dispute was resolved when Attorney General Warren Rudman personally intervened and convinced Corson that a less drastic position was necessary if all-out war between state agencies was to be averted. A revised water pollution permit was drafted in the attorney general's office in a series of closed negotiations between Rudman's staff and lawyers representing PSCO. The new permit contained language inserted to mollify Corson's biologists, requiring PSCO to undertake significantly more pre-operational biological baseline study than the Water Pollution agency had imposed on it, and that the company shut down and retrofit the Seabrook plant with a closed cooling system in the event that post-operational monitoring revealed significant environmental impacts. Rudman thereafter met in private with Corson and the Water Pollution agency in an effort to sell his permit. He succeeded.[20]

The Seabrook plant that received its major state permits was a plant without cooling towers. PSCO never attempted to convince the state siting committee that Seabrook *with* cooling towers was acceptable as well, and thus PSCO's future options, as it entered the then-unanticipated federal regulatory snarl, were limited.

The state proceedings ended with little fanfare. Though PSCO still needed a large number of lesser state regulatory permits (such as a "fill and dredge" permit to destroy nearly an acre of salt marsh in order to build a road to the plant site), they were provided without resistance. Word had spread among the agencies that the Governor was strongly in favor of the Seabrook plant—and issuance of the permits was made a matter of priority.

Thomson's campaign against the Fish and Game Department did not stop, however. Subsequent to the state proceedings, Fish and Game biologists continued to press for more stringent controls on the cooling system, but as consultants to the state attorney general, who had intervened in and become a party to permit proceedings being conducted by the Nuclear Regulatory Commission (NRC) and the U.S. Environmental Protection Agency (EPA). Thomson, in turn, continuously attacked the Department with whatever political weapon he could muster. By January 31, 1978, of the five key biologists involved in the Seabrook dispute on behalf of the Fish and Game Department, only one remained. Bernard Corson, after a bitter legal struggle, won the right to run his Department, but quietly retired early in 1978. Richard Seamans left the Department in 1977, accepting a position with the U.S. Fish and Wildlife Service. Arthur Newell, in failing health and the subject of merciless personal attacks by Thomson (who at one time actually issued an executive order aimed at preventing Newell from testifying in a Seabrook-related hearing), retired prematurely from the Department for which he had worked more than thirty years. Barrett had left the Department several years earlier to work for the New England Division office of the Army Corps of Engineers. The entire senior staff of the fisheries division had gone, and along with them many of the younger biologists fed up with budget cuts, eliminated programs, and harassment from Thomson and his commission members.

Conclusions

Though PSCO received a full license from the State of New Hampshire to build the Seabrook plants, it was not an honest license. The state siting committee, after eighteen months of hearings, issued a one-page, conclusory decision approving the project. That decision was later reversed by the state Supreme Court, which found it to be so devoid of findings and reasoning that it denied fundamental due process of law to the intervenors seeking to challenge it.[21] The Court remanded the matter to the Committee with instructions to write a decision that comported with due process requirements. The Committee, which had been authorized by then to retain its own counsel, hired an attorney to help it rewrite its decision. The reissued decision was little better than its predecessor, but it was not challenged by any of the intervenors, who by late 1975 had committed all of their meager resources to the NRC licensing hearings and had inadequate funds to mount another expensive appeal in the state courts.

The state proceedings also totally ignored public safety issues. The federal courts had held that regulation of nuclear power plants was preempted by the Atomic Energy Act and was reserved to the federal government. Moreover, even if it had felt that it had the authority to deal with public safety issues, the state agency simply did not possess the technical expertise to deal with them effectively. As a result, consideration of the acceptability of the Seabrook site from the standpoint of public safety was left to the NRC. The state did not even make an attempt in that direction.

Limited by a paucity of data and inadequate standards, the state site evaluation procedures in New Hampshire did little to narrow the issues or resolve public policy disputes in the Seabrook case. To those limitations were overlaid an unwilling decision-maker and a superficial, too lengthy string of hearing sessions that did little more than entrench the various actors in their rapidly polarizing positions. The state site evaluation committee refused to become involved in safety issues, even though the state law permitted such inquiry, and of the three issues that received a great deal of attention at the hearings, two were delegated to other agencies with more limited regulatory authority (the need and cost of the facility to the PUC and aquatic impact to the water pollution board), and one was made moot by PSCO at the last minute (wetlands ditching), for reasons that may have had nothing to do with the environmental issues raised before the siting committee. It never issued a reasoned opinion in support of its decision to license the facility.

The New Hampshire experience raises serious questions about the ability of small states to cope effectively with nuclear siting issues. Whether a state like New Hampshire can ever effectively adjudicate such cases is a question that requires serious consideration before additional responsibilities are imposed on it by Congress as part of a nuclear licensing reform package.

2
Regulatory Issues

The selection of a site for a nuclear power plant involves consideration of both the corporate and the public interest. The primary reason for the enactment of power plant siting laws in a number of states has been to create a legal framework within which various interests can be factored into the site selection and at an early time.[1] Ordinarily the selection process will evolve in three stages: (a) initial screening and selection by the utility, (b) review and certification under the state's power plant siting law, and (c) review by the Nuclear Regulatory Commission under the National Environmental Policy Act (NEPA) and the Atomic Energy Act. For reasons that will be set forth in some detail, it is suggested here that neither state nor NEPA review, as they are currently being carried out, has a significant impact on the choice of a nuclear power plant site or on the range of alternatives included in the candidate pool.

From the utility's standpoint, the important siting parameters are availability of the site for purchase, accessibility of adequate water for cooling the condenser, nearness to the load center, good transportation access for construction, and compliance with the NRC's suitability criteria.[2] The public's interest involves considerations that are more difficult to assess and includes the environmental impact of a power plant located on the site.* It also involves the impact that placement of a plant will have on the local economy, the local tax

*The use of the term "public interest" is not meant to carry any implication that the public at large has an interest that is necessarily different from or at odds with that of the utility promoting a particular project. There are, of course, many publics and many public interests, some of which will be in conflict with others. I use the term as a way to express concerns that are different from those which normally motivate the corporate management of a utility in making site or other decisions in a strictly business sense.

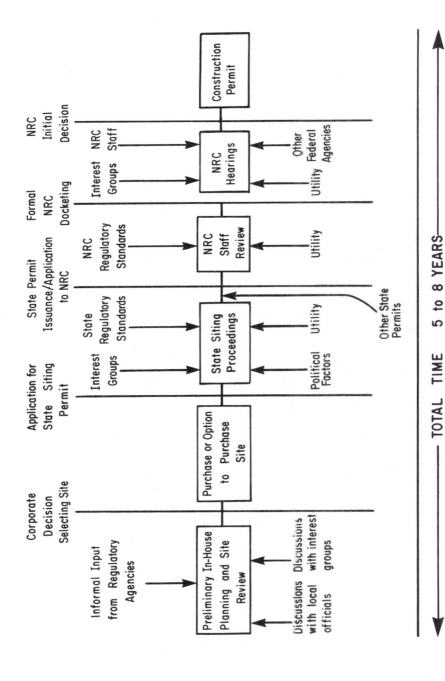

1. Schema of a typical site selection and licensing scenario for a nuclear power plant.

structure, or local growth; the cost to develop the site; and the cost to produce and develop the power.

Experience has demonstrated that a utility's internal site-selection process often will only imperfectly accommodate factors of concern to the public. Each utility's management goes about selecting a site in its own way. Public interest criteria are factored into the decision-making in the form of the utility's estimate of what will be required of it by local, state, and federal regulatory agencies. It accomplishes this by analyzing published regulations, by previous decisions of public bodies, and by informal contact with regulatory agency employees during the initial planning phase. Where there are active citizen interest groups, contact may also be made with them in an effort to gauge what areas are more sensitive than others.[3]

Site planning for a nuclear plant is complicated by the relatively long licensing and construction lead time (6 to 10 years). Figure 1 is a schema illustrating a typical site selection and licensing scenario. What appear—during early, prelicensing planning—to be guiding rules, policies, and criteria may change or turn out to be incorrect, leaving the utility that has relied on them with an unanticipated struggle despite careful attempts to consider the public interest. The Seabrook plant is a case in point. During informal discussions with state water pollution officials during the late 1960's, the management of the Public Service Company of New Hampshire was told that if an ocean-access site were chosen, it would not be necessary to construct cooling towers, which are used to prevent waste heat from being discharged into cold waters.[4] The utility, which did not favor the cooling towers because of their high operating cost, chose an ocean site; nevertheless, six years later, it was engaged in a regulatory battle with the EPA on the issue of whether cooling towers would be required for its ocean discharge of condenser cooling water.

The particular example cited is undoubtedly a product of the rapidly changing environmental standards of the early 1970's, caused in part by the imposition of new laws and in part by increasing scientific awareness of ecological impacts not heretofore understood. It is nevertheless also clear that no matter how thorough its internal screening process, a utility cannot anticipate every public interest concern and site and design a nuclear plant that will be totally free from challenge and the risk of regulatory rejection. Finally, utility planners may not perceive environmental or other concerns with the same sensitivity as regulatory personnel or environmental groups. Economic and other business considerations produce decisional biases that may downplay public interest factors in the internal decision-making process.

The first formal insertion of these factors into nuclear site selection is usually either in state site licensing proceedings (in states that have such laws) or before the staff of the NRC in its prelicensing review of the applicant's project. Whether at that point, after the utility has expended substantial resources on its chosen site, other factors can be adequately considered is a problem that needs exploring. A related issue is the extent to which states should be permitted to take over exclusively some of the regulatory functions heretofore dealt with by the NRC. A third and somewhat different issue is the extent to which comparative risk, a public interest issue heretofore largely ignored in formal licensing, can be included in the public decision-making equation.

Though some might argue that a utility's internal site selection process will at least result in economic optimization, it is doubtful that such is in fact the case. Since the electric utility industry operates as a licensed monopoly outside of the competitive private enterprise arena, whatever incentives exist in a competitive free market economy to foster careful planning for the sake of long-term cost minimization are largely irrelevant to it. Site-related diseconomies are passed on to the ratepayers under the prevailing rate-regulatory doctrine in most states.

The site of the Seabrook Nuclear Power Station, for example, has a major site-related diseconomy. It is over a mile from the ocean and nearly three miles from water deep enough to satisfy regulatory agencies as a location for the cooling water intake and discharge structures. Between the plant site and the ocean is a large salt marsh and a state park and beach complex. In order to bring cooling water to the site (whether or not cooling towers are required), the utility must construct bedrock tunnels eighteen feet in diameter from the site several miles to the points of ocean intake and discharge of cooling water. The increased cost to the ratepayers—a cost that would not be incurred at a site with more favorable access to the ocean—is at least several hundred million dollars.

The usual approach taken by states that have chosen to regulate the siting of utility plants has been enactment of state laws which require that the utility obtain a license or permit from a state agency before developing a site. Some of these laws require a two-level approval process: the first, ten to fifteen years prior to intended use of the site and the second when the utility decides on the size and design of its plant. This review ordinarily falls between the times the utility has made the choice of a site and its filing a construction license application with the NRC, although under a 1977 agreement experimental joint hearings were proposed for the state siting agency and the NRC in Massachusetts. Under the most typical state siting laws, the utility is required to present its site to the state agency, which must decide whether the site and the facility proposed for it are acceptable under whatever criteria have been established in the law. In most cases the utility must acquire numerous state and federal permits for other aspects of the project. Under some state laws the procedures for securing permits are coordinated with the siting proceedings or overridden by them, and in some they are not.[5] Problems created by overlapping or redundant permit requirements and the sometimes onerous requirements resulting from the environmental "permit explosion" are the subject of several recent studies[6] and federal legislation pending as this book was being written.[7]

Whether overlapping permits are good or bad is not always clear. Utilities and other major permit applicants usually argue against multiple levels of regulation, while environmental groups, and some academicians and government regulators favor multiple levels as a fail-safe protective mechanism, or as a way of providing meaningful control by various levels of government with different public constituencies, and for other reasons.

Virtually all the extant siting laws employ either a "reasonableness" standard[8] or require that the site be compared with alternatives and that its superiority to them be justified.[9] Siting laws of the first type provide only a crude measure for the site's acceptability and do not provide any basis for determining whether there has been optimization of parameters considered important to the public. They provide a mechanism for identifying the environmental and other impacts associated with development of the site and for judging, in a very general way, the magnitude of the identified problems. The New Hampshire law is a typical example of this first kind of state siting law. Under it, an applicant for a site permit is required to show that a plant built on the proposed site "will not have an undue adverse effect on aesthetics, historic sites, air and water quality, the natural environment, and the public health and safety."

The state siting agency in New Hampshire has no permanent professional staff; it is a committee made up of individuals who hold positions within various state executive departments. The agency is required to hold an adjudicatory (trial-type) hearing, at which the utility must produce witnesses to support its contention that its proposal meets the statutory criteria, and at which opponents are given like opportunity to present their case. It is significant that the statute requires only that the agency conclude that the site and facility will not have an "undue" adverse effect on the items of concern.

The term "undue" in the statute implies that a comparison must be made with some absolute standard. Yet the statute provides no guidance as to what the standard should be. For example, what if it is shown that a power plant located at site X will reduce the local clam population by 10 percent? Is that an "undue" impact? The answer to the question will, of course, depend upon the point of view of the decision-maker and will always be a subject of dispute. In the end such standards leave the decision to the discretion of the state siting board, whose expertise may be seriously limited and whose administrative procedures may be loose.

The nature of the inquiry is most often "all or nothing" insofar as the utility is concerned. It has selected its site and spent a substantial amount of money to produce data and studies to justify it. For example, the owners of the Seabrook plant had spent over a million dollars on the site up to the time of the state hearings. Management's mind set will be firmly behind the chosen site; hence, its ability to maneuver and compromise is limited. The adjudicatory hearing process, while providing the forum in which countervailing considerations can most effectively be raised by opponents, is expensive and cumbersome, and may effectively foreclose some groups from meaningful participation. Finally, an argument to its state regulator that a utility has spent millions on its project is no doubt at least a psychological deterrent to the agency's agreeing with opponents that the plant should be built elsewhere.

Ideally, the earliest formal site review process should provide, at the very least, incentives—and, at best, regulatory standards and policies—which aim at selecting the optimum site. Optimization in the political sense (selection of a site with which every player in the arena will be more or less happy, and which eliminates strong, vocal dissent) is an impossibility, but optimization in terms of providing appropriate weight to competing needs and concerns is a legitimate regulatory aim. If one accepts the premise that siting decisions should be made in the public sector rather than left to the utilities, and that all important public interest considerations should be weighed as early as possible, then the siting laws, like New Hampshire's, which leave issue development to the courtroom forum of an adjudicatory hearing held long after the utility has chosen its site and invested many thousands of dollars to justify it, are less than adequate to the task. By leaving the full examination of important issues to the opposing groups in a hearing, such a procedure can produce an incomplete review. Opposing groups will press only the issues they understand or can afford, and as a result many important concerns get lost in the ensuing shuffle.

During the state siting hearings for the Seabrook plant, the inquiry into alternatives was limited to one site, on which the utility produced very little data. The state siting decision (later, as noted above, overturned by the state Supreme Court because it lacked specific findings of fact) was based on a record lacking data on many issues that emerged as important ones in later proceedings before the NRC and EPA. Since the state law does not mandate minimum site standards, there was essentially nothing against which the state siting committee could measure the Seabrook site.

Some states have followed the lead of the NEPA[10] and have enacted laws that require state regulatory agencies to undertake an impact assessment of each proposal brought to them. NEPA and its state progeny require that for every "major" (state) action "significantly affecting the quality of the human environment," the "responsible official" produce a detailed statement on:

  (i) The environmental impact of the proposed action,
  (ii) any adverse environmental effects which cannot be avoided should the proposal be implemented,
 (iii) alternatives to the proposed action,
 (iv) the relationship between local short-term uses of man's environment and the maintenance and enhancement of long-term productivity, and
  (v) any irreversible and irretrievable commitments of resources which would be involved in the . . . action should it be implemented.

If one assumes that state siting officials will produce a thorough study under such a law and that they will base their decision on it, then that law could be considered a better means of factoring in public interest considerations than the state siting laws. Unfortunately, neither NEPA nor its state counterparts mandate that decision-making will be in accordance with the environmental assessment. Moreover, the quality of the environmental impact analysis produced under these laws is far from uniformly high. Furthermore, because of limitations inherent in the judicial process, it is unlikely that a biased Environmental Impact Statement (EIS) can ever be challenged successfully if it is procedurally adequate.

Another failing of state NEPA-like siting laws are that they do not (and probably cannot) mandate regional site selection and, to the extent some of them require a comparison of alternatives, that comparison usually comes long after the utility has made its site selection and hence is loaded in favor of the site chosen by the utility.

From the time a utility makes the critical in-house decision to choose a site, any further study of alternatives is necessarily negative in approach. Once sufficient corporate assets have been sunk into the chosen site to produce data adequate for state site review, the company's management has a large enough stake in it to resist suggestions that a full study of site alternatives be undertaken as a part of the state (or, for that matter, as a part of the NEPA) review process.[11] Hence, the company's methodological approach to evaluating alternates to the chosen site will always be oriented toward the desired conclusion: that the chosen site is superior. The company will accordingly have a tendency to look carefully at the negative aspects of an alternative and to underemphasize or ignore facts and circumstances that favor the alternative. Such a bias is inherent in any analysis that seeks to compare a preferred site with others; and as a consequence of this bias, such regulatory requirements will rarely result in a decision that the chosen site is inferior to some alternative.

By the time a utility's project reaches the NRC, which has a responsibility under NEPA to "study, develop and describe" alternatives, the company has invested substantial money and studies in its site and has already gained state approval. Any assessment of alternatives at this point cannot produce an optimum site, since NEPA methodology permits alternatives to be measured against the proposal.

In the ideal world the NEPA-type analysis at state level seems a step toward site optimization. Yet it does not appear that, in the real world, an adequate and sufficiently early consideration of public interest factors can be afforded under NEPA any more than under the more traditional regulatory laws used in states like New Hampshire in formulating siting decisions.

Decision-making models are designed to foster a multidisciplinary approach to problem solving and risk assessment in the selection of nuclear power plant sites. An example of one such approach has been developed by Keeney and Nair for the State of Washington.[12] The Keeney-Nair model integrates environmental, socioeconomic, and risk factors into a decision-making equation and subjects critical parameters to a sensitivity analysis before ranking candidate sites. Probabilistic assessments of impacts are made with respect to the following site attributes: site population (safety), impact of cooling system on aquatic organisms, other biological impacts, socioeconomic impact, environmental impact of transmission interties, differential site costs, and substrate stability in the event of an earthquake. The model also establishes screening criteria which are the bottom line for inclusion of a site in the model. For example, under the model only sites farther than three miles from populated places larger than 2500 persons and farther than 1 mile from smaller populated places are chosen for further, detailed analysis. Similar criteria were developed for other public and corporate considerations.

The Keeney-Nair model requires the selection of bottom-line eligibility criteria for such things as environmental impact, socioeconomic impact, or electrical system cost and reliability. That could be done by the state government, but could require the establishment of rigid threshold siting criteria by legislation. A methodology for sites that meet the threshold criteria could then be imposed on utilities by statute, with state review of a utility's selection process to assure compliance. Alternatively, ranking and selection could be undertaken in a public proceeding, by means of the same sort of hearing and permit-issuing procedure that goes on under existing state siting laws.

The model was designed for use by the state public power authority as a guide for its own site and facility planning. It could doubtless be adapted by a state like Maryland, whose siting law requires the state rather than private utilities to select and purchase power plant sites. Translation of the methodology employed by the Keeney-Nair and similar decision-making models into a regulatory context would be difficult and would not ensure that the decision-making would be less haphazard than it has been in the past.

Decision-making models are designed to provide a logical framework within which problem solving can occur. They do not ensure that the decisions made within the framework will be of substantive merit, and they do not eliminate political considerations, or extraneous factors, from influencing the ultimate conclusion.

Aside from their complexity, which makes their use in a politically charged atmosphere inherently difficult, decision-making models are only as good as the standards they apply and the decision-makers who use them. By adopting a decision-making model as an aid to nuclear siting adjudication, a state does little to solve the substantive problem facing it: to assess the various public and private costs and benefits of a site proposed by a utility.

My view is that the selection of a nuclear power plant site is of such tremendous public significance that initial site planning and screening ought not to be left to the utilities. The kind of social and environmental cost accounting required for a balanced initial assessment of, and development of, alternative sites should be done by a public body acting not as a reviewer of private choices, but as an active planner. At the same time, this initial site planning and inventorying by the public sector *should not* be devoid of an environmental assessment procedure like that fostered by NEPA; it *should* provide access to interest groups in a formal proceeding. Early site planning provides an adequate basis for threshold consideration of all the relevant public interest factors. However, a full examination of particular issues considered important by affected interest groups, including the utilities, can only occur in the context of an adjudicatory hearing. There should be provision for such a hearing at some point in the site selection process. An appropriate time would be when a particular site from the state's inventoried group is chosen for a particular facility (for example, some sites might be acceptable for a 300–500 mw facility, but not for a 1000–2000 mw facility). Figure 2 is a schematic representation of a state site evaluation procedure following these suggestions.

An important gap in the state and federal site selection process is the absence of any requirement that the sites be compared according to their public risk factor. For the purpose of this discussion, I define "public risk factor" to mean the number of potential human deaths and illnesses that would result in the event of a major nuclear

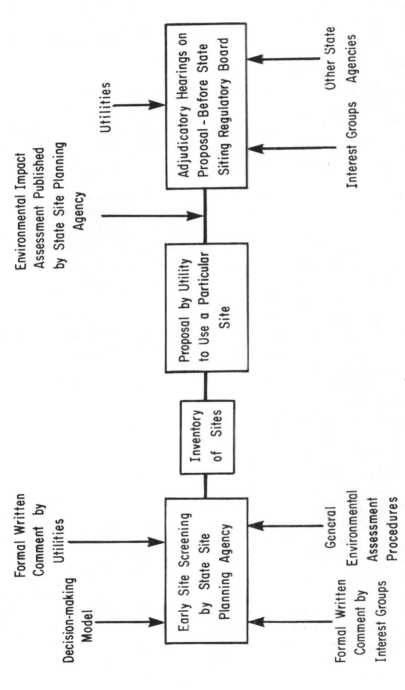

Formal Written
Comment by
Utilities

Environmental Impact
Assessment Published
by State Site Planning
Agency

Utilities

Adjudicatory Hearings on
Proposal – Before State
Siting Regulatory Board

Other State
Agencies

Interest Groups

Decision-making
Model

Early Site Screening
by State Site
Planning Agency

Proposal by Utility
to Use a Particular
Site

Inventory
of Sites

General
Environmental
Assessment
Procedures

Formal Written
Comment by
Interest Groups

2. Schema of an alternate scenario for site selection and licensing, with emphasis placed on early public involvement in the
site selection process.

accident occurring at the site, as calculated utilizing the prevailing methodology and assumptions—for example, utilizing the methodology used in the NRC's Reactor Safety Study[13] or some improvement on it.[14]

It has been demonstrated that the potential risk to the public resulting from a major nuclear reactor accident causing the release of fission products to the environment is in a large measure site dependent.[15] One of the major variables in the risk equation is the population density, downwind of the site, estimated to be present both at the beginning of and throughout the operating life of the proposed reactor.

Comparative site assessment is an effective means for screening sites only at the earliest site selection stages. Under present federal law there is no requirement for such an assessment to be done by the NRC. Although differences in theoretical public exposure are arguably within the NRC's obligation under NEPA to "study, develop and describe alternatives," it has never assessed them. Because of the low probability that a major accident will occur, the impact of including a theoretical risk factor in an NEPA cost-benefit equation would be negligible.[16] If, however, population distributions are compared as a threshold, it would seem to be a relatively simple matter to choose one site, or a group of several sites, having the lowest adjacent population, hence the least risk, for further study in a site selection program.

To what extent, without a change in federal law, states can legally undertake any sort of radiation-related risk evaluation is not clear.[17] The argument against state-mandated early comparative site evaluation is that since the NRC has adopted reactor site criteria, state action resulting in the rejection of sites that might be acceptable under the NRC's criteria is preempted by the exclusive regulatory scheme established under the Atomic Energy Act. The principal counter arguments are that since the NRC's site criteria do not establish rigid standards, there is room for state action, and what the state is doing is regulating land use rather than directly regulating the nuclear facility.

To include risk evaluation in early site screening at the state level would nevertheless raise problems of federalism and might require federal legislation. Since the risk of nuclear plants has traditionally been regarded as a matter of national policy, questions of site population, flooding hazard, and seismic qualification have been under the jurisdiction of the NRC for a long time. It might be argued, however, that risk assessment when undertaken as an aspect of site selection rather than plant design is indeed a proper state function, particularly in the face of the NRC's historic unwillingness to adopt meaningful site qualifications based on risk—a matter explored in detail in Chapter 3.

The value of any site selection process is also dependent upon the breadth of the pool from which candidate sites are selected. Where geographically small states are involved, development of a sufficiently broad candidate pool requires the inquiry to be on a regional basis. Barriers to regional site selection are partly legal, partly institutional, and partly perceptual; and removal of those barriers is a necessary component of any nuclear licensing reform scheme. Some states do not permit electric utilities to exercise the power of eminent domain (the power of the government to force the owner of land to sell it, at a just price, for public use) in the acquisition of land for a generating station; other states limit the exercise of eminent domain power to a utility's franchise area.

In the case of the Seabrook station, several sites with arguably better environmental and safety characteristics were dismissed by the utility because it did not possess the power of eminent domain in the states where the sites were located, and the sites were not for sale.

The Seabrook generating station was, because of economics and limitations of energy distribution, necessarily a joint venture. Much of the electricity generated at Seabrook would be consumed in Massachusetts, Connecticut, and Maine, and PSCO's co-owners were electric utilities in those states. All of these regional trappings, however, were insufficient under the existing web of state and federal environmental laws affecting the facility to compel a broader site search. Although the NRC ultimately ruled that NEPA required an analysis of alternate sites located in other states, the extraterritorial NEPA alternate site analysis was essentially an academic exercise. For region-wide site evaluation to be useful, it must be undertaken at a much earlier stage.

The problem of extraterritorial eminent domain can be solved by either of two methods. Congress could grant to utilities, under the supervision of the NRC or the Federal Power Commission, federal eminent domain authority to overcome the balkanization in this area which has occurred under state law, or all of the states in one integrated electrical system region could agree to provide eminent domain power to one another's utilities, for the limited purpose of siting nuclear generating stations. There are, of course, other legal problems. The Public Service Company of New Hampshire could not, for example, build a power plant in Massachusetts without obtaining a franchise from the Massachusetts Department of Public Utilities, and since the state is already divided up among a number of companies into existing franchise areas, the company in whose franchise area PSCO sought to build would have to consent to its presence. If the host is a member of the joint venture of which PSCO is the lead venturer, this is not a problem; but if it is not, and if PSCO wants to use a site for which the host has other plans, a legal problem arises in the competition between the two utilities for the site. The resolution of such a problem would normally fall on the state public utility regulatory agency, which might not be a dispassionate umpire in such a dispute.

Evaluation of Proposals for Change

Past and several present suggestions for reform of nuclear power plant siting laws have all, to one extent or another, included three basic assumptions: (1) control over public safety should be retained by the NRC; (2) responsibility for environmental site qualification should rest with the states, which would be responsible for undertaking environmental impact analysis under NEPA; and (3) early site planning should be open to public input and coordinated by utilities and states. For example, S. 935 and HR 4874, (93d Congress, 1973)[18] required utilities to undertake ten-year planning and provide state agencies opportunity to review and comment on the plans. They would have required utilities to apply to states for site approval three to five years prior to anticipated construction, and permitted a "coordinated" state-federal NEPA review, with the environmental assessment made by the state rather than by the federal licensing agency. States were not required to establish site certification agencies but were encouraged to do so, pursuant to standards promulgated by the Secretary of Interior. In the case of states having a certifying agency, a decision to authorize or deny construction on a given site would be "conclusive on all questions of siting, land use, public convenience and necessity [i.e. power needs], aesthetics, and other state and local requirements." It is not clear what was meant by the use of "siting" in that sentence, extracted from Section 7 of of the bill—specifically, whether public safety considerations would have thereby been delegated to the states. A similar approach has been suggested by the NRC.[19] Also, legislation reforming the licensing of nuclear power was submitted to Congress by the Carter administration in March 1978; it generally follows the same approach.[20]

Delegation of the responsibility for environmental assessment solely to the states may simplify the nuclear licensing process, but it would not necessarily improve the site selection process. Among the questions that must be addressed are the following:

(1) Are states inherently as capable as a federal agency to undertake the kind of balanced, interdisciplinary evaluation required in order to make a useful and complete impact assessment at the early stages of nuclear plant site evaluation? Or should Congress instead redefine the NRC's role, forcing it to undertake an early, comprehensive analysis of alternatives?

(2) To what extent would such a delegation limit the range of alternatives that must be considered? Clearly, a state that expects to receive revenue in the form of taxes on a nuclear facility will not look too hard at alternative sites located in neighboring states. Will the NRC be obligated to undertake its own wide-ranging analysis of alternatives, or will it be limited to a review of the state's work?

To an extent the problem would not be new. The Seabrook plant was approved by the New Hampshire site evaluation committee with a specific routing of the transmission line. When the NRC conditioned the license for the plant on a change in the route in order to avoid an environmentally sensitive area, the utility complained that it was locked into the original route and a change would necessitate lengthy state proceedings, with uncertain results.[21]

(3) On what basis would the NRC be able to refuse a state environmental assessment, and if a state assessment is procedurally or substantively inadequate, will the NRC be required to do the job itself? The states vary in their experience and capabilities to produce environmental or social impact assessments; hence a strong argument can be made for retaining a federal presence in the interest of promoting uniformity.

(4) Will the state component of the EIS be subject to scrutiny within the NRC's adjudicatory hearing process? Under present law the NRC staff personnel responsible for an EIS are subject to cross-examination on their work product during the course of licensing hearings. Would state personnel, or consultants, be subject to similar

treatment at the federal level, or is inquiry into their work product limited to the state proceedings?

These are obviously not easy questions to answer. The nuclear siting dilemma raises serious problems of federalism—the relative responsibilities of the separate levels of government in a federal system of shared governmental responsibility.

In addition, there are important flaws in the NEPA decision-making process as it has occurred in the federal government which could be magnified if responsibilities under the statute were left solely to the states. Repeated attempts to challenge the substantive conclusions of environmental impact statements have failed in court. It is entirely possible for the government to make very "bad" decisions based on procedurally adequate NEPA-based analyses.[22]

Whatever course the ongoing attempts at siting reform take, it is unlikely that the NRC will be replaced by the states as the principal decision-maker in the nuclear arena. It is important, therefore, to examine its decision-making processes closely in order to understand the nuclear problem. Further analysis of a state siting process is also required in order to place in its proper perspective the suggestion that the states play a greater role in nuclear licensing. The following chapters attempt to do both, by examining the licensing controversy surrounding the Seabrook Nuclear Power Station.

Conclusions

The principal points made in this chapter can be summarized as follows:

(1) Electric utility companies should not be responsible for decisions concerning early nuclear-site planning.

(2) Early site identification, evaluation, and inventorying is a public responsibility that should be undertaken by a public agency, with formal participation by utilities and interest groups, based upon criteria developed by the state legislature.

(3) Prior to the use of a particular site, the state should prepare a complete environmental assessment for it, and hold adjudicatory hearings on contested issues.

(4) Further effort should be made toward assessing the public risk of nuclear power plant sites.

(5) In areas like New England, characterized by geographically

small states and high energy demand, serious efforts should be made to develop regional site planning and evaluation.

(6) Nuclear licensing reform should focus on the quality of decision-making.

(7) There should be a continued federal presence in nuclear site selection, and the resolution of environmental problems should not be delegated entirely to the states.

3

Siting and Public Risk

Although the utility industry champions federal legislation designed to facilitate licensing and quell (or at least limit) formal opposition before the Nuclear Regulatory Commission in the hope that thereafter all will again be well for it, it is clear that a large segment of the public will not accept nuclear power until it is comfortable with the risks.

The NRC's controversial Reactor Safety Study (RSS)[1] attempted to measure the probabilities and consequences of reactor accidents, but disavowed any attempt to judge the acceptability of the risks it measured. Existing NRC regulations, I will argue here, establish a standard of acceptability by default.

The Atomic Energy Act of 1954 permits the establishment of siting criteria aimed at minimizing the risk of public exposure to radiation: 42 USC Sections 2133, 2134, 2201, and 2282 provide broad authority to the AEC (and to its successor, the NRC) to regulate the location, design, and construction of nuclear generating facilities.

The risk posed by a nuclear power plant is that members of the public will be harmed by exposure to radiation emitted from the facility as a result of a malfunction or accident. There are many types of accidents that can release radiation from a nuclear power plant, and the amount of radiation released will vary with the nature of the accident and the effectiveness of safety systems designed to cope with such occurrences.

For example, the rupture of a major steam pipe will cause the release of radioactive steam in large quantities into the secondary

40

reactor containment (the sheet metal building that houses the reactor). How much of that steam gets into the atmosphere will be determined by how much escapes and how much of the radiation is removed by filtering devices installed for that purpose, and by such unanticipated occurrences as whether a door has been left open. A pipe rupture will also cause the reactor vessel to be emptied of the water it contains. That water serves both as the moderator for the chain reaction of the nuclear fuel (without it the reaction will not occur), and as a coolant to keep the fuel from superheating and melting the reactor. When the water is removed, even though the chain reaction ceases, there is enough heat left in the reactor to melt the fuel and its assembly unless new water is injected in sufficient quantity. If the fuel melts, massive amounts of radioactivity will be released to the environment. Thus the amount of radiation released following a steam pipe rupture will depend on the adequate functioning of a safety system to reinject water into the reactor vessel.

The various types of accidents that could occur, their probability of occurrence, their consequences, and the effectiveness of the safety systems designed to cope with them are all subjects of heated debate by scientists supporting and critical of nuclear technology.[2] A similar debate is occurring with respect to the medical significance of exposure to low and high levels of radiation by individuals and population groups under the circumstances that would exist following a major plant accident.[3]

It is impossible to predict accurately the nature or consequence of a catastrophic nuclear accident, since one has not yet occurred. Although the probability that a major accident will occur is (the industry asserts) low,[4] that position is disputed by scientists critical of the industry. Even the industry has always conceded that there is some risk of several major types of accidents, and that, as a consequence of each, radiation would be released to the environment.[5] The 1979 Three Mile Island accident in Pennsylvania, though not catastrophic, was far more serious than the NRC had publicly predicted would ever occur, and it was hardly predictable at all, in that the chain of events that caused the ultimate release of large amounts of radiation included several which had never been foreseen, such as the obscuring of a gauge from the operator's vision by another operator's body or some tags attached to another gauge.

The presence of some risk, however small, of a large nuclear accident resulting in an offsite release of radioactivity caused the AEC to proceed with some caution in the early years of its power reactor program, and to develop site-suitability criteria intended to limit the risk to the public by providing regulatory control over nuclear plant site selection.

Part 100 of the NRC regulations, issued in 1962, sets forth general criteria for the location of nuclear reactors with respect to population clusters. It requires the identification of three areas or distances —an "exclusion area," a "low population zone," and a "population center distance." The exclusion area, over which the reactor owner must be able to exercise total dominion, surrounds the plant site and is usually a circle whose radius is determined by the inner boundary of the low population zone (LPZ). Under present NRC practice, the size of the LPZ is determined in part by the population center distance and in part by the reactor containment design. The population center distance (PCD) is the distance from the reactor site boundary to the nearest population center containing about 25,000 residents,[6] and it must be at least 1.3 times the distance from the site boundary to the outer boundary of the LPZ. The LPZ, finally, must be far enough away from the site that, in the event of a "design basis accident," a person standing on its outer boundary will not receive more than 25 rems to the whole body or 300 rems to the thyroid.[7] A typical configuration of exclusion area, LPZ and PCD is shown in Figure 3.

It is generally assumed that Part 100 "set down a procedure for relating plant size to distance from population centers—and thus formalized the 'remote location' concept, subject to modification through use of engineered safeguards."[8] There is in Part 100's history evidence to suggest that it was intended to encourage remote siting. For example, the "Statement of Considerations" that accompanied the text of the regulation in the *Federal Register* implies that the PCD concept was intended to mitigate the consequences of "accidents of greater potential hazard than those commonly postulated as representing an upper limit."[9]

Shortly after Part 100 was promulgated, however, the staff of the Atomic Energy Commission established a policy favoring engineered safeguards over remote siting, arguing in official publications that the distance factor could be "engineered out of existence."[10] Subsequently, the AEC and NRC's individual plant licensing decisions largely removed remoteness as the most important factor in the siting of a reactor. Large nuclear facilities were licensed at sites

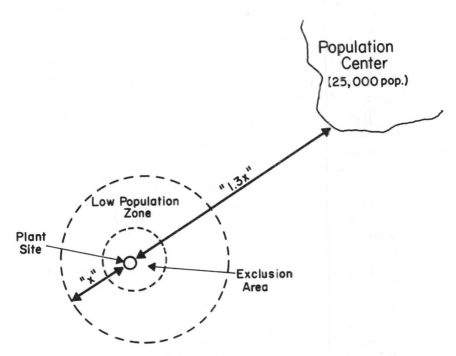

3.   Schema of the NRC's site suitability criteria, as set forth in 10 CFR Part 100.

close to such population centers as Chicago, Detroit, and New York City.

In actual practice inadequate consideration has been given to population, or to individual risk, in reactor siting decisions. In a paper published in the *Bell Journal of Economics*, Joel Yellin drew a rough safety comparison of two licensed reactor sites. Averaging wind directions around different reactor sites, and using methodology from the NRC Reactor Safety Study,[11] the average number of early fatalities resulting from a hypothetical core meltdown accident changes more than "a thousandfold" between the site of the Maine Yankee station at Wiscasset, Maine, and the Zion site at Zion, Illinois. Under this analysis, "the accident which caused on the average about one death at the site in Maine would be expected to cause about 1000 deaths if it occurred under the same weather conditions at the site in Illinois."[12]

The established AEC/NRC litany is that the Atomic Energy Act requires compound conservation to be applied to all criteria and decisions in the reactor program. Thus one finds in the regulations promulgated by the Commission and in decisions of its appeal board numerous references to the "conservatism" (by which we must assume is meant public protectionism) that theoretically underlies Commission decision-making. For example, the Commission requires reactor safety systems to function in the case of types of accidents for which there is an exceedingly low probability of occurrence, on the premise that there should be a "defense in depth" to protect the public from exposure to harmful amounts of radiation.

The utilization of conservative assumptions represents, if nothing else, a public position that there is a significant risk of harm from nuclear reactors, and therefore the government, in permitting their use for the production of energy, should, and will, err on the side of public protection. There is an assumption that risks will not be taken, that economic determiners will not, in this very special case, reign paramount.[13] They represent a cautious approach to a dangerous technology, the management of which and the potential hazards of which are only imperfectly understood. In the early stages of experimental power reactor development (a mere 20 years ago) this philosophy appears to have manifested itself in exceedingly "conservative" siting decisions. For example, the early, small Saxton, Pennsylvania, facility was located in a remote, desolate area that had years before been essentially destroyed by unregulated coal strip mining.

The same conservatism was articulated by President Carter shortly after he took office in 1977, when in his address to the Congress on his energy program he stressed the need to site nuclear facilities away from people and suggested underground siting as another level of protection.[14] This concern was repeated in a White House publication, *The National Energy Plan*, issued on April 29, 1977, in which the following statement appears:

> In addition, the President is requesting that the Commission develop firm siting criteria with clear guidelines to prevent siting of future nuclear plants in densely populated locations, in valuable natural areas, or in potentially hazardous locations. Proper siting will substantially reduce the risk of a nuclear accident and the consequences should one occur.[15]

By the time the Commission had decided the Seabrook case (1977), design had so completely eclipsed remoteness that a plant could be licensed within eye and earshot of a concentration of more than 40,000 summer residents. So long as the owner was able to demonstrate that, in the event of a "design basis accident" no one in the population center would receive more than 25 rems to the whole body or 300 rems to the thyroid, the site was "acceptable," regardless of doubts about the evacuability of the area.[16]

How this came about requires a brief review of the history of Part 100 and a close look at the Seabrook litigation.

Part 100—An Historical Review

Part 100 was produced by the AEC and has existed in substantially its present[17] form since the early days of the reactor program. The AEC solicited comments and testimony on the subject of developing siting criteria, and the matter was, during 1962, the subject of minor discussion in international atomic energy circles. It must be remembered that there was at that time little public understanding or even awareness of the emerging reactor program. Hence, none of the comments received by the Commission came from scientists or others who were not members of the relatively small nuclear development community in the United States or abroad.

There was, in 1962, and continues to be, a substantial lack of knowledge about the individual or population risks to humans who would be exposed to radiation emitted from a power plant under severe accident conditions. There has been and continues to be imperfect understanding, and a dispute among members of the scientific community,[18] as to the nature and size of radiation releases that should be anticipated and that thus would form the basis of population dose evaluation in an accident scenario.[19]

Some of the troublesome issues facing the AEC in 1962 and still being debated in international atomic energy circles, are:

—Should accident probability be considered in formulating siting criteria, or should sites be chosen based on an assumption that the maximum conceivable radiation release will occur?

—Should credit be given for total or partial functioning of the emergency core cooling system in the event of a double pipe rupture, or should siting criteria assume that releases produced by a full core meltdown are possible?[20]

—What consideration must be given to future population growth?

—To what extent should credit be given for "engineered safe-guards," like dual containment and filtration capacity?

—Whether individual dose or integrated population dose should be the limiting dose.

Rather than confront the difficulties of establishing siting criteria that attempt to resolve these and related issues, the AEC avoided them altogether and constructed Part 100 as a "flexible" guideline, capable of bending to meet emergent circumstances. The Commission is certainly not the only government agency ever to employ this kind of regulatory slight of hand, nor is Part 100 the only instance of its employment of an avoidance device.[21]

The practical economics of the enormously capital-intensive nuclear industry were destined to shape the course of siting decisions made by the Commission under Part 100. It is much more costly to construct a nuclear generating station remote from populated areas, for a number of reasons. It is, for example, more costly to fabricate a reactor vessel at the site than to purchase one already assembled from a vendor. Transportation corridors to remote sites are often inadequate for movement of large, heavy reactor vessel cargoes, hence on-site fabrication becomes necessary. Labor is generally more easily accessible in more populous areas, and it is costly to transport workers to a remote job site. Transmission lines are expensive to construct and maintain, and long transmission results in efficiency losses.[22] It is therefore not surprising that as more and more applications for construction licenses were filed by utilities, reactor sites crept closer and closer to dense population centers. Prior to about 1972, virtually all of the critical decisions with respect to site suitability were made by the AEC staff, in private consultation with applicant utilities. Licensing hearings were pro forma affairs, rarely lasting more than a day or two. Compliance with Part 100 became simply a matter of mechanistic application of the dose limits established for the outer boundary of the Low Population Zone in §100.11 (a) (2), limits which the Commission itself disclaimed in a footnote as not being "acceptable."

Table 1 summarizes the location of nuclear power plants licensed before 1970, in relation to population.[23] The Table does, indeed, imply that "population center distance and population distribution have had little to do with nuclear plant siting."[24] Moreover, power level and overall station capacity seem unrelated to population distribution or population center distance. Remembering the Yellin calculation discussed earlier, we note that the apparent ignorance on the part of the AEC of this obvious relationship is somewhat disturbing, especially in light of the fact that the fission product inventory, released fission products, and resulting population dose could be as much as five times greater in the case of a 2000 mw (thermal) reactor than for an 800 mw (thermal) reactor.[25]

Table 1 also raises questions about the use of the "population center distance" requirement of 10 CFR Section 100.3. For example, the Oyster Creek plant has a PCD listed as 25 miles, yet 38,500 people live within 0 to 5 miles of the plant. The Burlington plant has a PCD of 11 miles, but 119,370 people live within 0 to 5 miles of the plant.

Questions are raised by statistics like those in Table 1, but they are not answered thereby. It is important to look to the actual site-suitability decisions made by the AEC and by its successor, the NRC, for an indication of the reasoning process by which these and subsequent plants were licensed. The following section examines closely the Seabrook licensing proceeding, the only licensing case to date in which a major challenge has been made to the siting criteria.

The Seabrook Issues

Prior to *Seabrook*, the NRC rarely addressed Part 100 in its decisions or in those of its Appeal Board. In the case involving the San Onofre facility in California, an issue was raised as to whether the term "residents" used in the regulation included transients, such as beach users at a national park. The Commission's Appeal Board said it did.[26]

In licensing the Bailey Generating Station, a near-contemporary to Seabrook, the NRC addressed the "population center distance" required to be fixed by 10 CFR § 100.3(c). The rule, as you recall, requires identification of the nearest population center containing about 25,000 persons. The distance from the reactor site to this center fixes the maximum size of the LPZ. The question addressed in connection with the Bailey plant, first by the Commission's Appeal Board and later by the Eighth Circuit Court of Appeals was whether this distance was to be measured to the nearest political boundary of

TABLE 1.   United States Nuclear Power Plant Summary

Station	Licensed Station Capacity MWe Net	Exclusion Distance Miles	Population Center Distance Miles	Population 0 to 5 Miles	Population 0 to 10 Miles
Turkey Point Units No. 3 & 4	1302	0.85	20	0	42,000
Palisades	700	0.44	16	4,500	15,000
Browns Ferry Units No. 1 & 2	2130	0.76	10	2,800	30,600
Peach Bottom Units No. 1, 2, & 3	2170	0.48	21	6,145	23,550
Point Beach Units No. 1 & 2	910	0.7	13	1,241	20,845
Díablo Canyon	1060	0.5	10	10	
Monticello	471	0.3	22	3,942	
Oconee Units No. 1 & 2	1678	1.0	21	2,163	36,334
H. B. Robinson Unit No. 2	663	0.26	56	10,800	
Burlington	993	0.23	11	119,370	17 mi.-Phil.
Fort St. Vrain	330	0.40	14	1,951	8,420
Vermont Yankee	514	0.17	25	7,400	29,200
Quad-Cities Units No. 1 & 2	1430	0.23	5	5,369	
Indian Point Units No. 1 & 2	1128	0.32	1	53,040	155,510
Dresden Units No. 1, 2, & 3	1630	0.5	14	2,500	23,000
Connecticut Yankee	462	0.32	9	10,000	49,500
Oyster Creek	515	0.25	25	38,500	106,500
Nine Mile Point	500	0.75	6	1,900	30,900
Millstone Point	549	0.4	3	60,000	96,000
R. E. Ginna	412	0.29	12	1,500	8,000
Malibu	462	0.20	10	6,000	11,900
La Crosse	50	0.21	15	1,000	7,500
San Onofre	430	2.0	10	8,800	22,000

Shippingport	90	0.4	7	20,000	22 mi.-Pitts.
Yankee	175	0.5	21	2,000	30,000
Big Rock Point	72.8	0.5	135	5,000	9,000
Elk River	23	0.23	20	8,000	30 mi.-Minn.
Carolinas–Virginia	17	0.5	25	2,000	8,000
Enrico Fermi	60.9	0.75	7	9,000	61,000
Humboldt Bay Unit No. 3	70	0.25	3	35,000	40,000
Piqua	11.4	0.14	27	21,000	42,000
Pathfinder	58.5	0.5	3		

the population center or to the nearest densely populated cluster of habitation, or to some other point. This made a difference because the political boundary was much closer to the plant site than the nearest concentrated areas of population. The NRC opted to interpret the rule to permit measurement to the population cluster. The Court of Appeals reversed this decision, pointing out that the plain and unambiguous reference to "boundary" in the rule could not be construed out of existence.[27] Shortly after this decision the Commission, without a hearing, promulgated an amendment to § 100.3, redefining population center distance to make the rule support the staff's position with respect to the Bailey FCD.

Absent from the Appeal Board rulings in *San Onofre* and *Baily* or from the Court's opinion in *Bailey* or the Commission's *Bailey*-related rulemaking is any meaningful attempt to examine Part 100 in the context of its assumed purpose—the protection of the public, or, in regulatory parlance, the minimization of risk to the public. In none of these cases, moreover, was there an attempt to analyze land use patterns in order to determine where likely development would occur in the future, with respect to establishing a PCD responsive to the dynamics of population change. Curiously, the rule does not require that the inquiry go into the future. Although the AEC required inquiry into the "early years of reactor operation,"[28] no attempt is made to define just how many years that means.[29] Moreover, since the risk of a significant release of radioactive material is equally likely (indeed, it has been argued, more likely) in the later years of reactor operation, it would seem logical to compel at least some attempt to predict land use patterns twenty or thirty years into the future; and, if they cannot be predicted, to require that land use limitations be imposed. In the case of *Bailey*, for example, it would be more than useful to have some idea of the direction of population growth. Is it likely that the population will creep toward the rejected political boundary, or leapfrog into the LPZ? In the absence of such information, the truly conservative approach would compel setting the PCD at the nearest reasonable point of possible growth, and require siting decisions to be made on that basis.

It is not enough merely to look at the present population and assume that land use controls imposed by local authorities will limit population growth in the future. Control of population growth has been a difficult task; even if communities are willing to do so, they face constitutional limitations on their authority to exclude immigration. Moreover, one cannot assume that communities will always be willing to implement truly growth-limiting land-use controls in a growing urban area, especially if they perceive, as they often do, that by limiting growth, they freeze the tax base in the face of continually rising costs for such things as schools and other government services.

The Seabrook case involved two site suitability issues, which are critically related, although not treated as such in the licensing process. The first issue is: What should be the PCD, and what is the consequence to reactor siting of a PCD on the plant's doorstep? The second issue is whether under existing NRC regulations evacuation may be compelled (or even considered) outside of the LPZ.[30]

Figures 4 through 6, derived from exhibits filed with the NRC, depict the location and general relationship of the Seabrook site to its surrounding environs.

The permanent 1980 population of the area within a radius of five miles from the plant site as estimated by PSCO is shown in Figure 7. Figure 8 shows the 1980 maximum permanent plus transient population estimated by the applicant for the area; and Figure 9 shows the same population but with the transient population weighted to reflect its short-term period of occupancy, utilizing weighting factors adopted by PSCO and accepted by the NRC staff.

The area's land use patterns and population will be different after 1984, the date of scheduled operation of Unit 2.[31] Table 2 shows estimated population derived using various assumptions about land use changes up to 1995, derived from testimony by Charles Tucker, an intervenor witness and the only witness who produced such detailed testimony.[32] Neither the utilities nor the staff of the NRC produced meaningful evidence of land use change or composite population change beyond 1980.

Because of its location and the limited road network for providing ingress and egress, rapid evacuation of the Hampton Beach area is impossible during periods of heavy use. Based on the carrying capacity of the existing roads, and assuming the maintenance of a steady flow, traffic engineers employed by PSCO estimated an evacuation time of eight hours for a beach population of 128,000.[33] This estimate was questioned by a New Hampshire state police captain who had had experience with crowd control at Hampton Beach. In testimony during the NRC licensing hearings, he stated that he did not believe that the beach could be evacuated in the amount of time

TABLE 2. Table Showing Estimated 1995 Population Range Under Different Assumptions. Source: Testimony of Charles Tucker, Executive Director, Southeastern New Hampshire Regional Planning Commission

Assumptions	1995 Weighted Population– Beach Area
A. No significant redevelopment of Hampton Beach residential area; no filling of adjacent salt marsh.	27,000
B. Construction of large parking garage planned by Town of Hampton; conversion of some single family units to multifamily condominium units; no filling of adjacent salt marsh.	50,000
C. Construction of parking garage; extensive redevelopment of Beach residential area pursuant to renegotiation of 100–year leases (in 1990) into high-rise condominiums; some construction on adjacent filled salt marsh.	90,000

projected by PSCO. When pressed for an estimate of the length of time required for evacuation, he refused to hazard a guess.[34] Two of the four available routes of egress from the beach require either moving closer to the plant site, or skirting it at roughly the same distance as the beach before moving away from it.

The meteorology at the site is typically that of coastal New England. There are ordinarily periods of offshore and onshore winds each day. There are also prevailing wind patterns, and measurements taken by PSCO showed winds blowing from the plant site toward the beach during most of the year.[35] There is, therefore, a statistically significant likelihood that a radioactive cloud originating from an accidental release at the plant site would move toward the densely populated area of Hampton Beach.

The town of Seabrook lies on the far-out fringe of sprawling suburban development associated with the city of Boston. During the NRC licensing hearings there was at one point a frequent advertisement on Boston radio for a new apartment complex in Seabrook aimed at commuters. Interstate highway I–95 provides a 40-minute access to the Boston job market.

If the prevalent pattern of suburban development occurring north of Boston during the early and mid-70's continues into the 80's, or if the twelve-mile-long New Hampshire coastal zone experiences development associated with extraction of oil from the outer continental

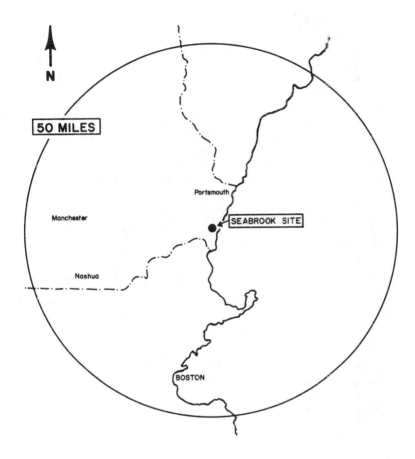

4. Regional geographic location of the Seabrook site, at a radial distance of 50 miles from the plant site.

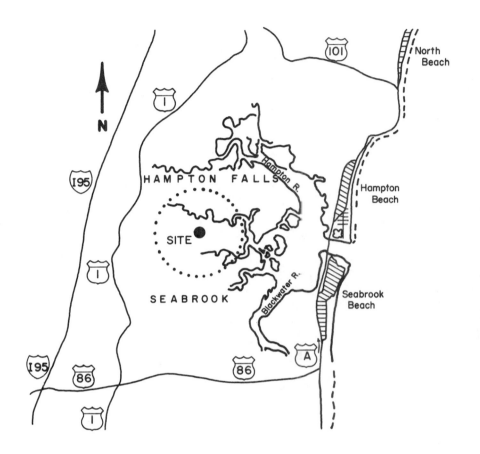

5. Local Seabrook site environs, showing the exclusion area and transportation corridors.

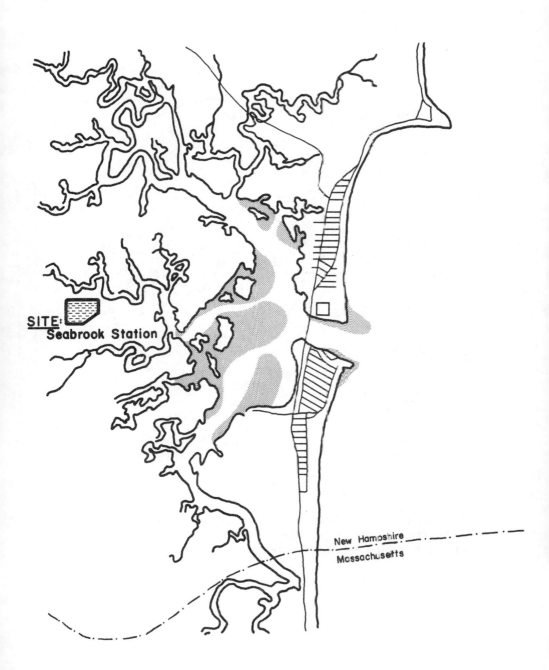

6. Seabrook site illustrating salt marsh complex and Hampton Beach area.

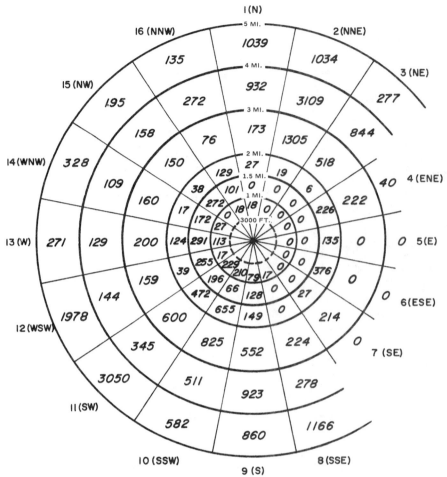

7. Diagram showing permanent resident population distribution 0–5 miles from the Seabrook site. *Source:* Applicant's Preliminary Safety Analysis Report (PSAR), U.S. Nuclear Regulatory Commission.

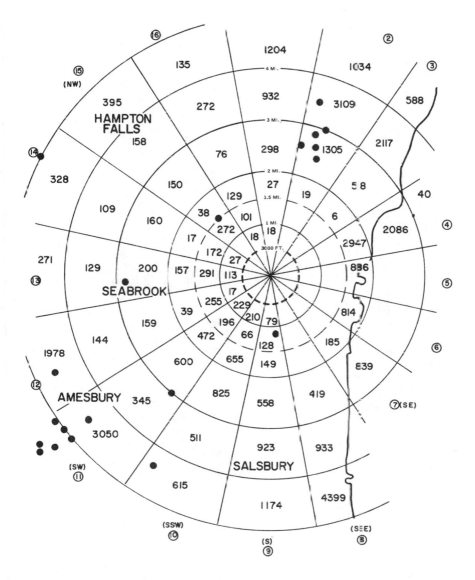

8. Diagram showing estimated 1980 population, including permanent seasonal, and transient population distribution 0–5 miles from the Seabrook site. *Source:* Applicant's PSAR, U.S. Nuclear Regulatory Commission.

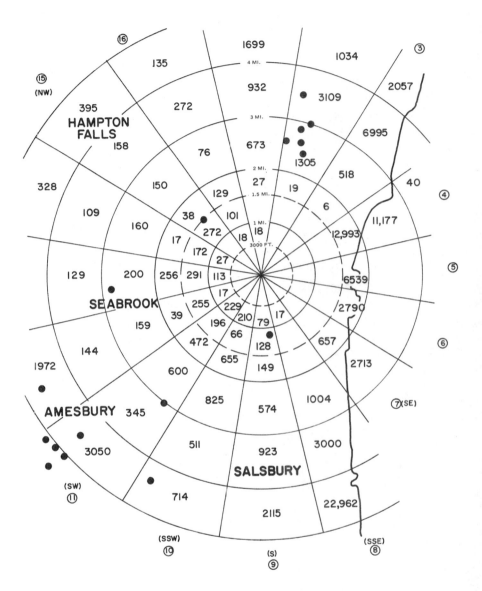

9. Diagram showing estimated 1980 population 0–5 miles from the Seabrook site, including permanent seasonal, and transient population, weighted to account for occupancy time according to methodology approved by the Nuclear Regulatory Commission. *Source:* Applicant's PSAR, U.S. Nuclear Regulatory Commission.

shelf in the Gulf of Maine, the towns of Seabrook and Hampton Falls may experience exponential growth. If there are growth pressures, moreover, the presence of the Seabrook plant in the town of Seabrook would tend to provide one significant economic incentive for growth to occur—an artificially low residential tax burden. Since under New Hampshire law virtually all of the tax revenue from industrial plants inures to the host town in the form of property taxes, the mere presence of the two-billion-dollar Seabrook facility will, during at least the first years of its life, reduce other property taxes substantially. Thus for at least several years following operation of the facility, the town of Seabrook will be more attractive than its Massachusetts neighbors as a place to develop land.

A conceivable growth scenario, then, would involve rapid residential development on the upland surrounding the large Hampton salt marsh, with commercial and industrial development continuing along U.S. Route 1 and I-95, both of which lie just west of the plant site. The Seabrook plant, intervenor NECNP argued, could become the hole in the center of a doughnut-shaped ring of dense population before the end of its useful life. Long-range plans projected by the Southeastern New Hampshire Regional Planning Commission seem to predict just such an occurrence, even without the added impetus of the plant's contribution to the local tax base.

The PCD Issue

Before proceeding to examine the site evaluation issues in the Seabrook case, it will be instructive to look again at the regulation itself and at the background of the regulation, to examine the AEC's public position expressing its initial intentions with respect to the use to be made of the reactor site criteria.

Section 100.3(c) of the NRC regulations requires the establishment of a "population center distance," which is defined as:

> "the distance from the reactor to the nearest boundary of a densely populated center containing more than about 25,000 residents"

The term "boundary" is modified by Section 100.11(a)(3) as follows:

> "The boundary of a population center shall be determined upon

consideration of population distribution. Political boundaries are not controlling . . ."[36]

The only specifically mandated use for the PCD under Part 100 is that it be "one and one-third times the distance from the reactor to the outer boundary of the low population area," with the distance increased where "very large cities" are involved (§ 100.11(a)(3)).

PSCO selected, and the NRC staff accepted and thereafter supported in the hearings, the City of Portsmouth, New Hampshire, as the PCD for Seabrook. Portsmouth is about twelve miles from the Seabrook plant site and contains a population of about 26,000. The population density of Portsmouth, a parameter not required under the regulation but given prominence in a staff working document discussed below, is about 1,600 people per square mile.

The Seabrook site, however, is only about a mile and a quarter from Hampton Beach,[37] which has a summer population density of 31,500 people per square mile. The attorney general of New Hampshire and NECNP urged on account of these facts that the beach be designated the PCD. Since PSCO had drawn its LPZ boundary to the edge of the beach, redesignation of the beach as the PCD would, by operation of § 100.11(a)(3), require that the LPZ boundary be redrawn closer to the plant. (The significance of this is discussed below, page 69.) NECNP further argued that at some point after 1980, the combined permanent and seasonal population of the individual towns of Seabrook, Hampton Falls, Hampton, and Salisbury, Massachusetts, which ring the plant site, would exceed 25,000, and since these towns have a similar socioeconomic base and even share some school facilities, the PCD should be the closest population cluster found in any of these towns.[38] This theory would have placed the plant site virtually in the center of a "population center," and became known as the doughnut theory.

Both of these intervenor theories required the inclusion of transient vacationers as "residents" under the Commission's rule. The Commission's Appeal Board, in an earlier decision,[39] had defined the term to include transients for the purpose of requiring "protective action" in the LPZ, so that there was clear (though perhaps inadvertent) precedent for the proposition that transients should be afforded protection under Part 100; hence the intervenor's basic premise was not seriously disputed. The problem became, "How much protection?" PSCO, seconded by the NRC's staff, argued that the transient population should be weighted to reflect occupancy time factors, and urged that each transient be counted as about one twelfth of a whole person.[40]

NECNP's doughnut theory was premised on an assumption that the "conservatism" inherent in Part 100 required identification of a "population center" regardless of the probabilities involved in all or any portion of its population receiving specific radiation doses as a result of the sort of accidents postulated as "credible" by the Commission.[41]

Further elaboration of the evidentiary dispute among the parties, while a potentially interesting academic exercise, is unnecessary here. For the purpose of assessing the Seabrook decision as a means of testing the value of Part 100 as a siting guide, limiting our focus to the Commission's final action is sufficient. In order to illustrate the curious cross-purposes at which the NRC's various levels function, however, let us look at the position taken by the NRC staff.

The staff had under study at the time of the Seabrook hearing a draft regulatory guide that estalished population density criteria for siting nuclear reactors. That draft guide, if it had been applicable to the Seabrook site, would arguably have required serious reconsideration of the Seabrook site in the event that the transient population was considered relevant for Part 100 purposes. It discouraged siting nuclear facilities in areas where the population density exceeded about 400 people per square mile. The thinking behind this draft guide had in fact prompted the staff initially to tell PSCO to look for additional alternate sites, although the request was not pursued by either PSCO or the staff with any perseverance.

This draft guide seems to constitute the preliminary beginnings of the "further study" the Commission had promised in 1962. In the Commission's rulemaking hierarchy, however, draft regulatory guides have no legal significance whatever. Formally adopted regulatory guides are considered as merely "guidance" documents, and non-compliance with a regulatory guide may not, the Commission has ruled, form the basis for regulatory decisions. Draft guides, then, amount to no more than the staff thinking out loud.

While one arm of the staff was thinking about proposing to discourage reactor siting to areas with present or reasonably anticipated population densities much less than the density anticipated for 1990 around Seabrook, another (that involved in the Seabrook licensing proceeding) was strenuously urging that population concentration around Seabrook virtually be ignored. Staff Project Director Staros-tecki and Staff Witness Grimes, in an effort to negate the beach area as a PCD, refused to concede that the area would experience population growth beyond 1980.[42] Grimes came up, in addition, with a device to reject NECNP's contention that the site was, or would be within a few years, in the virtual middle of a population center. He asserted that since the wind blows in only one direction at once, location of potential population centers must fall within the confines of discrete 22½ degree pie wedges radiating out from the plant site.[43] The staff had never before used this argument.[44] As it will become apparent, the approach seems also contrary to the heretofore assumed underlying premises of Part 100.

Grimes's position was adopted by the Licensing Board, appealed by NECNP, and ultimately adopted by the Appeal Board, which rejected the doughnut theory on the basis of Grimes's analysis.[45] The Appeal Board's reasoning is simple and straightforward. It represents the final adjudication of the issue and is binding precedent for future siting decisions. It reasoned:

> For any specific number of people, the highest projected total dosages to the population as a whole will result if they are all located in one direction from the plant (and the wind is assumed to blow constantly in that direction). Thus, for example, if 25,000 individuals were to be found in a population center located in one general direction from the plant and each were to receive a dose of "y" rem if exposed to the radioactive cloud for the entire period of its passage after an accident, the total population dose would be 25,000y. The same overall dose would not be encountered by two groups of 12,500 people living at the same distance but in significantly different directions from the plant. Assuming that, during the entire period of the radioactive cloud . . . , the wind shifted in such a fashion that each of the two groups was exposed to the plume for an interval of time sufficient to give it one-half of the maximum dose, the total population dose would be only 12,500y (i.e. 12,500 × ½y + 12,500 × ½y). In other words, a given number of persons who are congregated in one area are more significant, in terms of the rationale behind the population center distance concept than the same number of persons located at varying distances from the facility, all other things being equal.[46]

The Board subsequently reasoned that since, except for the beach area, it could not find 25,000 people within any one 22½° radial sector out to 2.5 miles from the plant site, it could not find that the combined population of the towns of Hampton, Hampton Falls, and Seabrook constituted a PCD.[47]

It is apparent that the Appeal Board was not entirely comfortable with this result. In a long footnote to the passage quoted above, the majority of the Appeal Board expressed "difficulties" with the lack of guidance in Part 100 and the "imprecision" of the PCD concept for establishing "tolerable" radiation exposure limits to people residing in a PCD. It felt "bound" by the "spirit of the concept" underlying the rule, which it understood to be that "cumulative exposure dose to the population as a whole" be "kept within bounds in the event of a postulated accident."[48]

One could perceive difficulty not only with the future implications of the result reached, but also with the Appeal Board's assumptions concerning the "concept" behind Part 100 that apparently led it to the result. The Appeal Board's reference to "postulated accidents" indicates its understanding that its responsibilities with respect to Part 100 are limited to exploring the consequences of accidents that are considered by the Commission to be probable or, in the terms used by the industry, "credible." Accidents of the "postulated" variety are those for which safety systems are designed, and are lesser in potential magnitude of radiation release than other possible, though less probable ("incredible") accidents, such as a core meltdown. It is clear, however, that the Commission intended no such limitation in connection with the PCD concept, for it said in 1962 that in creating the PCD concept it had in mind "accidents of greater potential hazard than those commonly postulated as representing an upper limit . . ."[49] Furthermore, by analyzing the PCD in terms of maximum doses, requiring designation of an area as the PCD only if it contains 25,000 people who will receive "y" rems, and refusing to designate another area because another 25,000 people will receive only "½y" rems, the Appeal Board substantially lessens the conservatism seemingly apparent in the concept of the PCD. It asks not whether the site presents a low "risk of public exposure," but rather whether anticipated amounts of radiation hypothesized to occur in the event of a postulated accident are acceptable.

The potential consequences for future siting under the Appeal Board's rationale are no less worrisome. They can best be illustrated by example. Figure 10 demonstrates one possible consequence of the

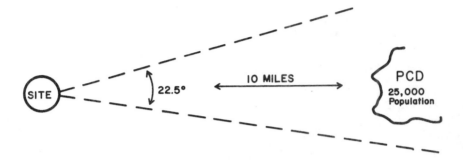

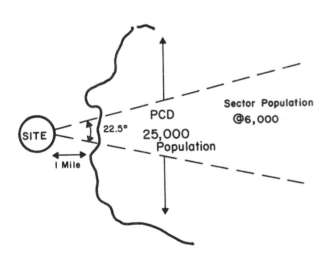

10.   Two diagrams illustrating how, under the Appeal Board's reasoning in the Seabrook case, a "population center" can be made to disappear by moving a site closer to it.

Appeal Board's decision in *Seabrook*. The U-shaped population cluster qualifies as the PCD in Figure 10 (above) because all of the cluster, with a total population of 25,000, lies within the 22½° radial arc when the plant site lies more than ten miles away from it. When the site is moved virtually to its doorstep, however, it ceases to qualify as a PCD. The PCD concept, accordingly, not only fails to discourage siting near large centers, but actually becomes irrelevant the closer one moves the site to a populous area.

To further illustrate this point, and to emphasize the crude nature of the Appeal Board's analysis, I shall apply its methodology to Figures 10 and 11. If we assume that the maximum hypothetical exposure in rems is y, and if we assume constant plume dispersion from the site to the population center, we might get a total population exposure of, say, $25,000 \times \frac{1}{4}y$, or $1/10y$, or some other amount substantially less than y, in the Figure 10 situation. In Figure 11, however, we are likely under similar conditions to get $8,000 \times y$. Merely doing a mathematical division to compare $\frac{25,000}{y}y$ with $8,000y$ (the Appeal Board's methodology) is not only absurd, but dangerous. If y is of genetic significance, but $\frac{1}{4}y$ is not, then quite clearly from the standpoint of population protection, a methodology that permits the $8,000y$ result should be rejected. Yet that is precisely the methodology accepted by the Appeal Board in *Seabrook*. So long as one accepts as basic regulatory premises that (1) the "design basis accident" is the largest nuclear accident that will occur, or (2) that 25 rems (whole body) or 300 rems (thyroid) are acceptable radiation doses for tens of thousands of humans, then the NRC's practice is arguably unobjectionable.

However, Part 100 explicitly disclaims that the "reference doses" 25 and 300 rems are "acceptable," even for the receipt by one individual, and the NRC encourages states to take "protective action" with respect to populations outside the LPZ in the event of a major accident. Moreover, the design basis loss-of-coolant accident is not the largest or most dangerous reactor accident currently expected to occur at a nuclear power plant. The RSS and subsequent NRC pronouncements make it clear that the probability of a "catastrophic" meltdown accident is greater than zero. While the design basis accident does not include a breach of the plant's containment and does not involve a release of more than 15 percent of the fission product inventory in the reactor vessel to the environment,[50] the RSS meltdown accident assumes both occur, and, further, that critical, engineered safeguards will fail. Once we accept these assumptions as a premise for regulatory practice, the NRC's Part 100 standard becomes questionable, and site-related risk assessment becomes imperative.

There is at least some evidence indicating that the NRC staff by 1972 no longer believed that a core meltdown would be an incredible accident. Speaking before a congressional group in 1979, following the Three Mile Island incident, John O'Leary, Deputy Secretary of Energy early in the Carter administration and formerly Director of Regulation at the NRC, made the surprising admission that the NRC staff in 1972–73 had *assumed* that there would be at least one full core meltdown within ten years. O'Leary's statement further erodes the basis of the accident assumptions on which the Appeal Board predicated the Seabrook decision and, for that matter, all other light-water reactor licenses issued by the NRC.

The Appeal Board's reasoning is even less palatable if one looks beyond postulated accidents into the realm of so-called incredible accidents, which I have argued were on the Commission's mind when it created the PCD concept. A core meltdown in the Figure 11 scenario, as at Seabrook, could have catastrophic consequences.

The Appeal Board's resolution of the controversy over the beach area raises additional doubts about the usefulness of the existing reactor-site criteria in providing the kind of conservative protection the Commission's public statements about them lead one to believe they afford.

The beach question dominates a significant portion of the Seabrook hearing record, and the specter of 40,000 bathers within sight of the reactor containment, with no place to hide in the event of an accident at the plant, will haunt the project throughout its existence.

The primary reason the Seabrook intervenors raised the PCD issue was their belief that the Commission's reactor-site criteria provided a mechanism for the disapproval of a site on the basis of risk, and that under the Commission's rules, it was accordingly possible to conclude that a site is too close to too many people to be acceptable. The Seabrook intervenors believed that Seabrook was such a site. Aside from the simple proximity of summer residents to the plant site were the questions of population growth of the surrounding area, and, particularly significant, the fact that the beach itself is relatively isolated from transportation corridors, and transportation in and out is difficult. Under the best of conditions, assuming the nonexistence of panic or other causes of extraordinary human behavior, PSCO's consultants estimated that it would take about eight hours to evacuate the beach area on a typical warm summer day.[51] As noted above (page 51), a New Hampshire state police captain, experienced in crowd control problems at the beach, disagreed that the beach could be so quickly evacuated, and refused to estimate how long it would take.[52] He did go so far as to say, however, that seven hours might not be enough time.[53] Such a site, the intervenors argued, is too risky.

The Licensing Board ignored the beach. The Appeal Board was clearly troubled by it, however, and identified three issues that would have to be resolved before the matter could be decided: (1) the permissibility of "weighting" summer residents and transients according to their length of stay and, by so discounting them, reduce the number of people considered effectively present; (2) the "adequacy and validity" of projections made concerning future population increases in the beach environs;[54] and (3) "the number of sectors (i.e., the size of the angle) which ought to be considered in defining a population center."[55] The first two issues were the subject of a severe difference of opinion between PSCO, the NRC staff, and intervenors at the licensing hearing stage. The third issue results from the Appeal Board's own ruling on NECNP's doughnut PCD theory and has been discussed above (page 63).

The Appeal Board chose not to resolve these issues, and—apparently in order to avoid the "nagging practical questions [of] what account is to be taken of the large number of people on the beach"[56] —the Board ruled that the "flexibility" of Part 100 was sufficient to permit it to treat the beach environs "as though they did constitute a population center,"[57] without actually designating it as such. The logic of the Appeal Board's position in juxtaposition with its rather inflexible use of the regulation in connection with the doughnut theory I leave to the reader.

Having designated the beach area as the pseudo population-center distance, the Appeal Board proceeded to negate the significance even of that act. It explained: "What this means is that the presence of the people on the beach now must be taken into account *in evaluating the adequacy of plant design*" (emphasis added).[58] The Appeal Board did *not* say that the designation of the beach as the PCD required a reevaluation of the reactor site; it merely required a mechanical reduction of the LPZ from a 1.5 to 1.25 mile radius from the reactor, which may or may not require the installation of additional "engineered safeguards" by the applicant in order for it to meet the Part 100 dose criteria for the outer boundary of the new LPZ (25 rem whole body total radiation and 300 rem thyroid iodine). These criteria limit the amount of radiation a person standing on the outer boundary of the LPZ will receive. The Atomic Energy Commission refused, and the NRC still refuses, to call those doses "acceptable."

What the Appeal Board has done is to relegate the siting criteria to the status of a gross determiner of the amount of hardware placed on the reactor to limit theoretical releases in the event of those "postulated" (i.e., "credible") accidents the NRC anticipates. It has eliminated any basis for protecting the public by requiring remote siting. Although the 1962 Statement of Considerations issued by the AEC with respect to Part 100 places careful site selection as the primary protective measure—placing "engineered safeguards" in a secondary role, subject to "further study"—it is plain that these functions are, as of 1977, reversed, although no amendment has ever been issued by the Commission to alter the initial concept. It is also clear that no consideration whatever is being given to "catastrophic" accidents, even though the potential occurrence of such an accident is at least in part behind the development of the PCD concept.

The Appeal Board's ruling allows the location of a reactor at the Seabrook site regardless of the number of people inhabiting the beach area. Whether 25,000 or 2.5 million people are crowded onto the narrow strip of land called Hampton Beach is immaterial because the number of bodies potentially receiving radiation is not a factor in the Appeal Board's equation. The Board said:

> The distance between the LPZ and the leading edge of the densely crowded area will, in essence, serve as a buffer zone; it will insure that the radiation doses the crowds might receive, by present definition not worrisome individually, will also not be of concern on a cumulative basis.[59]

That "buffer," in the Seabrook situation, is four tenths of a mile of flat salt marsh, containing no natural or man-made barriers to the movement of airborne radionuclides. The conclusion that the doses received will not be "worrisome individually" is premised on the Part 100 doses established for the outer boundary of the LPZ by § 100.11 (a)(2) [25 and 300 rems], which are absolute, and do not vary with the population at risk. Neither the Commission[60] nor anyone else, except, possibly nuclear industry spokespeople, consider those doses "acceptable." There is no explanation for, and no rational basis for, the Board's final assertion that the dose will be of no concern cumulatively. A 25 rem whole body dose received by 2.5 million residents theoretically camped just beyond the outer boundary of the LPZ may well be of concern, yet any inquiry is foreclosed by the Appeal Board's analysis.

The Commission's disclaimer stems from the fact that the "referent doses" were imprecisely derived limits for once in a lifetime exposure for nuclear industry workers. What is an acceptable lifetime dose for a nuclear industry worker, who assumes the risk of exposure and is paid well for it, and for an unsuspecting individual who would receive the dose as a whole in seconds seem necessarily to be different. In a British government report on recombinant DNA research we find the following:

> In discussing the hazards of these techniques we have to distinguish between the risk to workers in the laboratory and the risk to the public. Many scientists are engaged in potentially hazardous research (using radioactive materials, or unstable chemicals, or pathogens). They and those who work with them are trained to take precautions; accidents are rare and they do not spread. But if the danger is one which might not be contained within the laboratory, the need for precaution is much greater and the public have a right to seek assurance that they are not at risk.[61]

It might be argued in mitigation of the consequences of the Appeal Board's rule either that the capital cost of the "engineered safeguards" required under the Board's analysis will be sufficiently high to discourage siting the plant at the location, or that measures required by the NRC and state officials for protection of the populace at the PCD may be sufficiently onerous to discourage use of the site. Neither of these arguments is persuasive.

The design limits that the plant must be engineered to meet are based on the doses established for the outer boundary of the LPZ, by section 100.11(a)(1), and those limits are not population-dependent. Hence, the cost of the "engineered safeguards" is dependent only on the distance from the reactor to the LPZ outer boundary (meteorology and release rates are assumed to be at a fixed level under the rule), and is therefore easily predictable. The "engineered safeguards" are required only for the "postulated" accidents. In addition, capital expenditures of the magnitude required for these "engineered safeguards"are not troublesome for electric utilities.

The Evacuation Issue

The Advisory Committee on Reactor Safeguards, an independent body of scientists and engineers established by an act of Congress to advise the NRC, stated in a letter to the Atomic Energy Commission with respect to the Seabrook facility:

> Because of the proximity of the Seabrook station to the beaches on the coast and because of the nature of the road networks serving the beaches, the applicant has given early attention to the problem of evacuation. *The Committee believes, however, that further attention needs to be given to evacuation of residents and transients in the vicinity even though they may be outside the LPZ* [emphasis added] .[62]

Part 100 clearly requires that the number of inhabitants in the LPZ be so low that they can be safely evacuated in the event of an accident.[63] PSCO, however, drew its LPZ so that the outer boundary fell short of the beach area. Intervenors NECNP, the New Hampshire Attorney General, the Commonwealth of Massachusetts, and the NRC staff all argued that the LPZ, in a case like Seabrook, should not be an arbitrary limit to protective action. The NRC staff had, in fact, reversed a position on this point which it had held for many years, apparently somewhat nervous about all of the people sitting on the beach. It argued that both the individual and the cumulative risk of exposure required the development of an evacuation plan for the beach area.[64]

Whether the beach area is susceptible to evacuation rapid enough to ensure a "low risk of public exposure" is a much disputed question of fact. Some of the testimony related to this issue is discussed elsewhere in this book.[65] It is sufficient at this point to suggest that a requirement should be the capability of evacuating significant population clusters lying outside of, but close to, the LPZ, even though in some cases that would be a deterrent to siting a nuclear plant. It would accordingly be a "conservative" addition to the NRC's much-touted "defense in depth" concept. Whether or not Seabrook, or Midland,[66] is such a site is not necessary to argue here, because the NRC's Appeal Board decided in the Seabrook case that under the existing NRC regulations, no such action need or may be considered outside of the LPZ.[67]

In order to reach its conclusion, the Appeal Board's majority was required to adopt an exceedingly narrow and inflexible reading of Part 100. The majority's opinion rests on three major premises:

(1) in a long string of earlier decisions, the Appeal Board had, albeit mechanically, and often in dictum, ruled that no evacuation or other protection was required outside of the LPZ, thus establishing a kind of *stare decisis* binding the Board unless there were "compelling reasons" to change;[68]

(2) to change the "accepted" understanding of Part 100 would subject utility applicants to uncertainties, since they would be unable to forecast "whether the situation obtaining in the area beyond the low population zone (an area which, unlike the LPZ, has no fixed boundaries) might occasion the outright rejection of that site."[69] It would be "unfair," the majority argued, to reverse previous rulings that assured utilities that site suitability was not dependent upon an ability to take protective action with respect to people outside the LPZ; and

(3) since nothing in Part 100 explicitly compels the conclusion sought by the intervenors, and since there is express language mandating evacuation from within the LPZ, Part 100 does not permit the result sought by the intervenors.[70]

More should be said about this last premise. NECNP argued persuasively that section 100.10(b), together with the "flexibility" by which Part 100 was to be applied, provide authority for compelling evacuation beyond the LPZ. Section 100.10(b) requires that "population density, and use characteristics of the site environs, including the exclusion area, low population zone, and population center distance" be taken into consideration in determining the acceptability of a site. NECNP pointed to the word "including" and urged that the rule was clearly not straight-jacketed into a rigid formula limited to the exclusion area, LPZ and PCD, but rather must be read to accommodate the dynamic realities of population clustering. The Appeal Board majority never mentioned the "flexibility" explicitly required by the Commission in §100.1(b) as an integral part of the regulation, but stated that if the Commission had intended to consider people outside of the LPZ, "it would have said so expressly."[71] Since Part 100 is silent, the majority ruled, no such protection is available.

This ruling is inconsistent with the Appeal Board's reasoning on the PCD issue. There the Appeal Board, less than three months later, ruled that it could treat the beach *as if* it were the PCD without designating it as such because, inter alia, "significantly, in referring to the need to consider population density and use characteristics of the site environs, the Part tells us to include—but does not say to limit ourselves to—an evaluation of the exclusion area, low population zone, and population center distance."[72]

The Appeal Board had become a prisoner of its own past decisions, perhaps trapped by the imprecision of an inartfully devised regulation perpetuated beyond its time by a series of commissions too busy worrying about critics of its policies to reshape them to the needs of the mushrooming reactor program. The concurring opinion by Appeal Board member Farrar, which reads more like a dissent to the evacuation decision, is revealing:

> . . . there is much to be said for the view, pressed upon us here, that consideration need be given to the feasibility of protecting people located outside (as well as inside) a reactor's low population zone from radiation hazards in the event of a serious accident. . . .
>
> . . . we are being told, at least implicitly, that we may no longer take comfort in the thought that those outside the LPZ, whatever their circumstances, will be 'safe' from exposure to dangerous levels of ionizing radiation even if they take no steps to protect themselves. This was the linchpin of all our prior holdings; without it, we would have been unable to say that no concern need be expressed over those outside the LPZ. Now we are asked to consider whether the doses they might receive, even if less than the Part 100 guidelines, are sufficiently undesirable to require a showing that protective measures, such as evacuation, can be taken outside the LPZ.
>
> I emphasize that this matter cannot be taken lightly. . . .
>
> . . . we may have been too mechanical in the past in applying Part 100—we treated it rigidly, as though it necessarily furnished the last word for emergency planning. But my colleagues quite rightly point out that our decisions are on the books, that if followed they call unequivocally for rejection of the staff's position, . . . Beyond that, I perceive other difficulties with the staff's position.

These difficulties stem from an inability to discern the precise nature of the safety concerns which are motivating the staff here. Although Mr. Salzman's opinion carefully marshals the portions of the staff's oral argument which suggest that its underlying substantive position is that radiation doses below the Part 100 guideline levels should be avoided (see p. 748. *supra*), at one other point staff counsel appeared to reject any such suggestion. App. Bd. Tr. 112. And in its *Seabrook* papers, the staff appears to have studiously avoided taking a direct position on this point. Rather, it approached the problem obliquely, as exemplified by the following statements of its position: (1) there is a need to consider emergency planning outside the LPZ because the State might find it prudent to call for evacuation there; (2) there ought to be steps taken "to limit . . . on a timely basis" doses outside the LPZ (with no indication of the degree of hazard or the dose levels to be avoided); and (3) those outside the LPZ "might be endangered" by a nuclear accident.

My point is this—if the staff's experts believe there is a significant problem associated with accidental radiation doses at levels below those specified in Part 100, this should be said explicitly, so that the matter can be dealt with squarely, either in rule-making or in every adjudication. Instead, the staff has been vague. It has said throughout the *Seabrook* proceeding that the "facts of each case" will determine whether there is a need to be concerned about emergency protective measures outside the LPZ. Yet it has been unable to inform us with any precision as to what type of facts are to be deemed significant in making this determination. This is not surprising, for until one comes to grips with the questions of what dosage ought to be avoided, it is impossible to decide whether people in a particular area must be protected in some manner in a postaccident emergency. In this connection, it seems to me—and in this I believe I speak for my colleagues as well—that the same rule must apply in every case. Thus, for example, if whole body doses of 20 rem should be avoided, logic and consistency would require that in every case a board would have to determine that steps can be taken to protect individuals outside the LPZ from that dose—whether they be few or many, daytime bathers or nighttime dwellers. To be sure, the fewer the people and the better their shelter or the easier their access to a means of escape, the more readily might a board determine that adequate protective measures could be taken. But the inquiry would nonetheless have to be made in each case.

The Commission declined to review either the site suitability or the evacuation decisions of the Appeal Board. Thus the Appeal Board decisions stand as the prevailing policy of the Commission. They establish a policy that fails to discourage the siting of power reactors near large concentrations of people. It is a policy that favors technical solutions over cautious siting. It is a policy that permits the utility to establish the LPZ mechanically as a function of plant engineering, and requires no special protective action to be taken with respect to populations, no matter how large, nor how close residing outside of that LPZ. The NRC staff and the Appeal Board have, over the years, it seems, provided the refinements to Part 100 that the AEC as of 1962 refused to make without further study based on operating experience, and they have done so without the broad public exposure and comment that must accompany a formal change to the regulation. It has been a process of erosion of the conservatism, the ultimate level in the "defense in depth" concept, upon which the AEC sold the reactor program to the public.

The gap between the public image cultivated by the regulator of nuclear power and its actual practice is widening. If the economics of the energy industry continue to pressure for siting larger nuclear generating units closer and closer to the population clusters they serve, the absolute consequences in human risk growing out of the Seabrook site-related decisions will grow greater and greater. Especially in light of that fact, the processes of government would, it seems, be best served by either a modification of the existing criteria to a level of greater conservatism, or an honest acknowledgment by the Nuclear Regulatory Commission that, in fact, things are not what we have been led to believe them to be.

Indeed, the Three Mile Island accident may spell the end of the NRC's practice of not requiring evacuation plans for areas outside the LPZ. The TMI accident resulted in the release of large amounts of radiation that was carried well beyond that plant's LPZ. Evacuation of the City of Harrisburg, Pennsylvania, was considered but not carried out, and the congressional and public reaction when it became known that the NRC had not required Pennsylvania to develop such a plan was severely critical of the NRC.

Approaches to Change

Judging the acceptability of risk is not an activity that can be undertaken solely as a matter of scientific study. It is, in part (some would say in great part) a "normative, political activity,"[73] which must be carried out in an appropriate political forum. The choice of an appropriate forum is an issue of fundamental importance, complicated by the problem of how to present the issue fairly, clearly, and accurately to the decision-maker(s), and by the knowledge that it is a choice that is of necessity made as much by emotion as by reason.

The pool of candidate risk-assessors includes a range of decision-makers from the residents in the immediate vicinity of a proposed power plant, right up to state legislatures and the Congress. Who decides the issue will determine both the importance of competing types of information, and the standard by which acceptability is judged. For example, local decision-making would be likely to involve a purer evaluation, because local residents would tend to perceive the risk as more real, and would be less likely than a wider constituency to dilute or cloud its perception of the risk with notions of risk-benefit trade-off. Yet the transiency of many present-day local populations raises questions of "Who is deciding the fate of whom?"

Voters as Risk-Assessors

The fate of the 1976 California and Ohio citizen initiatives illustrates some of the difficulties one encounters when presenting as complex an issue as nuclear risk to the voting populace. The assessor must be given a clear, unbiased, and sophisticated understanding of the nature of the risk. Only then can the emotional responses that make up popular decisions be considered to be valid, so that the public can "define and debate the issues with sophistication."[74]

What is required are (1) an impartial presentation of the facts by the scientific community and (2) assurance that neither of the opposing advocacy viewpoints has at its command greater financial or other resources (and hence greater voter access) than the other. Neither of these conditions has existed in any recent citizen initiative. It is not clear that an initiative law restricting the opposing sides to equal expenditures would withstand a constitutional attack premised on the first amendment; hence the second of these requirements is of doubtful attainability.[75]

Moreover, as the debate over the conclusions of the Rasmussen Report demonstrates, definition of the problem is at present arguably impossible, at least in terms that do not require personal judgment about unknowns. Thus an impartial presentation of the issue is probably out of the question. Finally, even if the issue could be presented impartially, it is doubtful that it could be presented in so straightforward a way that the voter could make an intelligent decision based on the information presented. Abstract, statistical analyses such as "X persons will get cancer who otherwise would not," or "there would be a Y percent chance of an accident, which would result in A cancers and B birth defects" are of little use to the voter who must try to fit the issue into his or her own existential framework.

The nature of our electoral system limits us to presenting relatively simple "either/or" propositions to the electorate. Since risk measurements such as that attempted by the RSS are complex, and involve many assumptions and qualifications, formulating the data into a manageable unit for a popular vote would be a formidable task.

Finally, any judgment about the acceptability of a given risk to the public involves, ideally, a difficult assessment of the consequences of not accepting the risk. In the public debate that has been going on in the United States for some time, this issue has been treated crudely. The utility industry constructs simplistic doomsday models in its rhetoric, telling the public that without this or that nuclear plant all will freeze in the winter or sizzle in the summer; that the issue, stated most simply is nuclear plants or nothing. The opposition, on the other hand, lauds the merits of solar and wind technologies that may be years away from large-scale implementation.

Legislatures as Risk-Assessors

Congress has in the past wrestled with risk assessment. The Food and Drug Act, for example, contains within it food additive standards premised on a very stringent conception of risk acceptability.[76] It might even be argued that the present nuclear program, embodied in the Atomic Energy Act, represents a form of general risk assessment undertaken by Congress for the society at large, although one would have to term it assessment-by-default, since there is no evidence that the Joint Committee on Atomic Energy ever tried to grapple with the problem with any degree of sophistication.[77]

Legislative decision-making is often premised on personal influence, "horse trading" by powerful legislatures, and other considerations unrelated to the issues at hand. State legislatures sometimes suffer from a lack of professional staff personnel, and, particularly in smaller states, the mechanisms available for communicating information to members is often inadequate for a full exploration of complex technical issues.

The Standard of Acceptability

The methodology by which standards of acceptability are established will be determined in part by who evaluates the risk.

It is impossible to construct an empirical standard for use in a public referendum, since the voter's perception of the risk will in all cases necessarily be a subjective one. It makes no difference to the voter if his vote is to decide that the risk is reasonable or that the number of postulated deaths is insignificant. The voters will react to what is perceived by them to be the risk to them, and they will decide if they wish to accept the risk not on the basis of abstract notions of acceptability but emotionally.

If, however, the acceptability of risk is decided in a legislative forum, the decision-making process will involve the selection of a standard or guide. This could take one of two forms—the establishment of rigid acceptability criteria, based on the acceptable level of risk, or the development of more general standards to be applied by a regulatory agency like the NRC to specific sites. One example of the former approach was a proposed regulatory guide, developed by the NRC staff in 1972, which would have discouraged the siting of nuclear plants in areas having a population density in excess of 500 people per square mile over any radial distance up to 30 miles.[78]

Adoption of any such standard or guide requires the use of yet another standard—one that will permit the legislative body to determine for itself what level of risk is acceptable. Lowrence, in his study on risk, identified the following guides to acceptability: reasonableness, custom, prevailing professional practice, best available control, highest practicable protection or lowest practicable exposure, degree of necessity or benefit, zero risk, no detectable adverse effect, toxicologically insignificant levels, and the threshold principle. Any of these standards, except for those involving custom and professional practice, are available to legislative risk-assessors. Each will produce a different level of acceptable risk.

Reasonableness is a nonstandard and usually results in a risk-benefit approach to decision-making, as do "highest practicable" and "lowest practicable" standards. The danger of such approaches is that, in a case like a nuclear power plant where the benefits are concrete and easily quantified and the risks theoretical and in the future, a risk-benefit comparison is methodologically unworkable.

Zero risk or "insignificant level" standards would in all probability compel the elimination of all sites except for a few very remote ones, destroying the nuclear industry. We are left, therefore, with the threshold standard—asking the legislators in essence to tell us how many hypothetical deaths are acceptable.

The threshold standard can be applied, however, in more than one way. The most simple method of its application is the approach suggested by the NRC staff in its draft regulatory guide. However, it is possible that a threshold-type analysis can be combined with market economics to provide for a combined legislative-ratepayer risk acceptance scenario. In many cases the affected citizenry will also be utility rate-payers. If we are able to internalize the costs of risk, it is theoretically possible to have the rate-payers decide whether it is worth the commodity. The Congress, or state legislatures, could establish very conservative site criteria (almost zero-risk criteria) but permit utilities to place nuclear plants on higher-risk sites, provided that they establish a monetary fund for the payment of the damages that would be anticipated to result from the largest conceivable accident at the chosen site, and to include the costs of the fund in the rate base for the facility.

Unfortunately, for such a scheme to work one would have to devise a system whereby rate-payers as a voting bloc rather than state public utilities commissions approved rate increases. Another difficulty presented by it is the calculation of the costs of an accident, although such an activity is probably not any more impossible than revising the RSS to meet the criticisms that have been made of it. The advantage of such an approach is that it would eliminate the necessity for a legislative decision as to how many people it is acceptable to kill, while providing for the internalization of the true costs of risk.

Conclusion

The risk assessment calculus becomes exceedingly complex once it is brought down to the level of a specific project. Should the previous safety record of the plant's owner get factored into the risk equation? Such a consideration was not relevant to early plant sitings, since the industry as a whole had no record of experience against which to measure individual performance. Such experience is, however, now becoming available. A 1978 NRC study, for example, rated 51 operating nuclear plants for safety performance in 1975.[79] Should risk be calculated "conservatively," based on an assumption that the new plant's safety record will be equivalent to the industry's worst, regardless of the owner's own history?

Having examined the various methods of formal risk assessment, I am not confident that the risk posed by an individual nuclear power plant can ever be accounted for in a sufficiently rational manner to permit it to be factored into a logically constructed site-suitability equation. At the same time, I am convinced that it must somehow be accounted for, and that the present NRC site-suitability criteria are inadequate as they have been applied.

In view of the difficulties inherent in any sort of complex, site-specific risk assessment, the "remote location" concept that originally formed the basis of Part 100 should be reconsidered by the NRC. Its principal virtues are its simplicity of application and its ability to reduce substantially the significance of public safety in individual plant licensing decisions. There will always be concerns about catastrophic accidents, but the emotional significance of such accidents may be greatly diluted if the places at which they might occur are isolated from large clusters of human population.

The NRC must rethink its site-suitability criteria. Since remote siting avoids the need for complex, site-related risk assessment, which must in my view otherwise occur, it appears to be the only way out of the public risk dilemma, short of termination of the entire nuclear power program.[80]

4
The Licensing Procedure: How It Works

For a complete understanding of the material in Chapters 5 and 6, a preview of NRC licensing procedures is necessary. Moreover, the procedures have themselves become the subject of controversy, and a comprehension of the major issues that have arisen between the NRC, prospective licensees, and intervenors will be helpful for an evaluation of the nature and validity of attempts at reform of nuclear licensing.

Structure of the NRC

As a consequence of Congress' 1975 reorganization of the AEC,[1] its regulatory functions, along with those of its personnel responsible for them, were transferred to the NRC.[2] The promotional activities, with research and development employees, were transferred to the Energy Research and Development Administration (ERDA), which in 1977 became a division of the newly created Department of Energy (DOE).

Along with its regulatory employees, the NRC inherited the AEC's regulations, policies, practices, cases, and institutions. Indeed, the change occurred without interruption of ongoing licensing cases. The only thing that changed was the name of the agency typed at the top of all papers filed in licensing cases by the lawyers in them. While in the long run the policies and attitudes of the new agency may become different from those of its predecessor, it has been, in the short run, business as usual.

The NRC is headed by five commissioners who are appointed by the President and confirmed by the Senate. They are responsible for the agency's policies, which are most visibly reflected in its regulations, and they also act as a final appeal tribunal in the agency's quasi-judicial role.

The NRC, like most federal regulatory agencies, has, in fact, quasi-legislative, quasi-judicial, and purely executive functions. The quasi-legislative function, rule-making, is carried out by the commissioners with the assistance of the general counsel who advises them, and the staff under the Director of Regulation, which proposes regulations to the commissioners and provides technical assistance. The quasi-judicial function, deciding whether to issue a construction permit or an operating license, is carried out primarily by atomic safety and licensing boards and the atomic safety and licensing appeal boards, to which decision-making authority is delegated by the commissioners, with the commissioners acting as a final appellate body. Finally, the executive function, enforcement of the NRC's rules, is the principal activity of the regulatory staff under the Director of Regulation. There are, of course, overlaps; often the same individuals are involved in multiple functions. Thus, for example, lawyers on the executive legal director's staff are involved both in legislative and executive activities as well as being participants in adjudicatory licensing hearings.

Utilities must obtain a construction permit from the NRC prior to building a nuclear power plant and an operating license before the plant can be operated.[3] The two proceedings are separated by the number of years it takes the utility to build the plant, and the construction permit proceedings are more complex. They are also more important from the standpoint of their usefulness as a forum for resolving critical issues related to the plant's safety, its site, and its environmental impact.

The construction permit is the principal regulatory mechanism the NRC uses to address the matters it is required to consider under the Atomic Energy Act and National Environmental Policy Act (NEPA). Its basic statutory concerns are public health and safety,[4] the technical and financial qualifications of the applicant,[5] environmental impact assessment, and the balancing of costs and benefits under NEPA.[6]

The NRC is subject to the Federal Administrative Procedure Act (APA); and since its construction permits fall within the class of actions the APA calls "initial licensing," the agency is required to hold adjudicatory (i.e., formal, trial-type) hearings and its decision must be based on a record developed in those hearings. The Atomic Safety and Licensing Boards (ASLB's) are the key element of the NRC's formal licensing structure. They are three-member panels, chaired by a lawyer who acts as an administrative law judge. The other two members are ordinarily scientists or engineers, at least one of whom has a background in the nuclear energy or nuclear physics field. In theory, ASLB's should provide a mixture of objective legal and technical expertise sufficient for a thorough evaluation of the various questions arising in a nuclear licensing proceeding. Whether they function in such a manner is a matter of debate, discussed later in this chapter.

The AEC developed, and the NRC adopted, an elaborate process to carry out its APA-mandated initial licensing responsibilities. Figure 11, derived from an NRC report on intervenor funding,[7] is a schematic representation of that process. The time periods set forth in Figure 11 are not realistic in all respects, however, and should be viewed with that fact in mind. Contested hearings since 1970, for example, have seldom lasted as short a time as two months, and pre-hearing procedures have normally consumed less time than the fifteen months shown by the NRC in Figure 11. It does, nevertheless, demonstrate the process effectively from beginning to end.

Preapplication Review: The Critical First Year

At least one year before tendering its construction permit application, the hopeful utility and the NRC's regulatory staff initiate a formal series of discussions, and the utility provides the staff with detailed information about its project.

The staff evaluates the site, undertakes a technical safety-oriented review, and assesses the environmental impacts and environmental data. At the end of this review period the staff either accepts or rejects the construction permit application. If it is accepted, the application is docketed, public notice is issued, and the adjudicatory procedure commences.

It is during the preapplication review that the regulatory staff makes up its mind about the project. The staff reviews virtually all of the issues that will ultimately be placed before an Atomic Safety and Licensing Board in the adjudicatory hearing. After the application has been docketed, the staff becomes a mandatory party to the adjudicatory proceedings, represented in the hearing room by its lawyers and their witnesses, who urge the staff's position on the Licensing Board alongside lawyers for the applicant and the opposing intervenors.

The preapplication review is not a public proceeding. No public notice is issued informing the public of the filing of preapplication papers. The meetings are usually held in Washington, D.C., and are not open to the public. Since no notice is given, there is opportunity neither for intervenor groups to form, nor for their participation in this first third of the licensing process. The staff's position is accordingly fixed solely as a result of private, *ex parte* meetings with the applicant. During these meetings personal acquaintances and alliances of a sort may be formed, and by the end of the preapplication period, dealings between the staff and the utility generally take on a commonality of purpose—making sure the record is sufficient to support licensing of the plant as proposed by the utility.

The NRC staff and the applicant may, after the application is accepted, retain different opinions about specific issues that are not critical to the staff's determination that the application is acceptable. However, acceptance by the staff stamps the project with its seal of approval, and that means, at least with respect to all parameters the staff feels are significant, that the applicant has met its burden of proof. Having accepted the project, the NRC staff is prepared to defend it.

The actual impact of the staff's acquiescence in a project before it is formally placed before the NRC for licensing is difficult to assess. Several generalizations can be made, however:

1. Staff entrenchment in a position of support for the proposal prior to the time it comes before the Atomic Safety and Licensing Board for hearing and decision may result in a subtle shifting of the burden of proof at that point from the applicant, who is supposed to have it, to the intervenors, who are not. The licensing board knows that another arm of its parent agency has approved the project it is now being asked to approve. Instead of entering its judicial role with the attitude that "the applicant must tell us what is right about this project," the licensing board might have the tendency to ask of the intervenors, "What is wrong with it?" or "Show us why the staff was wrong."

2. The staff, under the NRC's rules, is responsible for producing the draft and the final environmental impact statement required by NEPA.[8] The staff begins working on this document in earnest only *after* it has decided to accept the application for docketing. Accordingly, its task becomes one of producing an EIS with respect to a

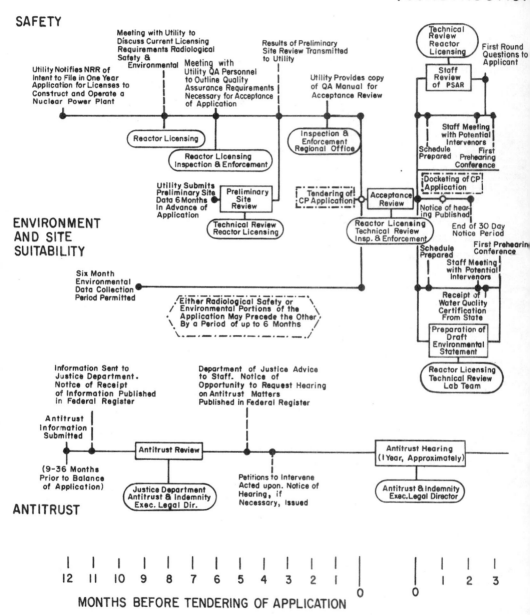

NUCLEAR POWER PLANT
(CONSTRUCTION

11. Diagram of the entire NRC Construction permit process, as of 1976.
Source: Boasberg, et al., Report to the NRC on Nuclear Intervenor Funding, US NRC (Official Document).

LICENSING PROCESS
PERMIT)

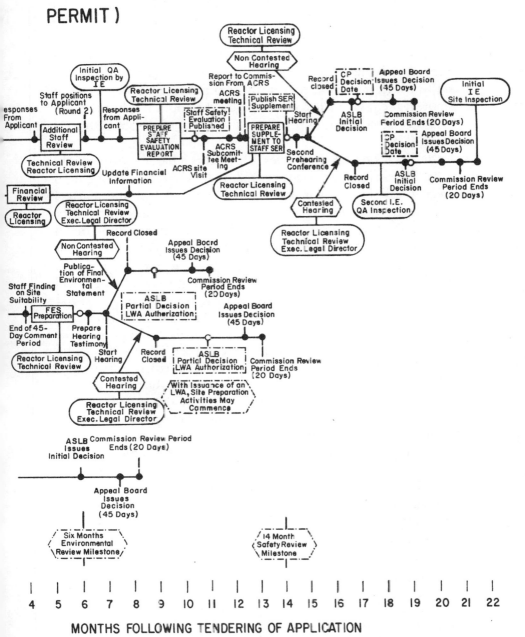

MONTHS FOLLOWING TENDERING OF APPLICATION

project it has already agreed is sound. The staff's ability to produce a sufficiently unbiased environmental assessment under such circumstances is clearly questionable. The staff is more likely to use the EIS procedure in such a way that the documents will be structured to justify the already made decision rather than as a means of reaching a decision to which it was not previously committed. Not only must an intervenor challenge evidence produced by the applicant, but the EIS must also be discredited (along with staff witnesses brought to testify in support of it).

3. Under Part 2 of the NRC rules, the staff is a party to the adjudicatory hearing before the licensing board. As such, it has a right to produce witnesses to testify on disputed issues of fact and matters requiring expert opinion, and to cross-examine witnesses who testify on behalf of all other parties. The normal order of presentation on all contested issues in the hearing is applicant-intervenors-staff. On most of those issues, and indeed all of them that are important to the fundamental viability of the project, the applicant and the staff will be in agreement. The order of going forward, accordingly, is at variance with that which prevails in court hearings in the American judicial system. In a trial before a judge or jury, all of the proponents of a point of view that carries with it the burden of proof must go forward first. Opponents are in the nature of rebuttors, and any further evidence produced by the proponents is strictly circumscribed —it is limited essentially to new subjects raised by the opponents.

In the NRC licensing hearings, however, the opponents (intervenors) are sandwiched between the proponents. The staff can, and often does, produce witnesses both to support the applicant's witnesses and to dispute the testimony of intervenor witnesses. The applicant thus gets two cracks at persuading the licensing board, and the intervenors find themselves in a lengthy, costly process in which their point of view is often buried in an avalanche of applicant and government-paid witnesses and lawyers.

Prehearing Procedures

In most cases the first notice received by potential intervenors that a nuclear plant is being proposed is the notice of the licensing proceeding published by the NRC after the application has been formally tendered and placed on the NRC's docket.[9] The hearing notice tells the public the name of the applicant, provides a general description of the projects, and invites interested parties to intervene, providing a deadline for filing petitions for intervention and the address to which petitions must be sent. The notice will also give a prospective intervenor his first taste of the cost of an intervention, for it requires that twenty copies of the petition be filed with the NRC in addition to the copies normally sent to other parties (at this point usually only the applicant and the staff).

Part 2 of the NRC regulations spells out the procedural requirements that are binding on all parties to the hearing process, including the staff. It establishes a rigid timetable, which commences with the issuance of the public notice and can be varied only by the Licensing Board, which assumes exclusive jurisdiction over the application once it has been docketed.[10]

The applicant is required by the NRC to file most of its supporting documents with its application, and, not atypically, one set of these documents will require a small truck to transport them to their destination. A set is placed in the NRC's public document room in Washington, D.C., and another is placed in a public location, such as a library, close to the site of the proposed nuclear plant. An individual or a group contemplating filing a petition to intervene must travel to one or the other of these places in order to examine the particulars of the proposal. The required filings by the applicant include (1) License Application, (2) Environmental Report (ER), (3) Preliminary Safety Analysis Report (PSAR) and (4) Reference Safety Analysis Report.[11]

Intervenors must review these documents and prepare formal intervention pleadings within sixty days of receipt of the notice. Aside from satisfying the usual requirement of requisite "interest," an intervenor must make at least one "valid contention"—that the proposed facility does not meet an environmental or safety criterion—backed up by a sworn affidavit in support of it.[12]

After the licensing board rules who is in and who out of the proceedings, discovery proceedings begin. "Discovery" is the method by which each party to an adjudicatory proceeding (or a trial in a court of law) is entitled to learn facts that are in the possession of other parties prior to the commencement of the actual hearings. The theory behind its use in adversary proceedings is to enable a free exchange of unprivileged information to provide either a basis to resolve disputes before trial or to make for a more orderly and speedy trial. In NRC cases this usually takes the form of each party serving written interrogatories on the others. Settlement of disputed issues has not been a normal product of discovery proceedings before the NRC. In the Seabrook case, several hundred pages of interrogatories and responses appear to have been put to little productive use.

The NRC staff drafts its environmental impact statement (EIS) and the Safety Evaluation Report (SER) during the prehearing period, and the beginning of the hearings is dependent on the timing of the final EIS, which must contain and evaluate the comments of the parties (and anyone else) submitted in response to the draft of the document. The EIS is totally a staff document, and because the staff has previously made up its mind about the project, it reflects that bias. It is also the natural starting point for the development of issues adjudicated in the hearings.

Characteristically, intervenors have attempted in nuclear licensing cases to discredit portions of the EIS with which they disagree. The applicant and staff attempt to reinforce its conclusions, and sometimes an applicant will produce testimony to challenge an EIS conclusion it considers damaging to its case. However the matter is approached, the EIS determines the course of the environmental segment of the hearings. It is a critical decision-making document, an important piece of evidence before the licensing board, and is accorded great weight by the board.

The staff SER serves a similar, though less significant, function with respect to the health and safety issues arising under the Atomic Energy Act. It is produced by a different group of NRC staff personnel than those who are responsible for the EIS, and the extent of the interaction between these two groups is unclear.

Prehearing conferences, (informal meetings between the licensing board and the parties) occur at least twice before the commencement of NRC licensing hearings. The first of these involves the admission of parties to the proceedings and sets a schedule for discovery. Several subsequent conferences may be convened to take up motions and other pleadings filed in connection with discovery proceedings. The final prehearing conference results in an order which (1) determines what issues are contested, hence which ones must be covered in the hearing, and (2) establishes a hearing schedule, including deadlines for filing testimony.

Issue formulation is generally an undisciplined affair. Though the NRC's rules technically require an intervenor to make out an offer of proof as to each issue the intervenor proposes, the offer need not be much more than a good faith statement of belief that there is indeed an issue. As a result, the final prehearing conference is not at all like a pretrial conference in the federal courts, which often results in forced settlements of a lawsuit whose weakness becomes apparent during discovery proceedings. Here many issues are permitted to go to the hearing room.

Although a more rigorous prehearing process might in some cases work to the detriment of underfinanced intervenors, it could also work to the advantage both of the system and some intervenors by narrowing the scope of the hearing to a few important issues. A well litigated case involving a few issues would make for a more ordered decision than a case poorly litigated because the intervenor was spread too thin, trying to cope with many issues. From the applicant's standpoint it seems to make no significant difference. It is not a hardship for an applicant to address many issues, and the hearing process does not seem to be lengthened appreciably by the present state of affairs. The quality of the administrative record does suffer, however, and concern for that fact should be shared both by applicants and by intervenors.

The Hearings

Under the NRC's rules all testimony must be filed, in written form, prior to the commencement of the hearings.[13] Ordinarily, much of the pre-filed testimony is of multiple authorship, and the hearings consist in large measure of panels of applicant witnesses being cross-examined by intervenor lawyers. The length of the hearings, in terms of the number of actual hearing days consumed, is determined, by and large, by the extent of intervenor cross-examination. The elapsed time from the beginning of the hearings until the issuance of an initial decision is, however, primarily a function of the general workload and of scheduling problems confronting the licensing board, which may be juggling three or four proceedings at once.

The efficiency of the chairman of the licensing board (that is, his ability to write an initial decision speedily) is also an important determiner of the length of hearings. In the Seabrook case, for example, it took the licensing board nearly six months to issue an initial decision, which then consisted of little more than a rewriting of the applicant's requests for findings of fact and rulings of law, supplemented by a short explanatory addendum. The document could have been written in a few days.

The utility industry has vociferously contended that the adjudicatory hearing process causes needless delays in the issuance of licenses.[14] They urge that the NRC streamline its proceedings and replace the hearings with less formal, rule-making-type hearings, and argue that the intervenors produce no useful evidence, simply serving to delay and confuse the process. Delay is, however, not necessarily a negative thing. As the NRC's Appeal Board has stated:

> In short, delay . . . attributable to an intervenor's ability to present to a licensing board legitimate contentions based on serious . . . problems . . . would establish not that the licensing system is being frustrated, but that it is working properly.[15]

The Seabrook proceeding is a useful example upon which to base an exploration of the delay issue. On the surface, the entire licensing proceeding appears unbelievably long. It began in 1973 and six years later was not complete (as of May 1979). (See below, Appendix II, page 178.) It is also true that if Seabrook had not been so hotly contested by intervenors, it would not have gone on for so long.

Much of the time spent in the course of the Seabrook case resulted, however, not from intervenor efforts but from inefficiencies in the NRC's way of doing business. The staff of the NRC, for example, was often late in filing documents and asked for numerous extensions of time. Moreover, the ASLB assigned to Seabrook scheduled and conducted the proceedings and moved them forward at a relaxed pace. This may in part have been caused by the individual desires of the members, but two characteristics of NRC licensing hearings appear to be the primary reason why, in *Seabrook*, the hearings before the ASLB, which consumed fewer than thirty total hearing days, lasted a year and a half. Similarly, much time was consumed by the Appeal Board in its deliberations.

The first characteristic is that the evidentiary portion of the licensing hearings is not conducted in one block, as would be the case in a court of law, but is generally fragmented, primarily because the licensing board members and NRC staff lawyers skip around the country from proceeding to proceeding, holding three or four days of sessions in one case, then going to another for a week, and so forth. This hopscotch is unnecessary. A licensing board could schedule one case and sit on it until it is completed before moving on to another. If the Seabrook board had chosen to do so, the hearings would have been completed before the end of 1975—in fact by mid-August of that year—instead of spring 1976.

As for the second characteristic, nearly twelve months were consumed in the Seabrook case while the parties waited for Licensing Board and Appeal Board decisions. The Licensing Board had an essentially complete record by late November 1975. It failed to produce an Initial Decision until June 1976, and the decision it issued was little more than a recitation of requests for findings of fact and rulings of law submitted by PSCO's lawyers five months earlier. The Appeal Board heard oral argument on all of the appeals from the Licensing Board's decision in December of 1976. It did not issue a decision on a majority of issues until August of 1977. As with the Licensing Board, there appears to be no reason for such a delay. Unlike an appellate court, which is burdened with many more cases and a multitude of different legal issues, the Appeal Board's mandate is narrow, and the subject matter and legal issues are familiar to it.

The Seabrook case did not involve frivolous issues. There is no evidence that the intervenors sought delay for delay's sake. Hence it cannot be said, at least about Seabrook, that the time consumed (except as noted above) was wasted time. Of more importance, I think, is the question whether the NRC's elaborate procedures produce *good* decisions. Other chapters of this book address this point in greater detail, but it is appropriate to observe here that the NRC's Appeal Board acknowledged that the actual decision produced by the ASLB in *Seabrook* was shoddy. Moreover, the quality of the day-to-day evidentiary rulings made by the ASLB in the hearings was poor. These deficiencies are not unique to the NRC, however, and cannot be blamed on the adjudicatory nature of the hearings. They stem from the quality of the decision-makers. That the transcript is longer than it need be, and contains much pointless cross-examination is, however, a fault that is attributable to the NRC's procedures.

During the hearings, procedural and evidentiary rulings are made by the board chairman, whose judicial temperament (or lack thereof) will color the proceedings. Rulings on the propriety of lawyers' questions or the admissibility of a witness's opinion can make for a sound, neat record or a sloppy one. Since in administrative proceedings the strict rules of evidence and other trial procedures do not apply,[16] there is a tendency toward a verbose record full of non-relevant material. In such a circumstance, licensing boards should take great pains to structure the record to keep it manageable. They seldom do so, and NRC hearing records are generally complex and difficult.

Intervenors in NRC construction permit proceedings, moreover, have also added to the length of the record by the way they have traditionally approached the hearings. Normally lacking sufficient resources to hire expert witnesses, whose function would include both giving testimony and separating the real issues from spurious ones, intervenors have attempted to develop a case by cross-examining utility and NRC staff experts. As a result, many pages of transcript are filled with useless questions and answers, bespeaking failed attempts by intervenor lawyers to uncover flaws in the testimony of uncooperative witnesses.[17] The Seabrook case contained more intervenor witnesses than most NRC proceedings, and the transcript still contains hundreds of pages of cross-examination excursions to nowhere.

Post-Hearing Proceedings

Once the licensing board has written an initial decision favorable to an applicant, the staff automatically issues a license that authorizes the beginning of construction, permitting the expenditure of large amounts of capital. This occurs—notwithstanding the fact that opponents have a right to appeal all or parts of the initial decision to the NRC's appeal board—because of the NRC's so-called "immediate effectiveness rule."[18] In order to halt construction, an intervenor must apply to the appeal board for an order staying the effectiveness of the initial decision. The NRC's standard for issuing a stay is difficult to meet.[19]

The one-two punch of the "immediate effectiveness" rule and the stay standard caused the U. S. Court of Appeals for the First Circuit to remark in connection with a *Seabrook*[20] issue:

We are unable to identify any other field of publicly regulated private activity where momentous decisions to commit funds are made on the strength of preliminary decisions by several agencies which are open to reevaluation and redetermination . . . [T]he risk of public agencies and courts accepting less desirable and limited options or, worse, countenancing a *fait accompli* are foreboding.[21]

Historically, the NRC has issued stays on intervenor requests in only a few instances, and then only under the most compelling of circumstances. In the case of the Seabrook dispute, the applicant had spent more than $350,000,000 on construction before all of the issues on appeal had been decided.[22] The likelihood that the appellate arms of the NRC would reverse the issuance of a license in the face of expenditures of such magnitude is slim, regardless of how compelling the intervenor's argument may be.

The NRC delegates authority to hear appeals to the Appeal Board. Unlike an ordinary appellate tribunal, however, the NRC's rules give the Appeal Board powers to rewrite ASLB decisions, filling in gaps upon a fresh analysis of the record. It is even permitted to hold hearings and take evidence to fill in gaps in the record revealed during the course of an appeal. One consequence of the Appeal Board's wide-ranging authority is that a litigant, after trying the case to an ASLB, identifying probable error and appealing the issue, can find itself faced with a new rationale supporting the decision, advanced for the first time by the Appeal Board.

The Appeal Board, in the Seabrook case, did not act swiftly to dispose of the issues presented to it by the parties. It established leisurely briefing schedules, and rendered decisions on a piecemeal basis, lengthening the administrative post-hearing process to well over a year, during most of which construction at the controversial site went on apace under the authority of the ASLB-authorized license that was the subject of the appeal.

The NRC's procedures need reexamination. The NRC staff should not have responsibility for initial site screening and preparation of the EIS and safety analysis documents, while at the same time acting as a party in the adjudicatory hearings before an NRC licensing board. Since it is unlikely that the agency could function if the staff were removed form the first two responsibilities, it should be removed from the hearings. The licensing applicant and intervening interest groups can adequately frame issues around competing concerns without the staff in a contested proceeding.

The rationale behind having agency staffs participate before the agency in the latter's role as judge stems from an era in which there was little active intervention by interest groups. The staff was injected to provide token opposition, or guidance for the hearing officer, which would otherwise be overwhelmed by one-sided presentations by the applicant. That historic function of the staff need not be abandoned. It should be permitted to enter licensing proceedings only if, like other intervenors, it presents contentions that are adverse to the applicant's position. In that way, issues not addressed by intervening interest groups but of concern to the staff will not be lost in the process. The staff should not, however, be permitted to shore up the applicant's position on contested issues, thereby lightening the applicant's burden of proof and prejudicing the process by its presence.

The NRC's Procedures, including its use of formal "discovery" techniques, do not narrow the inquiry sufficiently to prevent lengthy, largely valueless, on-the-record debates between lawyers and witnesses on broad issues that are simply beyond the power of the licensing boards to adjudicate. That is what occurred in the Seabrook hearings in connection with the cost-benefit balance required by the NRC's rules implementing NEPA. The issues were imprecisely framed early in the prehearing period—questions like "Whether the power will be needed" and "Whether alternative sources are available to meet the demand" form the basis of the issues on which evidence was presented at the hearings. The lawyers were never required to distill their clients' concerns to questions capable of a discrete, manageable factual inquiry.

Although part of the difficulty can be attributed to the broad standards set forth in the Atomic Energy Act and NEPA, which is unavoidable, considerable improvement can be made in the NRC's prehearing practices. The NRC's contentions rule could be enforced, with more attention paid to the specificity of the contentions made. The use of depositions as a means of laying expert opinions on the table and thus focusing areas of dispute should be encouraged; and the licensing boards should be required to exert more effort toward resolving issues that are not really in dispute—or that are not capable of reasonable resolution as framed—before the hearings begin.

Finally, the NRC's immediate effectiveness rule should be abolished. In the Seabrook case the various appeals from the licensing board's initial decision took two years to resolve within the NRC itself. Construction during most of that time was continuing, each day further limiting the possibility of reversal in the event the initial decision was found to be unsound. By eliminating its immediate effectiveness rule, the NRC would also encourage its appeal board to a quicker resolution of appeals. In the Seabrook case there was little incentive for the applicant or the staff to press for speedy resolution of the appeals, since at least from the applicant's standpoint, delay only served to further solidify its position.

5

The Licensing Procedure: Seabrook

The Seabrook plant became nationally prominent because it was the first American site of serious antinuclear civil disobedience, but there were other firsts associated with it. It experienced, for example, the first well financed, specific, issue-oriented intervention by an antinuclear intervenor. It also produced the first substantive dissenting opinion by a member of an ASLB, and some of the harshest criticism ever made of an ASLB decision by the Appeal Board.

The Public Service Company of New Hampshire (PSCO) formally tendered a construction permit application with the NRC, on behalf of itself and its joint venturers, on March 30, 1973. The application was initially rejected by the NRC staff, which sought additional information about alternate sites; a new application was tendered, and accepted by the staff, four months later. (The chronology of the licensing events, only some of which are discussed in the text of this chapter, is set forth as Appendix II, below, page 178.)

Petitions to intervene were filed by the State of New Hampshire and by the Attorney General of New Hampshire, the New England Coalition on Nuclear Pollution (NECNP), the Seacoast Anti-Pollution League (SAPL), New Hampshire Audubon Society (Audubon), Society for the Protection of New Hampshire Forests (SPNHF), Donald Ross, Elizabeth Weinhold, and the Commonwealth of Massachusetts.

The Attorney General of New Hampshire chose to intervene both on behalf of the State and in his own right, arguing that under the common law doctrines historically applicable to his office, he had legal standing separate and distinct from that of the State. This position was opposed by PSCO, but the Licensing Board agreed with the Attorney General and permitted his separate status as an intervenor.[1]

The Attorney General's position was in part dictated by political practicality. The Governor of New Hampshire was an ardent supporter of the Seabrook plant, and the Attorney General was concerned that if he intervened only in the name of the state, the Governor would at some point order him to withdraw, which the Governor had the power to do under the state constitution. The Governor had no such power over the Attorney General when the intervention was not in the name of the state.

Intervenor Ross, who described himself in his pleadings as a commercial fisherman, never appeared at the hearings except in the person of his attorney, named Norman Ross. During the course of the *Seabrook* case, the whereabouts of the phantom Mr. Ross became a standing joke among the parties.

The remaining intervenors, except for Massachusetts, are described in Chapter 1 (above, page 11). Massachusetts' intervention, in opposition to the Seabrook project, was an unanticipated blow to PSCO and the other utilities backing the project; and the project sponsors and construction trade unions that supported it exerted considerable political influence to remove the Commonwealth from the case—all without success. Massachusetts stayed until the bitter end.

The licensing board was convened for the Seabrook case in August 1973. Sixteen months passed before the issues to be raised in the hearings were established.[2]

Although the intervenors raised a large number of issues, dominant were:

1. *The suitability of the site.* This issue, discussed above in Chapter 3 (page 40), was raised by NECNP, the New Hampshire Attorney General, and Massachusetts; the issue involves compliance with the NRC's nuclear site suitability criteria. It brings into question the wisdom of permitting large numbers of people to inhabit areas close to the reactor site, and includes a subsidiary issue—whether under the NRC's rules evacuation may be considered an additional safety requirement for a large summer recreational community.

2. *PSCO's financial qualifications.* NECNP and Ross argued that PSCO was not financially qualified to own and operate a nuclear power plant. The intervenors' attempt to examine the NRC's financial qualifications regulation caused the agency to undertake a significant self-reappraisal, which is explored in detail in the next chapter.

3. *Seismic qualification.* Raised initially by Elizabeth Weinhold,

the "housewife intervenor," this issue was pursued by NECNP, which brought two of the country's leading earthquake theorists to the hearings to support its contention that the Seabrook reactor design was insufficient to withstand safely the anticipated ground movement from the largest earthquake considered probable. The NRC's reliance on historic records alone to establish the "maximum credible earthquake" was questioned, and as a result of information first brought out in the Seabrook hearings, the NRC later changed its seismic criteria (although the change did not affect the agency's position with respect to Seabrook).

4. *The need for power.* NECNP argued that PSCO and its partners could not justify the need for Seabrook to satisfy any reasonably anticipated New England or New Hampshire demand for electricity. This issue did not become important until after the 1974 energy crisis and the resulting national reduction in the growth of energy consumption. The issue narrowed to the acceptability or nonacceptability of PSCO's claim that need could be shown by a statement that Seabrook would be substituted for existing fossil-fueled generating units, claimed by PSCO to be more costly (an assertion disputed by NECNP).

5. *Whether Seabrook is the best alternative.* This issue was raised in various ways by NECNP, SAPL, Massachusetts, and the New Hampshire Attorney General. It involves an examination of how the NRC carries out a part of its responsibility under the National Environmental Policy Act of 1969. It has two elements:

(a) *Whether there is a better site.* At issue here is the adequacy of the NRC staff's independent evaluation of alternate sites. The issue became complicated when it became unclear whether Seabrook could qualify, under Section 316 of the Federal Water Pollution Control Act, as a "once through cooling" site. Hence, it became necessary for the NRC to compare Seabrook, as it would be with cooling towers, to other sites, and the adequacy of that analysis also became an issue.

(b) *Alternate energy sources.* The NRC s methodology was called into question here, since it seemed to address the issue myopically—asking only whether, for example, all 2,200 mw of Seabrook output could be replaced by solar energy or by coal or wood, etc. Intervenors argued (1) that a combination of energy conservation and solar and other small-scale energy technologies could meet the demand, and (2) that, in all events, a coal plant was more cost effective.

6. *Aquatic impacts.* PSCO proposed a "once through" condenser cooling water system, in which about 800,000 gallons a minute (gpm) of seawater would be circulated through the condensers, heated about 39 degrees, and returned to the ocean. SAPL contended that the impacts of this system, primarily because of entrainment and subsequent destruction of larval forms of fish and clams, would be unacceptable. This issue became incredibly complex when SAPL moved its fight to EPA. Although little attention was paid to the issue before the NRC (SAPL refused to come to the relevant hearing sessions), the issue formed the basis of a dissenting opinion by one member of the licensing board, who concluded that even PSCO's estimate of clam mortality was unacceptable.

7. *Cost-benefit balance.* In this NEPA issue, it was contended by NECNP and SAPL that the costs of Seabrook outweighed its benefits, and that it was more expensive than several alternatives.

8. *Transmission lines.* SPNHF argued that the Seabrook transmission lines should go around, not through, the Great Cedar Swamp, part of which it owned. The NRC staff agreed in principle with SPNHF, and the licensing board conditioned PSCO's construction permit on altering the location of the line. PSCO appealed the condition, first to the appeal board, then to the courts, maintaining that the NRC had no authority to mandate a new transmission line route in a construction permit condition.

Nearly two years elapsed before the commencement of hearings. While some of this time was being consumed by prehearing discovery—primarily the submission of written interrogatories to opposing parties—most of the delay was a result of the amount of time it took the NRC staff to write and issue an environmental impact statement and its preliminary safety analysis report. The NRC's rules properly prohibit the commencement of hearings until the final EIS has been released. The staff released its draft EIS in April 1974, and the final EIS was sent to the parties in December of that year. The PSAR was not completed until the following spring. Hearings began on May 27, 1975.

The fifty-four initial hearing days were spread out over a six-month period, a few sessions being held each month. This schedule was principally structured to enable the ASLB members and the NRC staff attorneys and witnesses to shuttle back and forth between the Seabrook hearings, licensing hearings being held in other parts of the country, and Washington, D.C.

The Seabrook intervenors approached the case on an issue-by-issue basis. Rather than to come in with a flat, unfocused opposition to the plant, they chose their issues carefully and limited the number of issues addressed, so that they could produce their own evidentiary case rather than having to rely upon difficult and historically fruitless cross-examintion as the sole means of making a record. They divded the issues, allowing a greater concentration of effort by individual intervenors on a relatively small area.

NECNP produced well qualified financial experts whose testimony contradicted much of that offered by PSCO and the NRC staff. They also developed highly respected seismic experts to attack the NRC's choice of seismic design standards for the plant. These witnesses were paid,[3] and their testimony was later acknowledged by the NRC's appeal board as credible and valuable, although it was virtually (and in the case of the financial expert, literally) ignored by the ASLB.

NECNP attempted in addition to make an evidentiary case for the proposition that there were adequate and cheaper alternatives to the Seabrook project. Its limited resources, however, did not stretch far enough, and it was forced in the end to rely upon a group of undergraduate students and their adviser from Dartmouth College, who did not demand much financial support. Understandably, NECNP's case was uneven and generally weak. A bright undergraduate student was obviously not as credible a witness as the professional energy planners produced by the utilities.[4]

SAPL produced no witnesses in the initial hearings. It had agreed to pursue the marine environmental impact issue, and decided at the last minute to boycott the ASLB hearings, electing to throw all its eggs into the basket of hearings set to begin in March 1976 before the EPA. Since EPA had direct regulatory authority over the Seabrook water discharges, SAPL reasoned, it would not be cost effective to produce the same testimony twice. The NRC's consideration of marine impacts was limited to its vaguely defined responsibilities under NEPA. SAPL's attorney did not even appear at the hearings on the day the marine impact testimony was to be given.

The important site suitability issue was not one that required the presentation of much evidence. It was primarily a legal issue, involving an interpretation of the NRC's regulations. However, the New Hampshire attorney general produced two important witnesses—a state police captain whose testimony demolished the notion that the Hampton Beach area was evacuable in the summer and a land use planner who projected population growth around the plant through 1990 (both noted above, pages 51 and 69).

The point that must be made is that citizen group and state intervention in the Seabrook construction licensing was not frivolous. It was not a waste of time, as it did not involve, as did many licensing proceedings earlier in the decade, endless hours of fruitless cross-examination of utility witnesses without discernible direction or point to be made.[5] The major issues were put forward well, the points made strongly, and as a result, the ASLB was provided with a record on which it could make a clear choice.

The full flavor of the hearings cannot, understandably, be portrayed here; nor can it be inferred even from a complete reading of the transcripts. As in any such proceeding, much of its interest lies in the theatrical nature of the oral and visual interaction of the parties in the hearing room. However, at least one aspect of the hearings does require further discussion for a complete perspective on the burden of public participation before the NRC.

One such matter involves the departure, prior to the end of the hearings, of the ASLB chairman and his replacement by an individual openly hostile to the intervenor groups. The original Seabrook ASLB was made up of a nuclear physicist, a lawyer, and a fisheries biologist. The latter, a university professor who served as a part-time ASLB member,[6] very early in the proceedings indicated concern about the environmental impact of the plant, and later dissented from the initial decision authorizing construction. This member and the original chairman made up a majority of the board on several preliminary prehearing issues, adopting the position taken by the intervenors. One such vote permitted the intervenors to introduce evidence bearing on the evacuability of Hampton Beach—which became an important issue in the case. The chairman, on another occasion, was the lone board member agreeing with the intervenors that the ASLB proceedings should have been suspended until the U.S. Environmental Protection Agency made a final determination as to the acceptability of the plant's cooling water system under Section 316 of the Federal Water Pollution Control Act.[7]

Had the original chairman remained, there is a substantial likelihood that Seabrook would not have been licensed. While one cannot, of course, be certain that the chairman would have sided with the dissenting member, turning his dissent into a majority decision, the intervenors felt strongly that the chairman was leaning their way.[8] This view was later corroborated when one of the other board members told an intervenor lawyer that he felt the original board might have denied Seabrook a license.[9] My own observations, made during the time I represented the State of New Hampshire in the Seabrook hearings, corroborate this view.

The original chairman, however, did not participate in the decision. About two thirds of the way through the hearings, the chairman announced one morning that he had accepted a position with what was then the Federal Energy Administration, and would leave the NRC immediately. The job he took was as expediter for energy regulatory proceedings—an FEA intervenor whose job it would be to speed up nuclear and other licenses. Following this announcement, an attorney for PSCO stood up to say that he felt obligated to state that an FEA official had called him and asked for his view of the chairman's abilities, and that he had recommended the chairman for the job. The attorney for SAPL expressed outrage, and asked rhetorically why the intervenors hadn't been asked for a recommendation as well. He also contended that a change of chairman in midstream would be illegal, and vowed to appeal any license issued unless the hearings began anew, so the new chairman would have the benefit of hearing all the evidence.[10]

The chairman was quickly replaced. Ironically, within a few months he returned to the NRC, Congress having abolished the position he had been hired to take. He did not, however, resume as chairman of the Seabrook panel. The new chairman was openly hostile to the intervenors, seeming interested in getting the hearings over with as quickly as possible. The overall tone of the hearings changed. Several outright angry exchanges occurred between the new chairman and intervenor lawyers. The main difference, however, was that the intervenors had become painfully aware that they simply didn't have a chance. The deck had, in their view, become stacked against them, and they wondered aloud whether the job offered to the original chairman had been a setup, engineered from within the NRC to reconstitute the Seabrook ASLB when it began to look as though a majority of the board would vote to turn the project down. There is no evidence supporting such a suspicion. Nevertheless, it would take strong exculpatory evidence to convince the intervenors otherwise.

Post-Hearing Developments

All of the Seabrook parties filed their written arguments by early February of 1976. The ASLB did not issue its decision until June 29, creating a five-month delay in resolution of the initial stage of the licensing controversy. The Board ruled in PSCO's favor on every issue except the location of transmission lines in the Great Cedar Swamp.[11]

Under the NRC's rules, a party dissatisfied with an initial decision may appeal to the Atomic Safety and Licensing Appeal Board for relief. The Appeal Board, established by the AEC in 1969, is quasi-independent and acts somewhat like an appellate court, although, unlike an appellate court, it has the authority to take an independent look at the administrative record and rewrite an inadequate licensing board opinion.[12] Prior to 1977, a litigant dissatisfied with an Appeal Board decision took his case directly to the U.S. Court of Appeals for the appropriate circuit. In that year the NRC amended its rules to permit appeal from the Appeal Board to the Commission itself.[13]

In the case of Seabrook the appellate process began in June 1976, within days of the Licensing Board's initial decision when all of the parties except SPNHF[14] filed exceptions to the initial decision. A list of issues appealed and the resolution of each appears in Appendix IV at the end of this book.

At the time the ASLB issued its June 29, 1976, decision, the EPA had not made a final decision on whether it could approve the plant's "once through" condenser cooling water system under the requirements of Section 316 of the Federal Water Pollution Control Act. EPA's regional administrator had tentatively approved the system in May, but his decision was automatically stayed under EPA's rules when SAPL asked for a full adjudicatory hearing on the matter. Hence, at the time the ASLB made its decision, it did not know whether EPA would allow Seabrook, as proposed by PSCO, to be built. If EPA ultimately said no to the cooling water system, PSCO and its partners would have to add cooling towers to the Seabrook plant, increasing both its capital and operating costs and introducing a not insignificant aesthetic negative into the cost-benefit calculus used in evaluating the project.[15]

There was, however, no evidence in the ASLB's record either as to the cost or the impact of cooling towers at Seabrook. In an attempt to deal with this problem without postponing its decision until EPA took final action,[16] the board stated in its decision that it was approving Seabrook *only* as proposed and that a subsequent change in the plant requiring cooling towers would automatically nullify the construction permit. It stated unequivocally that Seabrook with cooling towers was unacceptable.[17]

PSCO saw itself in a dangerous position. Needing to keep its options open, it appealed the portion of the ASLB decision rejecting the cooling towers, pointing out that it lacked support in the record. The intervenors also appealed the decision, fearing that it would have a tendency to influence EPA. They also asked that PSCO not be permitted to begin construction of the power plant until the issues being appealed were resolved. They were afraid that once PSCO and its partners invested millions of dollars in the Seabrook plant site, their chances of convincing the NRC or the court of appeals to overturn the decision would dwindle to zero, no matter how strong their case on the merits.

The intervenors' concern was not without foundation. Under the NRC's rules, construction could commence upon issuance of the initial decision and license, regardless of the pendency of an appeal of the decision. Only an order from the appeal board or the NRC itself staying the license would halt construction.

On several occasions, the Seabrook intervenors asked the Appeal Board and the NRC to stay the effectiveness of the initial decision, and each time the response was negative. Part of the reason for the difficulty in obtaining a stay is the NRC's adoption of the doctrine of *Virginia Petroleum Jobbers Assn.* v. *FPC*[18] as the standard for granting a stay. Under that doctrine a party seeking a stay must show (1) that he is likely to prevail on the merits of the appeal, and (2) that in the event a stay is not granted, irreparable harm will result of a greater magnitude than that suffered by the opposing party if it is granted.

Under ordinary circumstances, it is nearly impossible to satisfy the first requirement. Unless the defect in the Licensing Board's decision is obvious and egregious, it is unlikely that the Appeal Board will prejudge the argument on the merits. The NRC's "immediate effectiveness rule," allowing construction to begin immediately—before appeals are filed—tends to frustrate an appealing intervenor even if he can make the first showing. There are ordinarily two kinds of irreparable harm alleged by intervenors: (1) that the construction activity will irreparably harm environmental values and (2) that the public interest will be harmed by the expenditure of massive sums on the project, which might prejudice consideration of the appeal. On the other side, the permit holder can argue that losses in construction time, payments on idle equipment, and disbanding of the on-site labor force will prejudice it if a stay is granted.

In *Seabrook* the applicant blunted the intervenors' argument about environmental damage by quickly clearing the site before the argument on the intervenors' request for a stay was heard. Thereafter, all the intervenors had left was their public policy argument, which sounded weak against the applicant's parade of financial horrors that would occur if a stay was granted. On the day the initial decision had been issued, PSCO entered into construction contracts containing stiff penalty clauses, brought hundreds of skilled laborers to the site, and executed rental and purchase contracts for expensive equipment. For it to disassemble such a production would, it argued, be extremely costly.

In the Seabrook case, the impact of this procedure became painfully obvious. The Appeal Board denied the intervenors' requests for a stay of the construction permit. It did not pass on all of the issues on appeal until October of 1977, and the NRC did not complete its review until January 6, 1978. Construction began immediately on the issuance of the initial decision, and except for two brief suspensions it continued unabated during the pendency of the appeals. By March 1, 1978, PSCO had sunk about 350 million dollars into the project, while final resolution of the various intervenor appeals had not occurred.

A more equitable approach for the NRC would have been to delay the effectiveness of an initial decision at least until arguments had been made and a decision issued by the Appeal Board on the question of a further stay. It is arguable, moreover, that the stiff *Virginia Jobbers* rule is not appropriate in the context of administrative appeals. The Appeal Board, unlike a court, is not required by law to accord presumptive validity to Licensing Board decisions. In light of this, and because of the rather protracted appellate period within the NRC, a more reasonable standard for granting a stay would be one whose focus is the likelihood that construction would prejudice future decisions, and whether the appeals, on their face, raise serious issues that, if resolved in favor of the appellants, would require reversal or a remand of the Licensing Board's decision.[19]

The Commission's adherence to the *Virginia Jobbers* standard clearly tilts the process in an applicant's favor. The likelihood that the Appeal Board will nullify a construction permit is slim, no matter how compelling the intervernor's arguments and the equities are, if by so doing it knows that the result will be a one, two or, as in the case of Seabrook, three hundred million dollar loss.

I do not intend to discuss further here the substantive resolution of the various appeals. That is done in relation to specific issues, in other chapters. What is particularly interesting about the later proceedings is how the NRC's appellate process interfaced with EPA's permit proceedings for the Seabrook plant.

Figure 12 is a schematic representation of what happened to the Seabrook case after June 29, 1976. As the table demonstrates, the events subsequent to June 29, 1976, were a seesaw of decisions and reversals of decisions by each agency, complicated by the NRC's often delayed and apparently reluctant reaction to events at EPA. Each agency's decision-making process suffered from slowness caused not by delaying tactics employed by intervenors, but rather by the bureaucratic machinery of the agencies themselves. In the case of the EPA appeal, for example, the hearings were completed in May, but the decision of EPA's regional administrator was not made until November.

In November the regional administrator changed his mind and denied PSCO's cooling system a permit. He had apparently been persuaded that the absence of a clear understanding about what the Seabrook cooling system would do to the offshore environment was an adequate basis to refuse PSCO a permit under Section 316 of the Federal Water Pollution Control Act. Although PSCO had by that time compiled a great deal of relevant data about the offshore ecosystem, little information appeared in the hearing record on the effects of backflushing the system, and the impact on the local softshell clam population was uncertain, mired in a sea of statistical uncertainty and PSCO biological studies that fell far short of the state of the art.

PSCO elected to appeal the regional decision to the EPA administrator in Washington and succeeded in convincing him to reverse it,[20] but not before the NRC, caught between the temporary absence of an EPA permit which was required by law as a prerequisite to its own license, and an initial decision by its own licensing board that had been severely criticized by its own appeal board, halted construction of the plant.[21] The suspension lasted less than a month.

The EPA Administrator's decision was in part premised on his reliance upon a panel of scientists appointed by him to review the record. Certain areas of the record were deficient—lacking data or analytical conclusions—and were commented upon by the panel, which applied its own expertise to fill in the gaps. SAPL challenged the Administrator's decision in an appeal to the United States Court of Appeals for the First Circuit, which agreed with SAPL's argument. By relying on the panel of scientists to fill gaps in the hearing record, the Court reasoned, the administrator had denied SAPL due process of law, a fundamental constitutional right.[22] The Court, on February 15, 1978, overturned the administrator's decision and ordered EPA either to make a new decision on the record as it stood prior to being "fixed up" by the scientific panel, or to hold additional hearings permitting SAPL and other parties to introduce evidence and to cross-examine the members of the panel.

The administrator decided to hold further hearings and appointed a technical panel of three scientists to sit alongside the new Administrative Law Judge and act as a sort of inquisitorial panel. Those hearings began in June of 1978.

In light of the turn of events with the EPA permit, the NRC was again faced with a hard choice. Its licensing board, which had been ordered by it to issue two supplemental initial decisions, had still failed to produce a defensible environmental analysis of alternative sites.[23] The EPA permit, required to be in force as a precondition of NRC licensing of Seabrook, had been effectively revoked by the action of the Court of Appeals. The Seabrook project was ordered shut down a second time, on June 30, 1978.[24] But less than two months later, the EPA Administrator reaffirmed his previous decision to grant PSCO a permit, and the NRC reinstated the construction permit immediately.[25] Construction continued unabated while the various issues remained unresolved until well into 1979.

The "sunk" costs that PSCO and its partners were able to build up in the Seabrook project during the appeal process must have had an impact on the outcome of the intervenors' appeals. Indeed, as discussed in detail in Chapter 7, the NRC admittedly gave the Seabrook project an advantage over alternatives because of those sunk costs, once it recognized that the licensing board's initial analysis was deficient. That fact alone condemns the NRC's posthearing appellate process as one that permits an applicant with a marginal or in some

EPA

Adjudicatory Appeals Pending

6/29/76	9/30/76	10/9/76	1/21/77	1/24/77	3/31/77	4/18/77	6/17/77	7/7/77	7/26/77	10/30/77

EPA timeline events:
- **10/9/76** — RA reverses earlier approval – denies NPDES permit
- **1/24/77** — PSCO appeals RA's decision to EPA administrator in Washington
- **6/17/77** — EPA Administrator reverses RA re-instates NPDES permit

NRC

NRC timeline events:
- **6/29/76** — Construction License Decision; Construction begins
- **9/30/76** — NRC Appeal Board Denies SAPL motion to suspend Construction License
- **1/21/77** — NRC Appeal Board orders further hearings in light of EPA decision and inadequate ASLB decision orders halt to construction
- **1/24/77** — NRC reinstates construction permit
- **3/31/77** — NRC affirms appeal board orders construction stopped
- **4/18/77** — ASLB begins re-opened hearings
- **7/7/77** — ASLB issues supplemental I.D., approving Seabrook
- **7/26/77** — Appeal Board re-instates construction permits
- **10/30/77** — ASLB issues second supplemental I.D. approving Seabrook over all other sites

Change of U.S. Government Administration—Ford replaced by Carter as President / Russel Train resigns as EPA administrator, replaced by Douglas Costle

SAPL appeals EPA
decisicion to U.S.
Court of Appeals

Court of Appeals
rejects SAPL's
challenge to EPA
decision

EPA
reinstates
Seabrook
permit

U.S. Court of
Appeals Reverses
6/17/77 Decision
of EPA
administrator

EPA decides
to hold new
hearings
before a scien-
tific panel

N.H. Governor
Thompson
defeated
11/78

2/15/78	3/78	5/1/78	6/30/78	7/78	8/78	9/78	10/78	1/79	3/79	4/79

Appeal Board
finds supple-
mental I.D.'s
to be inade-
quate--refuses
to halt con-
struction

NRC orders
construction
stopped pend-
ing new ASLB
hearings and
final EPA
decision

NRC
reinstates
construction
permit

Remanded ASLB
alternate site
hearings begin

U.S. Court of
Appeals upholds
NRC construction
permit

PSCO asks U.S.
Supreme Court
to overturn NRC
transmission
line decision

U.S. Supreme
Court rejects
PSCO's
appeal

N.H. legislature
passes legislation
preventing PSCO
from taxing rate-
payers in advance
for Seabrook
construction

PSCO shareholders
vote to divest
the company of
48% of its
Seabrook shares

12. Chronology of permit and appellate events in the Seabrook Project, June 29, 1976, to April 1979.

way defective project to bootstrap its way into a license, effectively mooting opposition.[26]

Costs and Other Miscellany

The Seabrook licensing was expensive. Appendix V lists estimates of some of the vital statistics of the Seabrook saga. It demonstrates the extent of the record and some of the direct costs borne by the participants. PSCO and its partners spent more than thirty million dollars of rate-payers' funds to license the Seabrook project. The intervenors' costs were close to a quarter of a million dollars, most of which was raised by small donations from car washes, bake sales, and other such fund-raising endeavors.[27]

Appendix V does not attempt to impute licensing costs incurred by the United States, both in connection with the NRC proceedings and EPA's protracted struggle to issue a permit authorizing the plant's cooling water system. Those costs, including both government employee time and the direct cost of local hearings in New Hampshire, are enormous—well into the millions of dollars. The question one must ask about that component of the cost is whether it is well spent. The critical inquiry is whether the process yields a safer product in the end.

6

Financing: Who Bears the Cost?

With respect to CWIP, the company . . . attempts to prove that PSCNH is financially qualified to build Seabrook by showing that it is in "severe financial distress . . ."—Karin P. Sheldon, Esq.

This case has been widely depicted as a serious failure of governmental process.—U.S. Nuclear Energy Commission, 5 NRC 509 at 509 (1977)

The Law of Financial Qualifications

Congress, apparently perceiving a link between the financial capability of nuclear plant operators and plant safety, suggested in the Atomic Energy Act of 1954 that the AEC develop standards of financial suitability for applicants seeking licenses under the Act. Thus prior to issuing a license, the regulatory body was to determine "such . . . financial qualifications of the applicant" as it "may deem appropriate."[1] This directive was refined by another section of the Act, requiring that licenses be given only to applicants "who are equipped to observe . . . safety standards."[2]

The AEC thereafter identified safety as "the first, last, and a permanent consideration" of its licensing activities,[3] and promulgated its financial qualifications regulation with public safety in mind. As in the case of the site suitability regulations, the financial qualification regulations were written in the early sixties, and remained by the mid-seventies essentially unchanged. They are not precise, requiring only that the applicant show that it has the "financial qualifications . . . to carry out, in accordance with the regulations . . . the activities for which the permit (license) is sought," and that it "possess the funds necessary to cover estimated construction costs and related fuel cycle costs, or . . . has reasonable assurance of obtaining the necessary funds . . ."[4]

Either Congress or the AEC could have established strict, well defined financial criteria for entrants into the nuclear program. They could have, for example, defined eligibility in terms of net worth, or the ability to raise needed funds without having to resort to the money market. One could devise even more specific standards.

The AEC applied its generalized regulation on a case by case basis, stating the applicant must have such financial resources that it will not have to "cut corners in areas of safety concern."[5] The most succinct statement of this theoretical basis for the financial qualification criteria is this one, by a member of the NRC's appeal board:

> . . . there is a need to avoid a situation in which financial pressures on an applicant become so pervasive as to influence the manner in which the plant is constructed. If the struggle to obtain funds becomes too difficult, even the most safety-conscious utility company might succumb and, in its efforts to reduce costs, end up cutting corners in constructing the plant. Even where there is a promise that funds will ultimately be available in the future, financial constraints can have a heavy influence on day-to-day decisions . . . letting a financially strapped company go ahead with construction will inexorably result in decisions to do less testing, to use lower quality materials, to approve borderline workmanship, and the like. In insidious fashion, each such decision, even though not consciously designed or believed to do so, increases the risk to the public from an eventual accident. Repeatedly, companies which were not in financial distress have had to be prodded to adhere to quality standards. We can expect the problem to be exacerbated when the utility involved is being forced to save money at every turn.
>
> It is no answer to pretend that any deficiencies will be caught by the Commission's staff of inspectors and then corrected . . . the inspectors are not sufficiently numerous to oversee all work or even to review the documentation of more than a small part of it.[6]

It is accepted without question that compliance with whatever safety standards the Commission develops is largely a matter of faith. The NRC relies to a large extent on voluntary compliance, since it has insufficient staff to police every detail of reactor design, construction, and operation. Requiring that applicants possess a high degree of financial stability and substance is one way to make up for this inability.

The exceedingly high capital cost of a nuclear power station virtually assures that few if any license applicants will "possess the funds necessary to cover estimated construction costs." Were this not the fact, the inquiry under the regulation would be relatively simple. One would need only to verify the utility's cost estimates (no mean task, however, as discussed below), and then look at its balance sheet and income statements in order to determine its cash position. However, since few if any utilities can finance a nuclear plant with cash on hand, the critical language of the regulation is that there be "reasonable assurance that the utility can raise needed capital." What constitutes "reasonable assurance" that an applicant can obtain the necessary funds was a major issue in the Seabrook case, the first time the regulation was seriously examined since its adoption nearly twenty years before. It is my principal purpose here to discuss the social, political and safety implications of the "reasonable assurance" criterion.

Estimating Long-Term Cost

An analysis of a utility's ability to finance its project necessarily begins with the project cost. Construction costs for a nuclear power plant are affected by numerous variables, and in that sense they are no different from other industrial facilities. However, there are two things that make the handling of those variables more difficult in the case of a nuclear facility: the enormous size of the investment and the long lead time between planning and operation. Neither the AEC nor the NRC developed firm standards or methodological criteria for estimating construction costs.[7]

The cost variation resulting from long construction lead times are not insubstantial by any means. The significance of this phenomenon can best be illustrated by the Seabrook example. When first proposed to the New Hampshire Bulk Power Site Evaluation Committee, the Seabrook plant was estimated by PSCO to cost on the order of 900 million to 1.2 billion dollars. That was in 1972. This cost estimate was adhered to until 1975, when it was raised by PSCO during the initial nuclear regulatory licensing hearings to 1.6 billion dollars. At the time the evidence relevant to the financial qualificaiton inquiry was locked into the hearing record, 1.6 billion was the cost estimate, and therefore the decision by the Atomic Safety and Licensing Board (issued in the spring of 1976) assumed that it was evaluating the capability of PSCO and its partners to come up with that amount of money over the estimated construction period, 1976–1982.[8]

After the Licensing Board decision, however, PSCO did two things. It slipped the construction schedule for each of the two units by two years, and it revised the cost estimates. PSCO estimated in mid-1976 that the capital cost would be around 2.2 billion dollars. Late 1977 estimates pegged the cost at 2.6 billion.[9] Within two years of the initial NRC licensing decision, the cost of the Seabrook plants had increased by 2 billion dollars.

No doubt some of this cost increase can be attributed to schedule slippage, which can in turn be blamed to some extent on regulatory delay, particularly to a six-month construction moratorium during 1977 caused by a temporary disapproval by the EPA of the plant's proposed condenser cooling water system.[10] It is clear, however, that a two or even an three year delay is not solely responsible for cost escalation of the magnitude experienced by the Seabrook plant. More rapid-than-anticipated inflation also played a role, as the nuclear industry, a heavy user of concrete and steel, fell victim to rising energy-related material costs. Nevertheless, those costs were identifiable as early as 1975.

It is reasonable to conclude that much of the billion dollar post-licensing cost increase represents costs that could have been identified before the initial decision. Why, it must be asked, were they not so identified? Unless PSCO deliberately understated the costs during the licensing proceeding,[11] it is likely that its early cost-estimating techniques simply were not adequate to predict, within an 80 percent range of error, the actual costs that would be incurred.

An example of the unanticipated expense PSCO encountered came to light in 1977. PSCO had apparently assumed that construction laborers would be paid wages based on wage scales agreed to by New Hampshire unions. Most of the labor force, however, was recruited from Massachusetts and demanded the Massachusetts wage scale, 75 cents per hour higher than the New Hampshire scale. This resulted in total labor costs about 30 cents an hour higher than anticipated—$4.55 rather than $4.25. One might ask why the wage scale issue was not identified and resolved prior to the licensing decision. Presumably PSCO knew or should have known that most of its workers would be members of Massachusetts unions, and that there were different wage scales in Massachusetts than in New Hampshire. As a result of its failure to do so, PSCO underestimated the actual cost of the project to a significant degree.

Many of the major component costs for the project were fixed, or at least formulas for their computation were fixed by contracts entered into by PSCO as early as 1973.[12] Those costs were largely capable of reasonably accurate prediction, subject to some uncertainty about the rate of inflation.

Though it is not clear why the construction cost estimates provided to the licensing board by PSCO were a billion dollars too low, the margin is too wide to be passed off as unexpected inflation. While the licensing board might find PSCO qualified to build a 1.6 billion dollar plant, it might well not find it qualified to build one that cost 2.6 billion. One is compelled to conclude that the initial decision to license the Seabrook plant was premised on a fiction of sorts. That the regulations of the agency are apparently not sufficient to produce cost estimates within a reasonable range of accuracy, or at least to compel reassessment once a substantial aberration becomes apparent, is not a comforting thought.

There are ways in which construction cost forecasting can accommodate for unanticipated delay and other unanticipated costs. It is relatively easy to make "worst conceivable case" inflation assumptions, and to anticipate the type of delay experienced in the Seabrook case. Yet existing NRC regulations do not require such a forecast, and establish no enforceable guidelines for estimating costs.

It was not only the underestimated cost of Seabrook that plagued the project. PSCO had certain underlying financial weaknesses that allowed the project's opponents to mount a serious challenge to the company's ability to finance its share.

A detailed analytical discussion of the financial qualifications issue will be found in Appendix VI. It should be read by those readers whose interest is sufficient to delve into the matter deeply. What follows is a summary of the appended material, and a discussion of the political impact of PSCO's financial dilemma on the state of New Hampshire. The chapter concludes with a general discussion of the NRC's responsibilities in determining that an applicant is financially qualified. Footnotes are omitted from the summary, but are included in the supplement.

PSCO's Financial Dilemma

The Public Service Company of New Hampshire agreed to own and finance 50 percent of the Seabrook project. Under the NRC rules, it was required to demonstrate that it either had the funds on hand to pay for its share of the construction cost, or could demonstrate a "reasonable assurance" that the funds would be made available. PSCO did not have adequate funds on hand to pay for its share of Seabrook. The project cost more than two times the company's net worth. The issue accordingly became whether it could provide the NRC with reasonable assurance that it could raise the needed capital.

The traditional mechanism by which investor-owned utility companies raise capital for construction projects had been for them to sell medium-term debentures and additional stock. Construction costs would be paid in the first instance by borrowing short-term money from banks, which would be repaid out of the proceeds of the debenture and stock sales. Once the facility was built and operating, the utility would sell long-term (30–40 year) mortgage bonds, pay off the debentures, and amortize the bonds by increasing electricity rates to cover the principal and interest payments.

The NRC required nuclear project applicants to submit a financial plan showing how they intended to raise the capital needed for the project. PSCO's plan assumed that it would follow the course outlined above, and made certain critical assumptions in its plan which focused the attack of its opponents.

The company projected that it would raise most of the capital by selling debentures that would bear interest at 8 percent. It also assumed that it could sell a substantial amount of stock at or above its "book value" of around twenty dollars per share. Soon after these assumptions were made, it became obvious that they were not true. Utilities in general had not been able to float debt at interest rates as low as 8 percent for several years. PSCO was not an exception, and was also in worse financial shape than most utilities. Its stock was selling at less than its book value, its price/earnings ratio was poor, and it was unable, without substantial customer rate increases, to maintain a competitive rate of return on its common stock equity.

The Seabrook intervenors made a strong case, with the help of a knowledgeable expert witness, that PSCO could not raise the money it needed on the open market. They argued that the deeper the company got into the construction program, the poorer its earnings picture would look, to the point that when it was about halfway through the eight-year construction period, its stock and debentures would become unmarketable, and it would face the unpleasant alternatives of governmental financial bailout or bankruptcy. This, they argued, could lead to cost cutting and construction shortcuts that could compromise the plant's safety.

PSCO and the NRC staff were able to convince the licensing Board that things were not really that bad. They argued that the depressed economic condition of the utility industry was a transitory phenomenon caused by the 1973 oil embargo. PSCO, they urged, would bounce back. Though the company's bonds had been downgraded by the financial community in 1975 (rated for the first time in the company's history below "A"), the rating would, they claimed, be restored once the state Public Utilities Commission approved a rate package that guaranteed PSCO a 14 percent rate of return. The Licensing Board granted the Seabrook plant a construction permit on this promise.

During the time the intervenor's appeal was pending before the NRC's Appeal Board, PSCO's financial situation deteriorated even further. Its earnings continued to fall, and it became acutely short of cash. Though it continued to argue before the Appeal Board that it was financially sound, the Company's financial consultants were telling the Federal Power Commission and the state Public Utilities Commission that PSCO was in desperate straits, teetering on the brink of financial disaster. It was asking that it be allowed to charge its ratepayers enormously higher rates to pay for the mounting construction costs it incurred at the Seabrook construction site. Its argument was that it should be allowed to include what is called "construction work in progress" (CWIP) in its rate base, as a way to bail it out of its financial crisis.

When the NRC's Appeal Board learned of PSCO's true condition, it simply abandoned the findings of the Licensing Board, which were clearly no longer tenable. Rather than declare PSCO unqualified to build Seabrook, however, the Board reasoned simply that PSCO remained qualified so long as the rate-making "regulatory climate" in the state of New Hampshire remained favorable to it.

In reviewing the Appeal Board's decision, the NRC acknowledged the inadequacy of the Appeal Board's rationale. It formulated yet a third standard against which to judge PSCO's financial qualifications. It acknowledged that there was a link between a licensee's financial stability and nuclear power plant safety, but approved PSCO because there was an absence of evidence tending to show that the company's financial condition would lead to compromises of safety-related designs or equipment. In reaching that conclusion, the

NRC appears to have shifted the burden of demonstrating financial qualification from the applicant to the opponents of the project, requiring them to come forward with evidence that a weak license applicant will indeed build an unsafe plant. The NRC appears in its Seabrook decision to have rewritten the standards by which it judges a nuclear license applicant's financial qualifications in a way that lowers the standards significantly.

Subsequent events, which are discussed below, tend to support a conclusion that the NRC made a mistake with PSCO. The company's finances deteriorated after 1977, and the state regulatory climate turned hostile to it. Whether all of those factors will result in the creation of an unsafe reactor is a question whose answer must ominously await the future.

The State Politics of Utility Finance—The CWIP Battle

The ultimate burden of the Seabrook plant fell squarely on the shoulders of the New Hampshire ratepayer, whose protector is the state Public Utilities Commission. The PUC could not have anticipated, in 1973, that PSCO would be back four years later asking it to compel the ratepayers to finance the plant, or that it would cost as much as it now does. The PUC at that time had a small professional staff and did not employ an economist. The majority of the information before it at the time it "approved" the Seabrook facility came from the record of the state siting hearings, and that record contained essentially no financial information, and only PSCO's grossly underestimated cost figures and the company's bullish 11 percent projected annual increase in sales. Even in 1975, when PSCO finally received its rate increase, the company did not attribute its need to the Seabrook project and did not tell the PUC that the Seabrook plant would require rate-payer financing.

By 1976 the PUC had added to its staff an individual who had some knowledge of utility economics. In March 1976 that employee, David Lessels, produced an analysis of PSCO's financial situation that demonstrated: (1) PSCO's rates had increased by 112 percent since 1972; (2) it had greatly overanticipated future regional growth in energy demand; and (3) the consequent excess generating capacity created by the Seabrook plant would impose a severe economic burden on New Hampshire electricity consumers.[13] Lessels' study, though short and incomplete, was a warning of things to come.

However, the PUC, rather than acting on the study, effectively silenced Lessels by moving him to other duties.[14] This action may in part be explained as a result of pressure from the State's governor, Meldrim Thomson, who at about the same time issued a "gag order," in which he attempted by executive order to prevent state employees from speaking out against the project.[15]

It is reasonable to assume that the PUC would not have had to face assessing its ratepayers with its construction costs by the inclusion of CWIP in PSCO's rate base if the company had not chosen to undertake the Seabrook project. In all probability, PSCO would have been able to finance a coal burning facility in the normal manner, since the capital costs and the licensing delays and risks are far less.[16] Testimony filed with the PUC by a PSCO consultant seemed to place at least part of the blame for PSCO's poor earnings coverage ratio on extraordinary cash outlays for the Seabrook construction.[17] Faced ultimately with PSCO's request to insert CWIP in its rate base, the state PUC was confronted with a dilemma: If it denied PSCO's request, it risked: (a) watching PSCO scuttle the Seabrook project and face a hard choice as to who (as between the ratepayers and the stockholders) would absorb the sunk costs, or (b) precipitating PSCO's bankruptcy and a takeover of the utility's assets either by the state or by a larger utility. If it granted PSCO's request, it altered one of the fundamental premises of utility-rate regulation—that only the cost of assets "used and useful" (i.e., power plants already built and producing electricity) may be charged to the rate-payer—and thereby creating potential inequities among different rate-payers and, more fundamentally, drastically changing the historic relationship between the stockholder and the rate-payer. That is not a choice that any public utilities commission would willingly make.

The traditional utility doctrine that only assets "used and useful" are included in the rate base is premised on the traditional roles played by the stockholders of a public utility and the consumers of its product (in the case of an electric utility, electricity). The rate-payers are consumers of a product, and, as in the case of any manu-factured product, its price should and does reflect the costs the manufacturer incurs in its production—including the costs of constructing and financing the manufacturing plant or plants. The consumer expects to pay such a price, and if the manufacturer spends too much money in manufacturing the product, the consumer is free to reject it, or buy less of it, or seek an alternative. The stockholders are investors and as investors they are risk-takers. They invest money in a manufacturer hoping that the consumers will buy the product it makes, thereby allowing the manufacturer to provide them with a return on their investment. The investors are not forced to invest—they choose to do so, or not. If the manufacturer chooses to expand, to build more factories, it must do so either by withholding profits from its shareholders for investment (retained earnings), by borrowing the funds from willing lenders, who will be paid back out of the profits from the new goods, by raising the prices of existing goods or by selling more stock (or a combination of these). Both shareholders and consumers retain their freedom of choice.

Electric utilities (at least those in New England, which are not competitors) differ from the free enterprise model just described. The electricity manufacturing business is a natural monopoly. That is, it would produce chaos for there to be competing power companies in each community, each clamoring to string its own wires to households and businesses.[18] Hence, utility companies are given limited monopolies to sell their products exclusively to consumers within franchise areas ordinarily designated by the state. The consumers, if they want the product, must buy it from the franchised manufacturer. Since electricity has become a necessity, and will remain so until the occurrence of fundamental social and technological changes, the consumer's choice is limited to choosing, within the limits of energy conservation technology, how much to buy—there is no realistic choice to buy none[19]—and since there are no competing sellers, there is no opportunity to pick and choose the least expensive product.

The inherent limitation of the consumer's freedom to choose or reject the monopolist's product gives rise to the possibility that the monopoly owner will charge a higher price for the product—a price unrelated to the cost of production or established on the basis of inefficient production means—than would have been established in a competitive market. Thus the necessity to curb such excesses produced the Public Utilities Commission, whose function it is to establish the price of the utility's product so that it is "just and reasonable"[20]—that is, related to the cost of producing and delivering the product—and that the underlying cost is a realistic one.

By creating the electric monopoly, the state governments chose not to alter the fundamental roles ascribed to stockholders, money lenders and consumers. Shareholder-owned utilities were permitted to exist. The shareholders were still risk-takers, but the existence of a public rate-making body altered the nature of the risk. If the public utilities commission set the rates (the "prices" of the product) too low, a private utility might not make enough money on its product both to cover its costs and to pay its shareholders a return sufficient to compete for new shareholders against other industries not so regulated. Thus the courts have required public utilities commissions to allow the utility to charge a price for its product sufficient to allow it to compete successfully for investors, who will supply capital for the company's expansion and for the other uses to which capital is put.[21]

One significant role of the Public Utilities Commission has been to preserve the delicate balance between consumer and investor in the odd world of consumers who have little choice and investors who have little risk. It is generally accepted that utility rates involve four considerations—(1) they must reflect a realistic cost of service; (2) they must encourage an efficient delivery of service; (3) they must be sufficient to attract investors; and (4) they may in some cases be structured to deter unnecessary consumption.[22] Inclusion of CWIP in a utility's rate base permanently upsets the investor-consumer balance by eliminating from the investors the risk-taking aspect of capital investment and putting essentially all of the risk on the consumers and on the banks who lend short-term capital. Some perceive this situation as being from the far side of the looking glass, where investors are not investors but government-guaranteed depositors, and consumers are forced investors, who as consumers have no choice but to buy the product produced by the company in which they have been forced to invest. The consumers have no control over the company's management, such control remaining with the stockholders. The strongest argument in favor of inclusion of CWIP in a utility's rate base is that in a case like PSCO's the charge could save the ratepayers a great deal of money over the life of the plant.[23] Part of this theoretical "savings" is accounting gimmickry, but the real portion is substantial and arises out of the fact that the utility, with rate-payer generated cash, need not go to the banks for as much high-interest rate money; hence what is saved is interest on money that would otherwise have to be borrowed. Although this is indeed an argument in favor of CWIP from the utility's standpoint, it is at the same time an admission that the investor-owned utility may in fact no longer be viable as a business enterprise. For if the risk of construction must fall on the consumers, of what value to the enterprise (especially to the consumers) are the stockholders? All of those rate-payer savings induced by eliminating the free-market financing system would indeed be greater if the rate-payers were not forced to pay rates sufficient to provide a return to the now useless stockholders.[24]

There are other facets to the CWIP dilemma. Rate-payers who pay greater elevated electricity bills during the Seabrook construction period and who thereafter move to another state served by the plant in which CWIP is not allowed[25] not only fail to realize any saving from the scheme but also end by paying for it twice.

An even more difficult problem arises from the fact that electricity, like most other consumer goods and services, is price elastic—that is, as the price per kilowatt hour increases, there comes a point at which consumers will buy less; they will practice energy conservation and use substitute energy when available or, if they are industries, they may simply choose to locate where the cost of energy is less, such as in southeastern United States or the coal belt.[26] Let us assume, as is the case with the Seabrook plant, that it is designed so that when it has been built, it will meet an electricity demand equivalent to an 8 to 11 percent annual increase over that existing in the year of its conception. And let us assume, also, that as a result of national economic and energy cost factors, the actual rate of increase in demand up to the point at which CWIP is included in the rate base, is in the neighborhood of 4.7 to 5.6 percent.[27] If as a result of the massive rate increases associated with the inclusion of CWIP in the rate base, and of a continuing slump in the economy of the Northeast, the elasticity principle works to further erode PSCO's load growth, then additional rate increases will be required for continued plant construction. Upon completion, PSCO would have a plant for which there was inadequate demand, at which point the company would either have to sell a lesser amount of electricity at higher rates than anticipated, or market it to consumers in other states, who would get it at bargain rates at the expense of the New Hampshire rate-payers who financed the construction.[28]

These considerations led to substantial public opposition to PSCO's request to include CWIP in its rate base, sharpening the horns of the dilemma facing the State PUC, and indeed facing the NRC.[29] The CWIP issue also figured prominently in the unexpected defeat of PSCO's staunchest political ally, Meldrim Thomson, in the November 1978 gubernatorial election.

Thomson's support of the Seabrook project was complete, vocal and unwaivering. He had actively supported it from the time of his election as governor in 1972. His backing may have influenced the NRC's decision that PSCO was likely to be treated well by the state PUC. It would not have been unreasonable for the appeal board and the NRC commissioners to conclude privately that it would be unlikely for Thomson's PUC to defy him and turn down PSCO's requests for rate relief.

It became apparent by late in 1977, however, that Thomson's enthusiasm for the Seabrook project was not uniformly shared among the state's political leaders. Legislation was introduced in the state House of Representatives early in the 1978 legislative session by a member of Thomson's own political party that would have prohibited the PUC from allowing CWIP in PSCO's rate base. The bill was passed by the House. It was only as a result of substantial pressure by Thomson, including his threat to veto the bill, that the state Senate, a majority of whose members were generally sympathetic with the governor, shelved the bill in the last days of the session, effectively killing it.

During lengthy hearings before the PUC, a number of consumer interest groups had vigorously opposed PSCO's request. Lawyers for a legislatively established utility consumer advocate's office had begun to argue persuasively that CWIP should not be permitted, if at all, until PSCO revised its rate structure to discourage high electricity consumption and preferential treatment to its large corporate customers. They argued that if PSCO's rate structure was reformed, the company might not need Seabrook and the CWIP issue could be eliminated, or at least deferred. More significantly for Thomson, CWIP began to be called a tax on the wage-earning consumer to benefit PSCO and its larger customers. During the summer of 1978 it also became known that Thomson had attempted to stifle the consumer advocate's office by impounding money the legislature had appropriated to enable it to hire experts for the PUC's CWIP hearings.

Thomson had been elected governor and twice reelected on a platform containing nothing more than a pledge to veto any and all "broad base taxes." In New Hampshire, which remains the only state without either a general sales tax or a graduated general income tax, the "no tax" issue was dominant in state politics. The state's electorate also seemed sensitive to consumer issues. For example, John Durkin, considered to be a liberal Democrat, had recently been elected to the United States Senate by the state's predominantly Republican-registered electorate, on a platform in which he styled himself a consumer advocate, an image he had nurtured during the years when he was the state's Insurance Commissioner.

Thomson entered the race for his fourth term armed with opinion polls showing that a majority of the state's electorate either favored or did not oppose construction of the Seabrook plant. When CWIP arose as a campaign issue, Thomson quickly jumped to PSCO's defense. Although he later made an attempt to soften his position, his strong statements supporting CWIP were effectively turned against him. His opponent, Hugh Gallen, repeatedly accused Thomson of favoring a "broad base tax" in the form of CWIP, which would not benefit the general welfare, only PSCO. Thomson, who had been assumed to be unbeatable, lost the election.

There were other factors, including the presence of an independent conservative candidate, that undoubtedly also contributed to Thomson's defeat, and it would be inaccurate to place CWIP and Thomson's alliance with PSCO as the principal cause. Yet, it was without question a factor, for CWIP was a major campaign issue. A pundit could well conclude (and he would almost be right) that while the New Hampshire voters were at least tacitly willing to accept the presence of the Seabrook plant on their coastline, they didn't want to pay for it.

The end of 1978 and the first half of 1979 carried more financial bad news for PSCO. The state legislature passed a law shortly after it convened prohibiting the state Public Utilities Commission from permitting a utility to include CWIP in the rate base. The new Governor, in addition to signing the legislation into law, appointed an outspoken critic of PSCO's financing scheme to the PUC. Late in the spring of 1979, the reconstituted PUC decided that the new anti-CWIP legislation required it to reconsider its previous approval of rate increases based on inclusion of CWIP in the rate base (and on which the NRC had predicated its conclusion that PSCO was financially qualified). PSCO was forced to go to court in an effort to keep the PUC from reversing itself on the prior rate increases.

PSCO's own financial situation, moreover, continued to deteriorate. Its earnings coverage ratio improved somewhat, but the radical change in its local "regulatory climate" made future access to needed capital for the project doubtful. At its annual shareholders' meeting in 1979, the company decided to divest itself of nearly half of its Seabrook investment. Six months later, the company had been unable to find a buyer and announced that it would have to delay the project. The cost of the plant had climbed to three billion dollars.

Future Roles of the NRC and the States

Reevaluation of the NRC's role is a particularly difficult task, because its role has never been clearly defined. Obviously it is unfair that the state should be faced with a financial problem as large as PSCO's without being forewarned. Yet it was not entirely the fault of the NRC that such is the case with the Seabrook plant. The state PUC chose to hold its own certification proceedings prior to the NRC hearings, and it apparently chose not to keep a continuous watch over the developments before the NRC.[30] On the other hand, information about the cost and economics of nuclear facilities has traditionally been more within the grasp of the NRC than either the states or the utility industry.[31]

The issue is, however, more complex than simply the timing of regulatory decisions. The Seabrook case confronts the NRC with a very basic question: What is the nature of its responsibility in regard to financial qualifications? The inquiry must begin with whether an applicant's financial strength has any relationship to the NRC's safety responsibilities. If no such relationship can be found, then the question is, on what basis does the obligation rest? Finally, how does the nature of the NRC's responsibility shape its methodology, and is the approach taken in the Seabrook proceeding consistent with the Commission's responsibility as so defined?

The arguments made by the parties in the Seabrook case for and against a relationship between safety and financial qualifications were simplistic. The intervenors' position was that:

It is common knowledge that in high technology industries financial constraints affect the quality assurance of the product. As budgetary restraints bear down on project directors, so too do the pressures to cut costs. The pressures of financial constraints lead inescapably to decisions to run one less test, to utilize slightly lower quality material, to pass questionable welding thereby increasing the risk of failure.[32]

PSCO's rebuttal was to hide behind the regulatory shroud:

> To begin with in the world of nuclear licensing, the design and construction tests and materials are, in a large part, mandated by code and regulations. A decision not to do the tests or to use below-spec materials cannot be unconscious. To do it, a cold, hard decision to engage in fraud must be made by someone.[33]

The difficulty with the intervenor's argument is that it does not go far enough. What it fails to do is demonstrate how, within the existing regulations, a financially strapped licensee or license applicant might compromise public safety.[34] One might suspect that PSCO's rejoinder might portray the NRC's standards and enforcement as being stronger than they actually are, but it was incumbent on the intervenor to demonstrate that fact.[35]

A rather strong argument can be made establishing the linkage between a utility-applicant's financial health and an increased risk to public health and safety. It is, however, a subtle argument, which requires a critical analysis of the NRC's standard-setting and enforcement capability.

Contrary to the inference one might draw from PSCO's statement, quoted earlier and from the NRC's January 6, 1978, opinion, the NRC's equipment and design standards are general, and to the extent that they are refined to specifics, the task is left to the staff, which negotiates outside public scrutiny with vendors and utilities with respect to specific components.[36] In many cases, utility and vendor test data and other safety-related information are taken on faith, since the agency does not have the capability to make its own independent evaluation.[37] The NRC admitted in testimony before the Senate Committee on Government Operations in 1975 that it had too few qualified inspectors to carry out a full-scale sophisticated reactor inspection program adequately, and that it relied to a great extent on industry self-inspection.[38] Safety systems are only spot-checked by NRC personnel. Unless the NRC were to upgrade its inspection and enforcement capability substantially, the potential for a utility to compromise on the quality of safety-related components or sub-systems without being "caught" is ever present.

One need not, as PSCO argues, assume that a utility must break the law in order to install or fail to install a component or a system, or undertake or fail to undertake a procedure that might have adverse safety consequences. During the course of designing, constructing, and operating a nuclear reactor, many decisions are made that do not appear to be safety-related, but in fact are. The hiring of personnel is one example. Certain nuclear plant operating personnel must be licensed by the NRC, and others are not required to be licensed.[39] Many nonlicensed plant personnel might be called upon to act in a situation that could have public-safety significance, and the experience of those personnel may be a factor of the amount of salaries the utility can afford. Welders, for a specific example, are of different skill and experience. It is impossible to inspect each critical weld perfectly, and there are varying techniques available for inspecting welds, some of which are more costly than others. Nonsafety systems are not subject to as rigorous a regulatory scrutiny as are safety systems. A fire at the Browns Ferry nuclear plant crippled the plant's safety systems, and a serious accident was averted only by using a pump that was not intended as a safety device.[40]

The NRC staff also has in the past followed a curious practice of permitting nonconforming safety systems to be used by utilities while they are undergoing tests to determine compliance with NRC standards.[41] A utility seeking to cut costs may install an untested safety system without violating present NRC standards. Since testing for compliance could take a long time, the system could be operational for a substantial period while technically not in compliance with the NRC safety regulations. There are also questions of maintenance and replacement of worn or otherwise degraded components after a number of years of reactor operation, and the replacement of old safety-related components and systems with newer, more advanced, and safer systems as NRC standards change. The NRC has historically not required older plants to retrofit as standards are stiffened, leaving the choice essentially to the individual owners.[42] Replacement parts are not as strictly regulated as those included in the initial design.[43] As an operating plant ages, both the risk of component failure[44] and the opportunity for a utility's management to compromise safety systems increases.

It is therefore not implausible that a utility, by a series of apparently insignificant and unnoticed compromises, might construct and operate a nuclear plant that is not quite as safe, in the theoretical sense, as some other plant whose owner, with greater financial resources, chose to "overbuild" in the safety area. In this sense it can be argued that a utility's financial strength should be considered among the "conservatisms" used by the NRC in its defense in depth against radiation hazards.[45]

A less direct though no less important link between reactor safety and a utility's financial qualifications involves the consequences to a utility of severe corrective action ordered by the NRC. During 1975 the NRC ordered 23 BWR-type power plants shut down after it was learned that small cracks were developing in some of the pipes that carry water to the reactor area.[46] Late in 1977, following a request for emergency action by the Union of Concerned Scientists, the NRC shut down one reactor and considered wider action, requiring an investigation of possibly faulty electrical connectors within the reactor containment. These actions exemplify the fact that the NRC's safety regulations are broad and pervasive, and that nuclear plants are uniquely susceptible to unplanned shutdown, or down-rating as a result of government regulatory action. The economic consequence of such action will vary from utility to utility depending, among other factors, on the size of the utility's sytem and the affected plant, or on the percentage of its generating capacity that is made up of nuclear plants affected by the action, and on the utility's ability to purchase replacement power without seeking immediate rate relief.[47] To turn the argument around, the NRC should not permit itself to be placed in the position of having to consider the economic consequences of a safety order. An electrical system should not be made dependent on nuclear generation to so great an extent that after the addition of a new nuclear plant, both the cost or limited availability of replacement power might at some point result in a partial or complete power shortage as a consequence of a generic shutdown order. Faced with such a situation—of having to choose between the health or economic consequences of power outages and an enforcement order—the NRC's position as a regulator becomes untenable.[48]

This sort of problem falls under the general utility terminology of "system stability" or "reliability." It is, nonetheless, similar to the financial "lumpiness" problem created when a small utility undertakes the capital financing necessary to construct a nuclear plant. An inquiry that ought to have been made in the Seabrook case would involve the following questions:

What would be the impact on PSCO of a forced shutdown of both Seabrook units for a substantial period of time?

What would be the consequences to PSCO and its partners on the New England regional power grid of a forced shutdown of all operating PWR's for a substantial period of time (such as happened to BWR's in 1974–75)?

What would be the consequences to PSCO and its partners on the regional power grid of a shutdown of all operating reactors for a substantial period of time?

The analytical approach to each of these questions would have to be fine tuned. Among the consequences to PSCO would be power-replacement penalties and penalties incurred as a result of a poor cash position. The availability of replacement power would depend in some cases on the shutdown schedules of other regional generating plants, and a sort of "worst case" scenario ought to be developed, so that the NRC can be sure that in making future regulatory decisions it is not forced to choose between depriving the public of electricity (which presents certain risks) and exposing it to an increased risk of a nuclear accident.

Finally, an examination of the financial condition of a utility can reveal weaknesses in its management that can also be relevant to its ability to manage the nuclear components in its system safely. While the NRC does inquire into an applicant's "technical qualifications," its inquiry is rather superficial and relates, at the construction permit stage, primarily to the design and construction team, who are usually not employees of the applicant but are independent contractors. Since the risk to the public is at least in part determined by operating procedures and maintenance practices, a deeper inquiry would seem prudent. Whether the applicant's management has permitted its existing generating plant to run down, what its maintenance and plant upgrading practices are, how it has responded to environmental regulatory responsibilities in the past—all are of significance to an assessment of the responsiveness of the appliant's management to the concerns of nuclear safety.

A full examination of an applicant's managerial competence and of the other areas of concern outlined here can be undertaken meaningfully only at the construction-permit stage of the licensing process, before the utility's resources have been committed and the facility built. The present regulation, which requires only that an applicant show that it can raise the capital needed to build the plant, provides little of the needed information, although if it becomes apparent that an applicant will have difficulty raising capital, that fact, in and of itself, compels a further examination of the utility's financial condition.

A meaningful set of guidelines for analyzing an applicant's financial qualifications would address the following areas of concern:

(1) What difficulties will face the applicant (or specific individual members of a group of applicants) in its attempt to raise the capital to build the facility?

a. What percentage of the capital will have to come from the marketplace, and what is the likelihood that the applicant will be able to market securities proposed to be issued?

b. Does the applicant have a specific financing plan, and does it have commitments from underwriters? Is the plan feasible?

c. Under the proposed financing plan, will the applicant's "earnings" be composed of more than 10 percent AFDC?

d. Will the applicant require rate increases, and, if so, how large?

i. Will a fundamental change in the rate structure, such as inclusion of CWIP in the rate base, be required?

ii. Has the state Public Utilities Commission been made aware of the applicant's financial needs previous to the NRC hearings, and has it assented to the applicant's financing plan?

(2) If the applicant has been experiencing any financial difficulty, such as sagging earnings, what is the root cause of its difficulty, and is its difficulty in any way different from that being experienced by the industry generally?

(3) What percentage of the applicant's generating plant will be represented by nuclear plants of the type presently under consideration, if the proposed plant is built? What percentage is nuclear of any type?

a. What are the sources of replacement power, and what percentage of the replacement power is nuclear

i. of the type proposed, and
ii. any type?

b. What is the anticipated cost of replacement power, and its availability, if the nuclear plants on the applicant's system are ordered shut down at the same time?

(4) In what condition is the applicant's existing generating plant? What has been its practice with respect to maintenance and upgrading of facilities?

(5) What has the applicant's history been with respect to expenditures of capital for environmental pollution control and worker safety?

From each of these general topics, of course, detailed questions would have to be developed. Moreover, at least an attempt should be made to develop threshold standards for financial disqualification. For example, the NRC could prohibit a utility from constructing a nuclear plant if rate increases required to finance construction exceed some maximum annual percentage rate, which could be pegged to a regional average, to the applicant's past history, or to some other standard. A limit might also be placed on the percentage of the applicant's net assets represented by the proposed investment in a nuclear plant, thereby minimizing the impact both of the investment and of forced regulatory outages. A limit could be imposed on the amount of AFDC contained in the applicant's earnings. In sum, there are many ways the NRC might go about establishing a set of financial standards that are responsive both to its safety responsibilities and to the realities of rate-payer economics.

Finally, if the NRC's determination that a utility is qualified is based, as the Seabrook opinion suggests, on the state "regulatory climate," then the states must develop a means of assessing the costs, and reviewing the impact on the rate-payers before the case gets to the NRC. The federal agency should have a more concrete expression of state approval than was present in the Seabrook case. Its rules should require that the project be put before the state PUC in a realistic light, and if conditions materially change subsequent to PUC approval, the NRC should require the applicant to have its project reapproved in light of the new circumstances.

Since the Atomic Energy Act gives the NRC broad authority to construct its standards of financial qualifications, it could accomplish the task of remaking the existing nonstandard into a useful standard by means of administrative rule-making. The Seabrook decision casts doubt over the NRC's ability to succeed.

7

The Power Plant and the Environment

Prior to 1970, federal licensing of nuclear power plants involved only radiation safety-related issues, and ignored the impact of construction or operation of a plant on the environment.[1] The AEC's responsibilities were circumscribed by the Atomic Energy Act, which the federal courts construed as not permitting inquiry into environmental effects not directly involving public health and safety. The regulation of environmental impacts, such as those created by the introduction of waste heat to a water body, was solely a matter of state law.

In 1970 Congress enacted the National Environmental Policy Act (NEPA),[2] requiring federal agencies to consider the environmental consequences of their proposed actions and to submit in writing a detailed statement of environmental impact, assessing alternatives, prior to making critical decisions that might affect the environment. This statement (EIS) must analyze (1) the environmental impact of the proposed action, (2) any adverse, unavoidable environmental effects, (3) alternatives to the proposed action, (4) the relation of short-term uses of the environment and maintenance and enhancement of long-term productivity, and (5) any irreversible and irretrievable commitments of resources occasioned by the action.[3] The Act imposes several other duties, the most important of which for this discussion being a requirement that the agencies "study, develop and describe appropriate alternatives" to any "recommended courses of action" where the proposal involves "unresolved conflicts concerning alternative uses of available resources."[4]

Two years later Congress enacted sweeping amendments to the Federal Water Pollution Control Act, which had previously been little more than a grant-in-aid statute, providing money to states to encourage their water clean-up efforts. The Federal Water Pollution Control Act Amendments of 1972 created a federal permit program,

132

administered by the EPA, under which each discharger of a water pollutant was required to obtain a permit, which in turn compelled a reduction in the amount and concentration of the pollutants discharged, over an established time schedule, to the levels permitted by standards established by EPA.[5] Since the 1972 amendments included heat and radioactive materials within the definition of "pollutants," they added a new level of regulation to the nuclear industry.

This chapter discusses the effect of these laws on the Seabrook licensing scenario, and, in more general terms, the NRC's implementation of NEPA and its interaction with EPA.

Environmental Policy and the NRC

Many federal agencies found compliance with the National Environmental Policy Act difficult and burdensome. They did not possess the interdisciplinary staffs seemingly required by NEPA to produce EIS's, and were uncomfortable in their new role of environmental impact analysts. The AEC was no exception.[6] It took the Commission eleven months to issue implementing regulations,[7] which were promptly struck down by a federal court as inadequate.[8]

The AEC had decided that it would not consider any environmental issues in licensing hearings unless they were specifically raised by a party to the proceeding,[9] and it refused to consider any environmental impact resulting from any activity that was in compliance with existing "environmental quality standards of federal, state, and regional agencies."[10]

Calvert Cliffs Coordinating Committee v. *AEC*, cited above, stands as one of the most strongly worded criticisms of federal agency action ever lodged by a federal court. The Court found the agency's delay in compliance with the law, and its excuse for so doing, "shocking,"[11] its overall view of NEPA "crabbed,"[12] and its position with respect to other environmental standards an "abdication";[13] the Commission made "a mockery of the Act"[14] by placing the burden of environmental analysis on intervenors.

Shortly after *Calvert Cliffs*, the AEC was again before the courts, defending a conclusory, short, and unsophisticated EIS hastily produced with respect to its detonation of a nuclear explosive device in the Aleutian Islands.[15] In a successful effort to avoid a full scrutiny of its EIS by the Court, the AEC cluttered the litigation with procedural claims to the point that, with little time left before the scheduled test, the Court, in an opinion rife with frustration, complained:

> In our view the case does present a substantial question as to the
> legality of the proposed test . . . It is distressing that the case has
> come to require even limited judicial consideration at a moment
> when the time available for that consideration is even more
> limited . . . It is only within the past few days that important
> documents were produced by the Government. We are not to be
> taken as saying this in the spirit of assessment of blame. The
> Government's counsel were entitled to press its contentions—
> which were subsequently rejected—first that NEPA had been sus-
> pended, and second that "Executive Privilege" authorized it to
> withhold documents from the court.[16]

Nevertheless, the Court felt that its consideration of the merits of
the case had thereby been "drastically foreshortened."[17] It was left
with "difficult questions" about the validity of the EIS but felt that
it was unable to review several hundred pages of technical documents
in the time remaining before the scheduled test. The Court said:

> Our failure to enjoin the test is not predicated on a conviction that
> the AEC has complied with NEPA in setting forth the dangers of
> environmental harm. The NEPA process . . . has not run its course
> in the courts. We are in no position to calculate the dangers of the
> Canniken test.[18]

By scheduling a proposed action with little intervening time for
challenging its decision, then withholding the documents necessary
for review of the action, and finally releasing the documents only
after a court order to do so a few days before the action, the AEC
effectively sandbagged an attempt to challenge an EIS that was
probably inadequate.[19]

A year and a half later the AEC was again criticized by the Court
of Appeals for an "unnecessarily crabbed approach" to NEPA, this
time for its refusal to produce an EIS for its liquid metal fast breeder
reactor (LMFBR) program.[20] Though the Commission had performed
NEPA analyses on individual components of the LMFBR program,
such as the Hanford fast-flux test facility, it had failed to assess the
entire program, conceived in a ten-volume LMFBR Program Plan in
1968.

In defense of its inaction, the AEC argued that any detailed analysis of the overall program—its environmental effects and alternatives to it—would require it "to look into the crystal ball,"[21] and would be "meaningless."[22] The Court found such arguments had a "hollow ring" in light of the fact that the Commission had "already prepared a complex cost-benefit analysis of the LMFBR involving projections through and beyond the year 2000" which "notably lacks any attempt to quantify the environmental costs and benefits . . ."[23] Indeed, even though it admitted that by committing over $100 million per year to the LMFBR, the AEC was slowing down the development of alternative energy technologies, it still maintained that the time was not ripe for an EIS, a position for which the Court concluded there was "no rational basis."[24]

The GESMO,[25] Vermont Yankee waste management,[26] and Aeschliman[27] cases, discussed below, all involved policies originated by the AEC but carried forward and defended by the NRC after its creation in 1975. These cases not only illustrate the carrying-forward pattern of agency action with respect to NEPA begun earlier by the AEC, but also are interesting as examples of the widely divergent approaches to the role of administrative agencies and reviewing courts in NEPA cases taken by the courts of appeal and the Supreme Court of the United States. Moreover, the attitudes and approaches evident from *Calvert Cliffs* and these later cases are similar to those taken in the Seabrook licensing, which is discussed later.

The GESMO case involved the NRC's "generic" rule-making practice. By this device the Commission was able to examine and formulate rules with respect to problems commonly applicable to all or a substantial number of licensing proceedings. Rather than attempt to deal with such issues piecemeal in individual licensing cases, it established a practice whereby it convened rule-making proceedings simply to cover the problem, ultimately resulting in a decision (sometimes in a rule) applicable to all affected licenses and proceedings. Once a generic proceeding was begun with respect to an issue that otherwise would be dealt with in licensing proceedings, the NRC prohibited the licensing boards from considering it.[28]

Although not required to do so,[29] the NRC conducted adjudicatory (formal, trial-type) hearings in generic rule-making proceedings where substantial public interest and controversy existed, by which citizen groups and industry intervenors are permitted to present evidence and cross-examine witnesses in major generic proceedings.[30] Just how far the NRC had to go to accommodate intervenors in these types of proceedings was at issue in both the GESMO and Vermont Yankee cases.

The GESMO[31] hearings were structured somewhat more loosely than earlier generic adjudicatory hearings. They were convened to permit examination of the NRC's proposal to make a fundamental change in its nuclear fuel policy to permit the use of "mixed oxide" fuel, containing plutonium, in existing and future light water reactors. That the entry into the plutonium fuel cycle had potentially significant social and environmental impacts was not disputed by the NRC, which had produced a draft GESMO EIS in 1974, prior to the hearings. The draft, though voluminous, and well done in some respects, was criticized by the Court of Appeals, since it "did not reach any final conclusions on the question of safeguards" to prevent sabotage, diversion, accidental release or similar problems.[32] These defects were admitted by the NRC to exist.

Both the Council on Environmental Quality and the Environmental Protection Agency, each with statutory oversight responsibilities under NEPA, took the position that the NRC should issue no licenses for the use of mixed oxide fuel before it had completed its hearings and issued a final GESMO EIS, dealing with the important questions left out of the draft. Notwithstanding this fact, the NRC on November 11, 1975, issued an order in which it decided to license the use of mixed oxide fuel on an interim basis, prior to the completion of the GESMO proceedings, even though by so doing it was allowing the separation of plutonium and uranium from fuel waste, the reprocessing of spent fuel, fabrication of mixed oxide fuel, and its use and transportation on a commercial basis, all of which involve irretrievable resource commitments and all of which had potentially significant impacts. The NRC explained its decision as follows:

> While the Commission is properly mindful that certain licensing actions have the potential for foreclosing subsequent alternatives, it cannot disregard the equally hard reality that inaction or a blanket prohibition on fuel cycle related licensing actions could also foreclose or substantially impede realization of energy alternatives which may contribute to meeting national needs.[33]

Stripped of rhetoric, the NRC simply intended to proceed, for it was afraid that if it did not proceed until after the GESMO proceedings, the public might then not let it go ahead, on account of the hazards revealed in the hearings. NEPA be damned.

The NRC, apparently deaf to both Congress and the courts, relied in the GESMO case on an argument soundly rejected four years earlier. The court in the Calvert Cliffs case had held that:

The very purpose of NEPA was to tell federal agencies that environmental protection is as much a part of their responsibility as is protection and promotion of the industries they regulate. *Whether or nor the spectre of a national power crisis is as real as the Commission . . . believes, it must nor be used to create a blackout of environmental consideration in the agency review process.*[34] (emphasis added)

The Court of Appeals for the Second Circuit struck down the interim licensing order, finding the NRC's position untenable. Not only was its excuse for the action unacceptable but the rule on which the order was based was nonsensical. In order to justify granting interim licenses, the NRC had adopted several criteria, one of which was that the activity would not foreclose safeguard alternatives by committing resources.[35] The Court was "unable to understand how the Commission will be able to determine that a given activity will not foreclose safeguards when those safeguards have not yet been designed . . ."[36]

The *Aeschliman* case arose out of licensing proceedings for the Midland, Michigan, nuclear plant of the Consumers Power Company, and involved policies and issues that also dominated the Seabrook case several years later. The Midland case was as bitterly contested as *Seabrook*, though of somewhat less complexity, and is similar in that the opposition came from underfinanced intervenors who relied principally on cross-examination of power company and NRC witnesses to make their case.

The central issue in *Aeschliman* was the reemergence of a "threshold" test similar to the AEC rule struck down in *Calvert Cliffs*. The AEC had refused to consider energy conservation as an alternative to the Midland power plant in its NEPA analysis unless an intervenor raised the issue specifically and made an affirmative showing of its viability as an alternative. The AEC required intervenors to produce evidence that would "relate to some action, methods or developments that would, in their aggregate effect, curtail demand for electricity to a level at which the proposed facility would not be needed."[37] That is to say, not only did the Commission refuse to consider energy conservation unless an intervenor demonstrated its feasibility, but it would not look at it as an alternative unless it was demonstrated capable of eliminating the nuclear plant entirely.[38] This approach to alternative energy sources limited consideration to those which would alone be sufficient to eliminate the proposed plant and essentially ruled out a group of alternatives, such as a mixture of conservation, solar energy, and small non-nuclear generating facilities as one alternative to a nuclear plant.

The Court of Appeals for the District of Columbia Circuit, reminding the AEC that it had struck down a similar rule in *Calvert Cliffs*, concluded that the new "threshold test" was inconsistent with NEPA's basic mandate.[39] Although the intervenor had done little with respect to the issue, it had submitted comments to the AEC's draft EIS that the court found sufficient to raise a "colorable alternative not . . . considered therein," bringing "sufficient attention to the issue to stimulate the Commission's consideration of it." The Court also criticized the AEC for its refusal to consider alternatives that would reduce the demand for electricity, and its insistence on a showing that the alternative actually replaced the proposed facility, watt for watt.

It is not entirely clear just how heavy a burden the AEC was placing on the Midland intervenors. It contended in its administrative decision that it was not requiring that they produce a "prima facie case," common to civil litigation.[40] The Court of Appeals was critical, however, of the AEC's requirement that the intervenors make an *evidentiary* showing.[41]

The Supreme Court overturned the Court of Appeals decision in *Aeschliman*.[42] Justice Rehnquist, the author of the opinion, argued that an intervenor can properly be saddled with a heavier burden when "requesting to embark upon an exploration of uncharted territory."[43] Energy conservation was to Rehnquist "uncharted territory" in 1972 when the Midland EIS was written, because, he argued, the Council on Environmental Quality had not mandated consideration of it as an alternative until August 1973.[44] The AEC, he concluded, was not behaving arbitrarily or capriciously when it refused to consider energy conservation even though urged to do so by intervenors, because it could legally require them to do more than simply raise the issue, and in *Midland* the intervenors did no more.

Were the facts simply those set forth in the Supreme Court's opinion, it would be unquestionably correct, and the result merely a logical outgrowth of the bootstrap litigating attempted by the Midland intervenors. The lesson: in order to force the AEC to embark on an "uncharted course," the intervenor must produce competent evidence that it will not be a voyage to nowhere. Innuendo and lawyers' arguments are simply not enough (though they were historically the primary weapons in the nuclear intervenors' arsenal).

There were other facts, however, the existence of which casts the Supreme Court's opinion in a different light. For example, it ignored the fact that the AEC still had the energy conservation issue before it in its administrative process as late as 1974, when energy conservation was no longer "uncharted territory" but of recognized significance, and the agency still refused to consider it. Instead, Justice Rehnquist looked narrowly at the Licensing Board's *1972* deliberations when the record before it was relatively devoid of energy conservation information, concluding that its refusal to consider the alternative was at that time defensible. While he recognized that "the concept of alternatives is an evolving one requiring the agency to explore more or fewer alternatives as they become better known or understood,"[45] he failed to look critically at the fact that the AEC, according to its own rules, had the authority to modify both the *Midland* EIS and the Licensing Board's findings, yet simply refused to do so, even after the importance of energy conservation became plain.

The Supreme Court seems also to have failed to understand the significance of the AEC's "threshold test." The Court's opinion nowhere acknowledges the fact that NEPA does not establish different burdens of proof for alternatives that are "well known and recognized" and for those that are more obscure, but which may nevertheless be significant. The opinion points to no established legal doctrine that would support such a dual standard, and it glossed over the Court of Appeals' careful analysis of the practical significance of the rule as severely narrowing the scope of inquiry into alternatives, simply accepting as adequate the AEC's self-serving statement that it did not intend that intervenors present a prima facie case.[46]

At the end of the opinion, Justice Rehnquist added a gratuitous statement, quoted here in part:

All of this leads us to make one further observation of some relevance to this case. To say that the Court of Appeals' final reason for remanding is insubstantial at best is a gross understatement. Consumers Power first applied in 1969 for a construction permit—

not even an operating license, just a construction permit. The proposed plant underwent an incredibly extensive review. The reports filed and reviewed literally fill books. The proceedings took years. The actual hearings themselves over two weeks. To then nullify that effort seven years later because one report[47] refers to other problems, which problems admittedly have been discussed at length in other reports available to the public, borders on the Kafkaesque.[48]

The Court's implication that a construction permit is somehow less significant than an operating license indicates a fundamental misunderstanding of the NRC's licensing process. The construction permit is in fact the *critical* stage for raising most safety and environmental issues. Once the plant has been built and billions of dollars have been spent to build it, even the most significant of issues can be lost in a sea of economic waves. The fact that the reports generated by the applicant "fill books" is of no significance either, unless the reports are of substance and critically unbiased. In this regard the Court's opinion ignores any distinction between quantity and quality. The same is true of the Court's characterization of NRC's procedures ("The proceedings took years").

The message sent down by the Supreme Court in *Aeschliman* is that the Courts of Appeal simply may not look beyond the procedural surface of NRC licensing decisions. They may not, as the Court of Appeals in *Aeschliman* had done, look behind the volumes of "books" generated by the agency to determine whether the pages contained straightforward data and analysis, or biased gibberish. They may not peer into the record of the NRC's licensing hearings to analyze its content.

By the time *Aeschliman* reached the Court of Appeals for the District of Columbia Circuit, the Court was clearly disturbed by the NRC's apparent refusal to abide by NEPA's ground rules and those established by the Court in *Calvert Cliffs* and its progeny. The Court's impatience with the AEC may well have invoked an opinion in *Aeschliman* that probed more deeply in to the AEC's substantive decision-making than is appropriate for a reviewing court, hence it may well be that the Court in several instances violated the time-honored prohibition against substituting their own judgment for that of administrative agencies over matters committed to the latters' expertise.

However true this may be in the *Aeschliman* case, Justice Rehnquist's sweeping and vituperative rejection of the Court of Appeals' approach to the NRC creates a danger of going too far in the other direction. It is, if not an outright command, at least an open invitation to the judiciary to review NRC and, for that matter, all similar federal agency decisions with tunnel vision, focusing only on the procedures leading up to the decision, without making a meaningful attempt to determine whether a rational basis for the decision exists, as a matter of substance. It is at least arguable that the Court of Appeals in *Aeschliman* was *not* second-guessing the AEC but had instead caught the agency at a deliberate obfuscation of its responsibilities. To what extent the Supreme Court's opinion will effectively remove meaningful judicial scrutiny from the NRC's activities is a question that remains to be answered.

Seabrook and NEPA

Under the NRC's regulations, the agency's regulatory staff has primary responsibility for carrying out the analysis required under NEPA. The staff is responsible for producing the Draft and Final EIS and for defending its conclusions before the Licensing Board.[49] The Licensing Boards may modify the EIS in licensing decisions, to reflect new material introduced into the record of the licensing hearings,[50] and are responsible for striking the cost-benefit balance required under the Commission's NEPA rules. Both the Appeal Board and the Commission itself, in exercising their appellate review functions, can add their reasoning to the record and thereby indirectly alter the staff or licensing board's NEPA analysis.

In *Seabrook* the staff delegated its initial responsibility to prepare a working draft EIS to Oak Ridge National Laboratory, a federal research facility then operated under contract to the NRC by Union Carbide Corporation.[51] While Oak Ridge technical personnel produced most of the analytical material in the EIS, critical conclusions and subjective evaluations were made by NRC administrative personnel housed in Washington.[52] Since the EIS is produced *after* an application is docketed, hence after the staff has decided to support the project, there is a great deal of institutional pressure on the administrative personnel not to produce a negative EIS.

The Seabrook site possessed several disadvantages. It had high population density, was located in a productive and arguably fragile estuary, and took in and discharged its cooling water to near shore waters adjacent to the estuary. It had a difficult transmission-line access. That there was a clear need for a hard search for an alternate site was stated by the Advisory Committee on Reactor Safeguards (ACRS) early in the proceedings, and the NRC staff informed PSCO to expand its inventory of potential alternate sites, shortly after its application was docketed. It was clear from early in the proceeding that a major, if not *the major*, NEPA issue would be whether their alternatives to the Seabrook project, which have a smaller environmental cost, were viable.

NEPA requires the NRC to "study, develop, and describe" alternatives.[53] The NRC staff made no attempt on its own to seek and evaluate alternative sites. It relied on sites selected by PSCO. The initial selection of alternate sites was limited to locations in New Hampshire (and one in Maine), most of which were located on rivers whose capacity to absorb the massive amounts of heat rejected by the Seabrook reactors was questionable.

Though PSCO did expand its listing of alternate sites, it did little or no investigation of the environmental and other attributes of the alternate sites it chose. It boldly concluded that the Seabrook site was superior to each, on the basis either that the alternate was not owned by PSCO and not for sale and could not be taken by eminent domain,[54] or that the sites might have economic or environmental costs in excess of those encountered at Seabrook, although in each case PSCO made no effort to study the alternative in sufficient detail to determine whether the claimed impediment actually existed or could be mitigated.[55] In the case of inland riverine sites, which required "cooling towers" to avoid environmental damage, PSCO "compared" them with the Seabrook plant under the assumption that it would not require cooling towers (a distinct economic advantage), although at the time PSCO undertook the comparison it could not have been certain that the EPA would approve the Seabrook plant as proposed. On its face, EPA's regulation would have required even Seabrook, located near the ocean, to have cooling towers.

The NRC staff was urged by intervenor groups to undertake its own independent analysis of alternative sites. Instead of doing that, the staff did what it termed a "reconnaissance level" review of the alternate sites listed and rejected by PSCO.[56] When asked under cross-examination what a "reconnaissance level" review was, staff witnesses Geckler[57] and Zittel[58] admitted that they did no more than fly over or drive past most of the sites and walked around on one or two of the sites for not more than ten minutes[59] and made no independent attempt to evaluate the reasons advanced by PSCO to reject the alternatives as inferior to the Seabrook site. The staff's approach to comparing the Seabrook site with alternatives appears to have suffered from some of the same flaws that affected PSCO's.

One of the primary reasons the ACRS required PSCO to undertake a wider search for alternate sites was that the Seabrook site had a population density greater than that recommended by the staff in its own regulatory guide.[60] The staff admitted that a number of the alternate sites identified by PSCO had population densities less than that at Seabrook, and most did not have the massive summer population that was perched on Seabrook's doorstep.[61] In each case the lower population density represented a benefit to the alternate, or a cost to Seabrook, which properly should have been factored into the staff's comparative assessment. The staff, however, ignored these factors in its analysis.[62] The Licensing Board, moreover, effectively prevented the intervenors from raising the issue by refusing to allow them to present evidence quantifying the population difference between Seabrook and alternate sites, in terms of potential human lives lost in the event of a major accident.[63]

The only alternate site that PSCO analyzed in any detail was a parcel of land it owned, called the Litchfield site, located on the Merrimack River in south-central New Hampshire. Both PSCO and the NRC spent a greater effort on it than on any other alternate site. PSCO rejected the alternative for essentially the following reasons: (1) it would require closed-cycle cooling and therefore be more expensive than Seabrook, (2) it might have foundation problems, which could be expensive to overcome, and (3) the needed closed-cycle cooling system might have adverse impacts on the Merrimack River.[64] The staff did not require PSCO to refine or quantify these objections, but accepted them largely without question. Lengthy cross-examination revealed the following: (a) Neither PSCO nor the staff had compared the added cost of cooling towers at Litchfield with the cost of pumping water from the ocean to the Seabrook site, even though rough calculations appeared not to favor Seabrook; (b) No attempt was made to quantify the cost of the alleged foundation problem (apparently raised because the Litchfield site is underlain with glacial till rather than bedrock); (c) No attempt was made to compare the claimed possible environmental impact on the

Merrimack River with that anticipated to occur as a result of the operation of the Seabrook plant's "once through" cooling water system. Moreover, whereas PSCO and the staff almost uniformly discounted or played down unknown or poorly understood aspects of the Seabrook plant's impact, they assumed the worst with respect to Litchfield.

The staff took the position that it could reject an alternate site unless it was found to be "obviously superior" to the Seabrook site.[65] The Licensing Board adopted this approach as well. Of the nineteen sites offered by PSCO, the Licensing Board analyzed only four.[66] With respect to the Litchfield site, for example, the findings of the Licensing Board were as shown in Table 4. No further analytical treatment of the issue was done by it.

Several things should be readily apparent with respect to the Licensing Board's analysis. There is no way to compare the Seabrook site with Litchfield, based on the information provided. Disadvantages numbered 1, 3, 5, 6, 7, 8, and 9 are speculative, can to a great extent be quantified with additional study, and could turn out to be minimal. Disadvantage number 2 is at best misleading and possibly a deliberate obfuscation of the real population issue. The population within a ten-mile radius may indeed be greater at the Litchfield site, but the population within a five-mile radius and a two-mile radius is much greater at the Seabrook site. Moreover, a quick glance at a map reveals that most of the Litchfield-associated population is near the outer edge of the ten-mile radius, while the population at Seabrook is mostly close to the plant. Finally, the population number used for the Seabrook site (72,000) appears not to include transients, a decision which the NRC's appeal board later reversed for Part 100 site suitability purposes but which remained throughout the proceedings as an assumption for NEPA purposes.

The above brief discussion is intended to provide the reader with a sense of the alternate site issue in the Seabrook case. It is not intended as an exhaustive analysis of the issue as a substantive matter, which is beyond the scope of this text. The overall EIS produced for the Seabrook project is a generally adequate NEPA document—far from the best produced by the NRC, but by the same token by no means the worst. It is fairly typical of EIS's produced by the AEC/NRC during the 1973-76 period, and a full discussion of it would be neither useful nor possible here.

It is not unfair to conclude, however, that the NRC bungled its

TABLE 3   Findings Made by the NRC Licensing Board Relative to the Litchfield Site

A. *Advantages*	B. *Disadvantages*
1. Less Miles of Transmission Lines. —The Litchfield site would require about 37 miles of 345 KV line compared to the Seabrook requirement of 86 miles.	1. The site as proposed is located on a flood plain. This would result in increased safety-related costs. If dikes were required for safety reasons, a choking effect on the river could result during floods.
2. Less Cooling Water Requirements. —The two nuclear units with cooling towers would require makeup of about 30,000 gpm as compared with the once-through cooling requirements of 780,000 gpm at the Seabrook site.	2. Population. —There is a population of approximately 140,000 in a ten-mile radius of the site, approximately twice the population for the Seabrook site (72,000).
3. Small Impact on Biota. —Since the cooling requirements are an order of magnitude less than at the Seabrook site, the potential impact of both the intake and the thermal discharge should be less at the Litchfield site.	3. Consumptive Water Uses. —The consumptive use of water would be larger than at the Seabrook site.
	4. Cooling Tower Costs. —The cost for cooling towers would be approximately comparable to the once-through cooling cost at the Seabrook site. If the cooling towers were moved out of the flood plain, canal might be required, additional costs would accrue
	5. Cooling Tower Impacts. —The impacts commonly associated with cooling towers, drift, fogging, and icing would be present to some degree.
	6. Loss of Farmland Productivity. —The Litchfield site is composed to a large extent of productive farmland. This is to be compared to the Seabrook site which is not an area where farming is carried on.
	7. Proximity to Manchester Airport may require hardening of design.
	8. Aesthetics. —Cooling towers would have an aesthetic impact because of the size of the towers required and other typical characteristics such as frequent plumes.
	9. Diversion Requirements. —The site would require consumptive use of Merrimack River water. Present plans indicate that the Merrimack River will be a major source of domestic supply (ER, § 9.2.3.2). Use of water by a power plant would limit such usage to some degree.

Source: LBP–76–26; ASLB Initial Decision, 3 NRC 857 at 907.

attempt to "study, develop, and describe" alternatives to the Sea-brook project. The Appeal Board determined that the licensing board's alternate site analysis was grossly deficient.[67] Its analysis was characterized by a member of the Board as "superficial and incomplete,"[68] of "poor quality," built on "hurried, careless analyses" by the NRC staff.[69] The defects were found by the Appeal Board to be "serious."[70] The Commission itself could not accept the alternate site analysis done by its staff, and ordered the Licensing Board to conduct new proceedings in which it was to (1) examine alternate sites located in southern New England (and not among those suggested by PSCO), which it had previously refused to consider, and (2) reexamine all of the alternate sites in light of the possibility that the Seabrook plant would have to have closed-cycle cooling (i.e., cooling towers).[71]

Although the NRC and the Appeal Board both concluded that the Licensing Board had grossly violated its obligation under NEPA, however, the terms on which the issues were sent back to the Licensing Board virtually assumed no better result. The NRC first clung to the "obviously superior" standard used by the staff.[72] (Though the Appeal Board mistakenly has called this a "new" standard,[73] it is clear that the staff has consistently refused to consider alternatives except those which, as presented by the applicant, appeared obviously superior to the primary candidate). The Commission also ordered the Licensing Board to consider, as a penalty against all alternate sites, the costs of construction already sunk into the Seabrook project (at that point about $300 million) and the "delay" that would result from starting anew at a different site.[74] It did so in spite of the fact that PSCO had not made a convincing showing that by delaying the project, it would risk failure to meet its obligation to supply any anticipated demand for electricity.

It may be recalled that the Licensing Board had authorized PSCO to begin construction in June of 1976. Three days later several of the appealing intervenors requested the Appeal Board and the NRC to stay the effectiveness of the decision, and the agency refused, utilizing a stringent burden-of-proof rule that was effectively impossible for an appellant to meet.[75] PSCO had subsequently moved forward, pouring hundreds of millions of dollars into the project. The Commission, in no apparent rush to decide the issues appealed to it, did not render its first decision on the alternate site issue until March 31, 1977, over two months after the Appeal Board's decision, which it affirmed with minor modifications. It then allowed PSCO a "credit" or preference against alternate sites for the time and money it had spent. As a result, the NRC made it nearly impossible for the Licensing Board to reject the Seabrook site in favor of an alternative; its licensing scheme became at that point a clear *fait accompli* and its appellate review process essentially meaningless.

The Licensing Board held new hearings during May of 1977, in accordance with the Commission's remand. It considered two issues: whether any alternate site was obviously superior to the Seabrook site as a "closed-cycle" site, and whether certain southern New England sites were obviously superior to the Seabrook site. The Licensing Board refused to evaluate sites other than those which had been previously listed by PSCO. Little new evidence was introduced by PSCO, and most of the evidence submitted by the NRC staff to justify rejection of southern New England sites was stricken from the record by the Licensing Board as incompetent and devoid of reality,[76] leaving the staff's entire case on the subject with "nothing more than [a] few glittering generalities respecting the 'serious economic and scheduling disadvantages, as well as institutional and legal uncertainties' which purportedly [are] inherent in siting a reactor outside of the state in which the applicant is located."[77] The staff's position was not supported by anything and later was soundly criticized by the Appeal Board.[78]

The Licensing Board stuck to its preference for the Seabrook site, issuing two decisions nearly six months apart, both of which, on April 28, 1978, the Appeal Board again ruled were legally insufficient. The Appeal Board's decision was upheld by the Commission in June 1978, a full two years after the plant was licensed and construction begun.[79]

Rejection by the Appeal Board and the Commission of the Licensing Board's attempt to produce a defensible alternate site analysis the second time around resulted in an unprecedented maneuver by the Appeal Board, apparently calculated to put an end to the Seabrook litigation. On August 18, 1978, the Appeal Board reconsidered ALAB-471 and decided that it would convene itself as a licensing board and take evidence comparing the Seabrook site with nineteen alternate sites, assuming the Seabrook plant required cooling towers (even though by that time EPA had decided that it didn't), and first including, then not including, as a "penalty" imposed on alternatives, the sunk costs attached to the Seabrook project.[80]

It appears that the Appeal Board (and the Commission, which did not overturn this procedure) had completely lost confidence in the licensing board assigned to the Seabrook case. The notion that an appellate body can metamorphose itself into a trial court is unique and not particularly encouraging to those who look to the licensing boards as the primary NRC decision-maker. Of course, one is compelled to ask how valid is a license issued by a decision-making body so inept that it must be replaced by its superior? The Appeal Board did not ask itself that question.

Judicial Review of the NRC's Seabrook NEPA Decision

All of the appeals from the NRC's Seabrook decisions were consolidated and heard by the United States Court of Appeals for the First Circuit, which sits in Boston. The Court issued a brief opinion on August 22, 1978, in which it addressed all of the contested issues.[81] Since the NRC was still groping with the alternate site issue, however, the Court limited itself to a general analysis of the acceptability of the "obviously superior" criterion and the NRC's requirement that sunk costs in *Seabrook* be considered as a penalty attached to alternatives.[82]

The Court refused to address the "obviously superior" criterion rule because it concluded that it did not have any authority to "interject itself within the area of discretion of the executive as to the choice of the action to be taken."[83] The Court reasoned that since the "obviously superior standard" goes not to how the NRC undertakes its environmental analysis, but to "what the Commission will do with the findings that the studies generate,"[84] the standard is simply not one the Court has authority to review. Underscoring this conclusion was the fact the "NEPA does not require that a plant be built on the single best site for environmental purposes."[85]

Unfortunately, the Court's narrow reading of its responsibilities seems to have avoided or ignored the problem with the "obviously superior" standard, since the NRC staff used the criterion not so much for a basis to conclude that none of the group of studied alternatives was preferable to Seabrook, as for a reason to reject potential sites without detailed evaluation or analysis. The Court appears not to have understood this critical fact, hence its review of the Seabrook decision-making process, on this issue, missed the point.

The Court plainly avoided dealing with the sunk costs issue, stating that it was too early to review the issue in depth, since it was still before the NRC, and "other courts have decided that the Commission may give an already-developed site an advantage when comparing it to alternate sites."[86] It was not unconcerned, however, and leveled what appears to be a warning to the NRC:

> In the abstract . . . the standard is a realistic way of dealing with existing circumstances, for instance, the fact that certain preliminary costs must go into preparation and studies of the site before the Commission can even consider it.
>
> The problem becomes serious where, as here, the Commission has allowed the applicant to go beyond the relatively minor, necessary investigatory expenditures and to sink large sums into actual construction. That raises the second problem, the advisability of allowing construction permits to issue before final approval of the site. If the Commission is careful about granting such permits, and if the Commission wisely uses its power to stay such grants, situations in which sunk costs predetermine comparative site analyses, rendering them meaningless . . . can be avoided.[87]

Unfortunately, it does not appear that the NRC was either careful about granting its permit for the Seabrook project or wise in the use of its authority to stay the license once granted. The expenditure of somewhere between three hundred million and five hundred million dollars before an acceptable alternate site analysis was carried out would seem to demonstrate that failure, without need for any further inquiry.

The NRC staff's position was constantly changing. At the beginning of the proceedings, it told PSCO that it would have to widen its search for alternate sites. When PSCO failed to do so in a meaningful way, the staff agreed with PSCO that Seabrook was indeed the best alternate. After PSCO's license was granted and the appeal board was asked by the intervenor to reverse the licensing board because it failed to consider the Seabrook site as a closed-cycle cooling site and failed to consider southern New England alternatives, the staff argued that the wider scope was not required—that, indeed, a second comparison of the Seabrook site with the "old" alternatives was warranted—but that Seabrook should be rejected only if there was an "obviously superior" alternate. Moreover, the staff argued, Seabrook must be given the benefit—a credit against alternatives

—equivalent to the sunk costs PSCO and its partners had invested in it.

When the Appeal Board adopted the staff's position and remanded the case for the first time, the staff's position was that there were no alternatives superior to Seabrook and none obviously superior. The Licensing Board refused at that point to permit consideration of southern New England sites.

On the second remand the staff finally conceded that there was in fact an alternative superior to Seabrook. It argued, however, that the site was not "obviously" superior, since it was not sufficiently superior to overcome Seabrook's $300 million sunk cost "advantage."

The staff hit a low point in its factual presentation in the remanded hearings before the licensing board. In order to buttress its argument that it would be inappropriate to consider any sites in Connecticut as alternatives to Seabrook, the staff produced as an exhibit a map on which it depicted a transmission line running from Seabrook to Southern Connecticut. It argued that any power plant constructed in Connecticut would have to be connected by a new transmission line running all the way to Seabrook, in order that PSCO's power needs be serviced. It failed to note that there was already a high voltage transmission grid in place in the corridor, which PSCO was proposing to use to deliver about 20 percent of the Seabrook output to Connecticut! According to the staff's testimony, which the licensing board, ordinarily deferential to it, flatly rejected, electricity could flow south over existing transmission lines, but not north.

So transparent was the staff's attempt to make the Seabrook site appear superior that even PSCO found it impossible to support it. PSCO, clearly embarrassed, did not oppose a motion by the New Hampshire attorney general to strike the staff testimony from the record. The motion was granted, effectively rendering the staff's participation in the remanded hearings valueless. That episode must be regarded as one of the worst performances by a government agency to take place in a public forum.

The Seabrook Cooling System

Although most of this book is devoted to problems that arose because the Seabrook plant is a nuclear plant, the project's cooling system, not peculiar to nuclear plants, caused it significant difficulty. The project ended, literally and figuratively, in a lot of

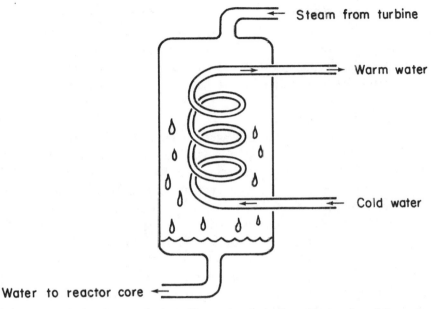

13.   Diagram of a condensor, illustrating how heat is transferred into the secondary cooling water system.

hot water, because of PSCO's choice of a "once through" system for cooling the Seabrook condensers.

There are at present two widely used methods for disposing of the heat absorbed by the condenser cooling water. The water is either returned to the water body from which it came ("once-through cooling"), or is cooled by evaporation in "wet" cooling towers and recirculated with some new water to make up for evaporated losses ("closed-cycle cooling"). In the first case the receiving water body acts as an intermediate heat sink, with the heat ultimately dispersed into the atmosphere, and in the second case the heat is ejected directly into the atmosphere.

The Biological Significance of Cooling Water Systems

Heat has for a long time been known to kill or injure certain types of aquatic organisms. Several things can happen to fish and other water dwellers when subjected to sudden or long-term temperature increases. Death can occur as a result of thermal shock—stress placed on the organism by exposure to lethally high temperatures, which are in some cases as high as 4 or 5 degrees above normal habitat temperatures. Death by starvation or reproductive failure may also occur as a result of the speeding up of metabolic activity caused by long exposure to warmer-than-usual temperatures in an organism's habitat. Occasionally fish have been killed by "reverse thermal shock," when they are lured into living in a warm discharge plume after the time they ought to have migrated to southern waters, and are subjected to cold temperatures in the ambient water when the power plant is shut down.

The other end of a cooling water system is not without biological problems. The withdrawal of massive amounts of water from an aquatic ecosystem also removes (entrains) large numbers of plankton, fish, and benthic larvae, which are small (sometimes microscopic) and float more or less passively in the water column. In cases where the temperature differential is sufficiently high, these organisms will be killed by the billions as a result of either thermal shock or pressure changes.[88] In addition to entrainment of small organisms, larger animals, such as fish, can become entrapped in the intake, suffering death either from pressure changes or trauma inflicted on them by the traveling-screen or "trash rack" devices used to remove debris from the intake pipes before the water enters the power plant. There have been numerous cases of entrapment and death of millions of schooling fish that, for reasons not fully understood, swim into power plant intakes.[89]

The Federal Water Pollution Control Act Amendments of 1972[90] define the term "pollutant" specifically to include heat. The EPA, which was given the power under the Act to issue permits to the dischargers of pollutants, was mandated by the FWPCA to require, for existing sources of pollution, the installation of the "best practicable control technology currently available" by July 1, 1977, and the "best available technology economically achievable" by July 1, 1983.[91] The "national goal" of the Act was elimination of all pollutant discharges where feasible.[92] For "new" sources (those whose construction began after the publication of proposed "new source" standards by EPA), the permits would require that the "best available demonstrated control technology" be achieved immediately.[93]

The electric utility industry succeeded in securing an exemption from EPA's thermal discharge standards by an amendment to the law specifically addressing thermal discharges. As it emerged from the House of Representatives, the FWPCA contained a provision that allowed a particular discharger to avoid compliance with any EPA-imposed effluent limitations if the owner or operator could demonstrate to EPA that the regular limitations were "more stringent than necessary to assure the protection and propagation of a balanced, indigenous population of fish, shellfish and wildlife"[94] in and on the water body into which the effluent is to be discharged. In such a case EPA could accept a less stringent, alternative limitation.

Following a recommendation by a House-Senate Conference Committee, Congress adopted the "Section 316(a) exemption," as it came to be called, but also added a new provision, not previously in the bill, bringing cooling water *intake structures* under EPA's authority. The new provision, Section 316(b),[95] unlike the remainder of the FWPCA, regulated not the discharge of a pollutant but the intake of water from the natural environment. Section 316(b) is deceptively simple. It states:

> Any standard established pursuant to Section 301 or Section 306 of this Act and applicable to a point source shall require that the location, design, construction and capacity of cooling water intake structures reflect the best technology available for minimizing adverse environmental impact.

Section 316(a) inherently requires a case-by-case approach to its application. EPA promulgated guidelines for the selection of representative organisms to study for effects on indigenous populations, but determination of an applicant's qualification for the exemption was left to be established on a case-by-case basis in the hearing room.

Section 316(b), on the other hand, required refinement by agency rule-making. Because of the generality of its language, EPA was compelled to provide guidance for the identification of the "best technology available" for minimizing adverse structure-related environmental impact. Had the Statute been limited to considerations of design and construction, this task would have been relatively simple. There is a "state of the art" for underwater construction, and for such things as fish deflection and removal devices. But the Statute requires, in addition, that the "location" and "capacity" of the intake also reflect the "best technology available." These are inherently site-dependent factors. For example, the significance of the location of an intake is its proximity to large numbers of organisms that could be entrained. Avoidance of that impact is not so much a matter of technology as it is the cost to move the intake and locate it elsewhere. Thus EPA's inquiry will always necessarily end in a dispute over whether the relocation cost, a known, economically quantifiable cost, outweighs the environmental costs of the original location, which if estimable at all, will be imprecisely quantified.

Intake "capacity" involves a similar problem. The term relates to the volume of water flowing through the intake at any given time, expressed usually in gallons per minute or cubic feet per second. At a given population of small organisms per liter of water, their total continuous destruction by entrainment becomes an obvious function of the capacity of the intake to ingest them. Although a reduction in intake capacity does involve certain technologically defined limits, those limits are not significant, since the capacity can be reduced nearly to zero by employing cooling towers, a known and available technology that nearly closes the cooling water system, insulating the aquatic environment from it. The limit is again not the availability of technology but the economics of cooling towers and other constraints (such as aesthetics) on their use.

In each case Congress appears to have required a form of regulatory analysis that is at odds with the basic thrust of the FWPCA, which was to provide for the establishment of technology-based standards that did not require EPA to evaluate the biological impact of the activity on a particular water body, an exercise generally felt to be impossible or at best fraught with uncertainty.

The best design technology available for minimizing environmental impacts can be established. It is the "state of the art" in intake design. It requires no particular analysis of the impact at specific sites but could be established by EPA as a more or less uniform standard and applied nationally. Not so for "location" and "capacity." Whether a particular intake location or capacity minimizes environmental impact is a question that demands an analysis at the site of the proposed structure. The meaning of the term "minimize" becomes important, and its subjectivity makes it a difficult standard to apply in such a manner.

The statute accordingly raises questions like: "How much is too much to require utility X to spend on moving its intake location in order to achieve a given level of 'impact'?" Or, "What level of impact is acceptable?", and "On what basis is acceptability to be determined?" Section 316(b) provides no guidance, leaving the decisions instead to EPA in its role as judge in the issuance of individual permits to thermal discharges. That EPA would run into trouble playing this role in the Seabrook case was easily predictable.

EPA's Permit and Appeal Procedures

The establishment of Section 316(a) alternative effluent limitations and a determination of compliance with Section 316(b) occur as a part of EPA's review of the power plant owner's NPDES permit application, submitted to it under Section 402 of the FWPCA.[96] An applicant must ask for the exemption, and submit documentation intended to justify the requirements of the statutes and EPA's implementing regulations. Applications are submitted to EPA's regional offices, which schedule a hearing to which the public is invited.

The initial hearing is of the legislative variety, conducted informally without the trial-like atmosphere of adjudicatory proceedings. The hearing record constitutes documents and oral testimony submitted by the applicant and other interested persons, together with any material generated by EPA's regional office internal review process.

Under the EPA regulations in force at the time of the Seabrook proceeding, once a decision had been reached on all aspects of the permit review, an initial permit determination was made by the regional administrator (RA), who released the permit in the event that the decision was favorable to the applicant.

Under EPA's rules any interested[97] person could then request an adjudicatory hearing if dissatisfied with the initial determination. That proceeding was more formal and was conducted like a court trial before an administrative law judge (ALJ). The adjudicatory hearing involved a totally new examination of the issues placed before the ALJ. At the time the Seabrook case was heard, however, the ALJ was not permitted under EPA's rules to decide the issues or even write a recommended decision. His function was simply to conduct the hearing, compile the record, and send it to the regional administrator (who, as one recalls, rendered the decision in the first place).[98]

A participant unhappy with an RA's second decision could appeal to EPA's Administrator, who considered the matter on the record made in the adjudicatory hearing but could conduct further hearings if he deemed it necessary. Thereafter, a dissatisfied applicant or intervenor could seek relief from the appropriate United States Court of Appeals.

Shortly after passage of the FWPCA, it became apparent to EPA and the NRC that some attempt should be made to coordinate their respective licensing activities. Since a decision by EPA with respect to a plant's cooling system could materially change the facts on which the NRC based its environmental analysis and its licensing decision, need for water pollution review and approval prior to NRC licensing was obvious.

In an attempt to resolve the interagency difficulties presented by the FWPCA, EPA and the NRC produced a "First Memorandum of Understanding," and later a "Second Memorandum of Understanding," by which they intended to coordinate their licensing activities.

The agencies basically agreed:

1. That EPA would make its NPDES review of nuclear power plants during the NRC's construction permit licensing stage;
2. That where the power plant was a "new source," the NRC would be the "lead agency" for NEPA purposes, and EPA would not write a separate Environmental Impact Statement;
3. The NRC would delay licensing until an EPA permit had been issued.
4. The agreement would be applied to plants already being evaluated only to the extent that it was practical to do so.

The NRC chose not to subject Seabrook to the third requirement of the agreement because, it argued, licensing was under way when the Memorandum was entered into, and it was not practical to delay licensing the plant. The result of that decision is discussed in pages 160–164.

Seabrook

The Seabrook plant is sited on an upland promontory at the landward edge of a large salt marsh. The estuarine complex of which the marsh is a part is in excess of 5,000 acres in size and contains, near its mouth, the largest soft-shelled clam habitat in New Hampshire. The estuary is home not only for clams but many varieties of fish associated with the offshore coastal ecosystem.

The power plant was conceived and designed to have a "once-through" cooling water system. In its original plan, PSCO, as noted, intended to dig a 50-foot-wide ditch across the salt marsh and bury in the peat its intake and discharge pipes, intended to carry water about 2 miles to the plant and return it to the ocean. This scheme was dropped quickly during state siting proceedings when it became apparent that under the New Hampshire wetlands law PSCO would not be granted permission to dig the ditch.

As submitted to EPA, the Seabrook cooling system originated

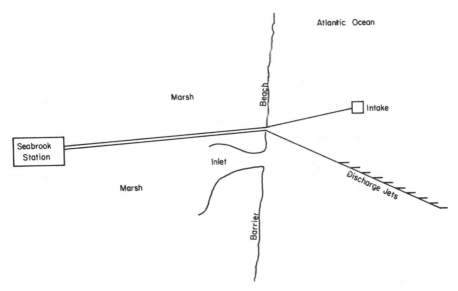

14.   Schematic representation of Seabrook station and cooling water intake and discharge pipes leading to the Atlantic ocean.

about 3,000 feet offshore and just to the north of the inlet to the estuary. Ocean water was to be conveyed about 2 miles to the plant via bedrock tunnels 18 feet in diameter and returned to the ocean to the south of the inlet via similar tunnels. Water heated to 39° above the ambient temperature would be mixed rapidly with ocean water by means of multiport diffusers, which eject streams of water at a high velocity into the ocean over about a thousand feet of ocean bottom. A schematic of the system is depicted in Figure 14.

Biofouling of the intake tunnel was to be controlled by periodic backflushing of the system. At predetermined intervals, the system would be reversed, with water taken in through the discharge ports and returned to the ocean via the intake structure. By exposing fouling organisms to warm water, they would be killed, avoiding the use of chemical biocides.

Since PSCO had an imprecise understanding of the existing aquatic ecosystem, evaluation of potential impacts had to be theoretical. By the time its application for an NPDES permit was filed in 1975, the company had expanded its baseline data studies and had undertaken some analytical evaluation of the data but had not done a complete study of the ecosystem.[99]

One of the major issues that evolved in the Seabrook case was the anticipated impact of the intake on the local clam population and other aquatic organisms, particularly those related to the off-shore commercial fishery. It was generally agreed the the Seabrook plant would kill larval clams, but among the interested parties there was a great difference of opinion as to how many would be killed and what the resulting impact on the estuarine ecosystem would be. The issue first surfaced in the state siting proceedings, two years before EPA got into the act.

PSCO initially took the rather naive position that the plant would have no impact at all. Since it was withdrawing only an infinitesimal percentage of all the water in the Gulf of Maine, the company argued, how could it ever entrain enough larvae to mean anything? This argument was challenged by John Clark, a well-known marine biologist, who testified on behalf of the Seacoast Anti-Pollution League, that the evidence produced by PSCO was equally supportive of a conclusion that the estuary and the nearby coastal waters operated as a closed system, and that larvae produced by clams within the estuary were simply carried out and back in as the tide rose and fell. In such a case, he argued, after a while all available larvae would be consumed by an intake that lay within the closed system, destroying the indigenous clam population. There was no way, Clark argued, to tell whether PSCO's intake lay within or outside of this system.

The intake issue was ignored by the state authorities. The NRC staff attempted to undertake a more sophisticated analysis, based on PSCO's data, and concluded that about 4 percent of the stock of clam larvae and 5 percent of the stock of lobster larvae would annually be destroyed. The NRC staff and PSCO argued that these losses were insignificant.[100]

By the time it had applied to EPA, PSCO had done further studies. Larvae that provided the source of new clams to repopulate the Seabrook and Hampton clam flats were hypothesized by PSCO to originate principally in clam beds in Maine, from which the larvae floated southward in a "neritic band," a sort of river of clumps of immature clams, carried along by the southerly coastal currents of the Gulf of Maine. Young clams are released only in the summer months, and float for from ten to twenty days before becoming heavy enough to "settle out" to the bottom of the tidal shallows, where they spend the rest of their lives (which usually lasts until they are dug up by a human predator).

The intake was positioned west and slightly to the north of the entrance to the estuary (see Figure 13) and, SAPL argued, between the clam larvae and the clam flats. It contended before EPA's regional administrator that since PSCO could not demonstrate that a significant number of clam larvae destined for settling in the estuary would not be destroyed by the power plant intake, it did not meet its burden of proof under Section 316(b), and a permit should be denied.

SAPL also argued that PSCO failed to demonstrate that warm water that was backflushed through the intake to control biofouling would not damage a biologically rich nearby area called the outer-sunk rocks.

EPA's licensing proceedings had barely begun when the NRC license was issued and construction began. SAPL and other intervenors had unsuccessfully urged the licensing board to suspend the NRC proceedings until EPA had completed its work. Following a standard NPDES hearing held during the spring of 1975, EPA's Boston regional office told PSCO that it qualified for a Section 316(a) exemption from EPA's normal requirements for cooling water systems for existing[101] sources. However, it denied PSCO's request for a permit, because it concluded that the Seabrook intake location was not sufficient to "minimize adverse environmental impact," as required by Section 316(b) of the FWPCA. It told PSCO either to move the intake 2½ miles offshore (to a point everyone agreed was beyond the "neritic band" of larvae) or study the matter further and present a revised intake location.

Two months later, PSCO proposed a new intake site, 4,000 feet further offshore than the originally proposed site. The new site coincided with the farthest offshore location at which PSCO had good geological information about the substratum, hence it was the farthest point to which it could extend its bedrock cooling water tunnels without undertaking further exploratory operations, costly to it in terms of time. In July 1975 and without further public hearing, EPA's regional office approved the new intake location. That decision was promptly appealed by SAPL, which requested an adjudicatory hearing. PSCO also requested an adjudicatory hearing with respect to the requirements that it place its intake farther offshore.

Formal adjudicatory hearings were held before an EPA administrative law judge during April and May of 1976—nearly six months after the appeals were filed. Under EPA's rules, the ALJ's sole function was to compile a record which he then turned over to the Regional Administrator for a decision. The Seabrook hearings actually lasted about two weeks, and produced a voluminous record. Late in the summer, the ALJ sent the transcript and exhibits to EPA's Regional Administrator. The RA, however, impressed with arguments made by SAPL that the proceedings were subject to the Administrative Procedure Act, [102] which requires the hearing officer to prepare a recommended decision, sent the record back to the ALJ, asking him to write a recommended decision. To this the ALJ replied that EPA's own rules prevented him from so doing, and he sent the record right back to the RA, who delegated the task of reviewing the record and preparing the decision to a staff lawyer.

While EPA was busy deciding who would decide SAPL's appeal, the NRC's Licensing Board issued a construction permit for Seabrook, even though the aquatic impact data it had was based on the originally proposed intake location, which had been clearly rejected by the RA. That decision was made on June 29, 1976, while the adjudicatory hearing record was being passed around between the EPA regional office and its ALJ.

The rest of the EPA story is complicated and long. It is not so much what happened in EPA's permit proceedings that is important, but what didn't.

A case could have been made that the plant's cooling water system was unacceptable. PSCO's early baseline studies suffered from serious inadequacies. For example, the report of one of its consultants concluded that there was an absence of a certain type of fish residing in the area. A close analysis of the study revealed that the consultant had sampled at the wrong time of the year and with the wrong kind of net. Its later studies were better but still substantially less than the state of the art. A well structured attack on these studies could have raised substantial questions about the validity of PSCO's contentions about the plant's benignity. Coupled with credible expert testimony arguing that the plant would harm selected indigenous organisms, such an attack could have forced EPA to reject PSCO's "once through" system. No such attack was mounted by the opponents.

Except for studies produced by PSCO, most of the hard evidence in the first EPA hearings was produced by EPA itself. SAPL produced two scientists, one who chose to talk only about shipworms (a pest of no great significance in an area like Hampton) and one who had not done enough homework prior to testifying, so that PSCO's lawyer was able to shake the witness's credibility badly upon cross-examination. (For example, he claimed that PSCO's consultant had misread a text when, in fact, he himself had done so.)

It became apparent during the course of the hearings that there was a wide difference of opinion among EPA scientists about Seabrook. Jan Prager, an EPA scientist employed at the agency's Narragansett Laboratory, gratuitously began his testimony with a statement that, in his opinion, the Seabrook site was a poor one for a nuclear power plant. He was admonished by a lawyer for the Agency to keep his testimony to the narrow issue at hand. The RA, following the hearing, sought the advice of an independent biologist, who apparently convinced the RA that PSCO had not met its burden of proof.

The Administrator, reviewing the RA's determination, relied on a panel of EPA scientists whose recommendations included filling in deficiencies in the record which supported a decision by the administrator favorable to the power plant. The string of events leading to the Administrator's reversal of the RA resulted in a rebuke by the Court of Appeals (discussed above) and a charge by one of the scientists who advised the RA that his testimony was intentionally suppressed by the Administrator.

SAPL got caught up in the procedural morass generated by the Administrator's review of the RA's decision, and by the time it took its case to the Court of Appeals, it had little in the way of a substantive complaint to make. Rather than attempt to convince the Court of the inadequacy of the baseline data to form the foundation of a determination under Section 316, a task made formidable by SAPL's failure to produce relevant supporting evidence in the hearings, the intervenor took the easier course and spent its legal resources to challenge the Administrator's reliance on his panel of scientists.

SAPL got the result one would expect. The Court of Appeals simply remanded the Administrator's decision back to him, giving him an opportunity to consider the matter further in light of a properly developed record. The Administrator's second round of hearings presented SAPL with a second opportunity to develop an evidentiary basis to support a contention either that PSCO's studies were inadequate or that the plant would indeed have a deleterious effect on the marine environment.

The Administrator instructed the EPA staff to remain neutral in the remanded proceedings. As a result it produced only enough evidence, subject to SAPL's newly won right of cross-examination, to fill in the gaps in the old record. SAPL did not rise to the occasion. It produced little testimony of its own. Later, appealing the Administrator's second decision supporting PSCO's permit, SAPL again relied principally on a procedural argument—that it was unlawful for the Administrator to order staff neutrality—this time to the Court's deaf ear; it found nothing wrong with the Administrator's neutrality order, and SAPL did not have the facts to back up its claim that his decision to grant the permit was wrong as a matter of substance.

It may well be that it is impossible to predict with any degree of certainty the aquatic impacts of a power plant like Seabrook. Indeed, much of the dispute in the EPA proceedings involved scientists who disagreed with one another's guesswork about what might or might not happen when the plant is switched on, eight or ten years hence. Such a situation makes regulatory decision-making particularly difficult.

There are undoubtedly cases in which a utility possesses sufficient information to convince even conservative biologists of the likely impacts of a cooling water system, but there are also many more Seabrooks waiting in the wings. Section 316(a) has the potential to produce protracted and often inconclusive administrative litigation. Section 316(b), equally important in terms of its environmental significance, first tried in the Seabrook proceedings, proved to be standardless and difficult to apply.

What becomes obvious, however, once one juxtaposes EPA's Seabrook decisions with the status of construction under the NRC construction permit, is that the EPA Administrator was under enormous pressure to reverse the RA, whose decision would, in all likelihood, have killed the Seabrook project, which by mid-1978 had consumed nearly half a billion of the economy's dollars. Given a record that could arguably support varying interpretations, it is not at all surprising that the Administrator decided to approve the project.

EPA was subjected to scathing editorials in the *Wall Street Journal* and the *Washington Post*.[103] New Hampshire Congressman James Cleveland, a long-time Republican member of the House of Representatives and ranking minority member of the House Public Works Committee, was openly critical of further delay of the project and had asked the General Accounting Office to investigate EPA's Seabrook procedures. He held two days of hearings on the matter during the Administrator's review of the RA's decision.[104]

These pressures should not have been placed on EPA. It should have been able to exercise its role in an atmosphere of dispassionate objectivity. That it was not able to do so appears to have been caused partly by the NRC's refusal to suspend its construction permit before substantial financial commitments were made for the project, and partly by PSCO's lateness in requesting its exemption. It requested its Section 316(a) permit in 1975, and probably could not have done so much earlier because it did not possess sufficient supporting data prior to that time (most of PSCO's significant aquatic ecosystem studies were performed in or after 1976). Had PSCO not been allowed to begin constructing the plant in 1976, it, at least, would have had a greater incentive to speed the EPA procedure to completion. As it was, the company made no apparent effort to move the EPA proceedings quickly; rather, it seemed content to allow them to move slowly while the construction bill mounted. The two short stays issued by the NRC had little effect on the rapidly mounting construction costs.

When one looks at all the factors at work in the Seabrook regulatory soup, one begins to get an uncomfortable feeling that the truth, in the sense of substantive rectitude, is a matter that became secondary to a more compelling need—the termination of a process that had gone on far too long.

As is often the case, environmental harm is impossible to quantify and hard to perceive. The Seabrook decision presents an ominous precedent for energy-related environmental decision-making. Where the thirst for energy is large and the economic commitment to a project significant, the government's ability to say no based on speculation about future damage to an ecosystem must be doubted. The lack of immediacy of threatened harm distinguishes most environmental regulatory decision-making from that more closely related to public safety or health. Neither we, as a society, nor the government, as our protector, are likely to react enthusiastically to stop an energy project on the basis of evidence of what it might do, under postulated conditions, to organisms other than humans. The undeniable long-term nexus between such harm and human survival seems beyond the grasp of our regulatory schemes.

8

Public Perception of Civil Disobedience

In the waning days of the Seabrook licensing controversy, after almost five years of hearings, pleadings, decisions, and court appeals, after most of the evidence on which the ultimate fate of the project would rest had been submitted, and, for the NRC at least, after the record was pretty much closed, the continuing dispute gave birth to the Clamshell Alliance, and *Seabrook* ceased to be just another contested licensing case. It became the national symbol of the escalating political battle over the future role of nuclear power in the United States.

Civil disobedience to protest nuclear power plant construction in New England did not begin with the Seabrook plant. A small group of antinuclear activists in western Massachusetts had undertaken isolated acts of civil disobedience opposing a proposed plant at Montague, Massachusetts, during 1975.[1] The first public demonstration against the Seabrook project occurred during April 1976, when about 40 members of a group called Greenleaf Harvesters Guild marched from Manchester to Seabrook and one of them climbed a weather tower at the site and sat on it for a few days.[2] Several members of both groups later became active organizers of the Clamshell.

Seabrook became a major political issue in 1976. Early in that year a group of individuals who had previously supported SAPL's efforts to win a licensing victory became disenchanted with the legal process and began vocal public criticism of both the project and the process.[3] The Clamshell Alliance was formed in that year, and on August 22, 1976, it massed about 800 demonstrators, who marched to the Seabrook site in an attempt to stop the construction that had begun on July 7 following the issuance of the NRC permit at the end of June.[4] One hundred and seventy-nine persons were arrested and charged with trespass and violating the terms of an injunction against occupation of the site, issued by a state superior court judge.

The Clamshell Alliance, stepping up its activities following the August 1976 demonstration, planned an occupation of the site for May 1, 1977. So vocal was the group that many individuals, including some members of the press, mistakenly ascribed legal actions taken by the various Seabrook intervenors to the Alliance. By late April the Alliance had trained about 1800 persons in nonviolent civil disobedience tactics, according to its own counting.[5]

Individual members of the Alliance, a loosely knit organization, sometimes espoused widely divergent reasons for opposition to Seabrook. For example, Guy Chichester, a former SAPL member turned Clamshell organizer, contended that the organization's purpose was to protect the local clam population.[6] The dominant theme of the group's mass demonstrations, however, appears to have been fear of radiation.[7] Many of its early attempts to address the more subtle environmental issues involved in the Seabrook controversy were characterized by confusion or misunderstanding.[8]

On May 1, 1977, about two thousand people entered the enclosed confines of the Seabrook construction site,[9] ignoring a state court injunction against such activity. State police arrested over 1400 demonstrators at the site, most of whom refused to post bail, leaving the state in the embarrassing position of having insufficient jail cells in which to house them.[10] The demonstrators, kept in armories, cost the state well over half a million dollars before they finally agreed to post bail.[11] The affair brought the Clamshell Alliance to national prominence.

In June 1978 the largest site-specific antinuclear demonstration in the United States took place at the Seabrook site, without arrest or other major incident. Between nine and ten thousand demonstrators occupied a portion of the site made available to them by PSCO under pressure from the state attorney general, leaving after having spent a weekend listening to antinuclear speeches and music. This demonstration had more the character of a media event than the confrontation-oriented demonstrations of the previous years. Though impressively large and in that sense a high point in the expression of popular antinuclear sentiment, the affair caused a split in the leadership of the Clamshell Alliance. The demonstration had been carried off without major incident because a majority of the membership of the group had agreed with the state that the demonstration would be officially limited to a designated area and for a specific period of time. Dissention within the group resulted when some members contended that such an agreement was contrary to the group's fundamental purpose—to halt construction—and to the principles of free exercise of individual conscience.

The Clamshell Alliance, though ideologically fragmented following the 1978 demonstration, has become increasingly institutionalized, and even periodically publishes an antinuclear tabloid containing arguments on such wide-ranging topics as nuclear disarmament and medical uses of radioactive isotopes. Its original focus on Seabrook as a specific, unacceptable, power plant appears to have diffused into a national outlook.

Whether civil disobedience, as it has emerged in western jurisprudence as a theoretically supportable act of conscience,[12] can be justified when applied to situations like the Seabrook plant is an intriguing issue for further examination. It will not be explored here except for the suggestion that there are, indeed, problems. Traditionally, civil disobedience is justifiable because the law that is violated is thought by those who disobey it to be in violation of some higher law, such as the constitution or moral or "natural law."[13] Thus, for example, the "freedom riders" disobeyed state law prohibiting black people from sitting in the front of busses because they believed (in that case correctly) that the laws deprived them of basic constitutional rights. The Seabrook demonstrators disobeyed common trespass laws, choosing to enter PSCO's property without its permission and remain there after being asked to leave.[14] That is a harder case to justify.

The demonstrators would argue that their trespass was justified as a means to stop what PSCO was doing (building the nuclear plant), which they would say offends a higher moral law.[15] Thus the trespass laws become irrelevant in the face of their right to protest against the unlawful activity. The difficulty with this position is that there are undoubtedly limits to the use of civil disobedience, and one of those might be that there must be a direct nexus between the law broken and the higher law that it offends. Such a nexus exists in the freedom rider case but does not in that of the power plant.

The demonstrators might also argue that the power plant was not lawfully licensed; therefore, construction is going forward illegally, and the trespass laws may not be utilized to frustrate conscientious protest of the unlawful action. That argument seems stronger. Although PSCO holds a construction permit for the Seabrook project, the adequacy of the NRC's regulatory program is clearly not above serious question. Moreover, the NRC itself had admitted serious defects in the way in which the Seabrook plant was licensed. While those defects might not be sufficient to permit a court to overturn the permit, because of the exceedingly narrow scope of such review permitted under the applicable statute, the demonstrators might well believe that the decision itself, the NRC's regulations, or the Atomic Energy Act violates a constitutional provision (such as the prohibition against deprivation of life without due process of law), or some higher moral law. These arguments, too, are not without their difficulties, but they are at the same time not clearly indefensible.

The demonstrators and the organizations which intervened in the Seabrook licensing proceeding, though they share, to some extent, a commonality of purpose, clearly differ in their perception of the way to achieve their goals.[16] Both agree, however, that in their view the NRC does not undertake its role as a regulator with adequate objectivity, that it does not listen to intervenor arguments, and that it deals with license applicants at less than arm's length. These criticisms are made with varying levels of severity and with varying amounts of justification. The issues discussed in the previous chapters point out some of the inadequacies in the NRC's reactor licensing program. The agency must eliminate such inadequacies if it hopes to win sufficient public confidence to avoid another Seabrook. While a tougher, more openly objective regulatory program obviously would not eliminate antinuclear dissent, it would assure a better safety program and would remove from public debate the aspect of the dissent which focuses on the NRC.

Conversely, it seems that attempts to speed licensing by reducing public opposition within the licensing process will cause it to increase outside of the process. Just such a course has been backed by the NRC in legislation it has endorsed,[17] and its action seems unwise. There are signs, however, that the Commission is seriously interested in changing some of the past practices that have eroded its public image. For example, it has publicly disavowed the widely criticized Rasmussen report on reactor safety.[18] It is an agency which, at this time, seems uncertain of the direction in which it should go.

That the future of nuclear power is uncertain now is a state of being that must, at least partly, be laid at the door of the NRC. The Seabrook story is not a pleasant one, and does not speak well of our attempts to regulate the private uses of nuclear energy. It raises questions not just of the ability of the people who are charged with safeguarding the public, but of the competence of the institutional structures within which they work.

Appendixes

I

Nuclear Regulatory Commission Reactor Site Criteria

Title 10 Code of Federal Regulations

PART 100—REACTOR SITE CRITERIA

§ 100.1 Purpose.

(a) It is the purpose of this part to describe criteria which guide the Commission in its evaluation of the suitability of proposed sites for stationary power and testing reactors subject to Part 50 of this chapter.

(b) Insufficient experience has been accumulated to permit the writing of detailed standards that would provide a quantitative correlation of all factors significant to the question of acceptability of reactor sites. This part is intended as an interim guide to identify a number of factors considered by the Commission in the evaluation of reactor sites and the general criteria used at this time as guides in approving or disapproving proposed sites. Any applicant who believes that factors other than those set forth in the guide should be considered by the Commission will be expected to demonstrate the applicability and significance of such factors.

§ 100.2 Scope.

(a) This part applies to applications filed under Part 50 of this chapter for stationary power and testing reactors.

(b) The site criteria contained in this part apply primarily to reactors of a general type and design on which experience has been developed, but can also be applied to other reactor types. In particular, for reactors that are novel in design and unproven as prototypes or pilot plants, it is expected that these basic criteria will be applied in a manner that takes into account the lack of experience. In the application of these criteria which are deliberately flexible, the safeguards provided—either site isolation or engineered features—should reflect the lack of certainty that only experience can provide.

[27 FR 3509, Apr. 12, 1962. as amended at 40 FR 8793, Mar. 3, 1975]

§ 100.3 Definitions.

As used in this part:

(a) "Exclusion area" means that area surrounding the reactor, in which the reactor licensee has the authority to determine all activities including exclusion or removal of personnel and property from the area. This area may be traversed by a highway, railroad, or waterway, provided these are not so close to the facility as to interfere with normal operations of the facility and provided appropriate and effective arrangements are made to control traffic on the highway, railroad or waterway, in case of emergency, to protect the public health and safety. Residence within the exclusion area shall normally be prohibited. In any event, residents shall be subject to ready removal in case of necessity. Activities unrelated to operation of the reactor may be permited in an exclusion area under appropriate limitations, provided that no significant hazards to the public health and safety will result.

(b) "Low population zone" means the area immediately surrounding the exclusion area which contains residents, the total number and density of which are such that there is a reasonable probability that appropriate protective measures could be taken in their behalf in the event of a serious accident. These guides do not specify a permissible population density or total population within this zone because the situation may vary from case to case. Whether a specific number of people can, for example, be evacuated from a specific area, or instructed to take shelter, on a timely basis will depend on many factors such as location, number and size of highways, scope and extent of advance planning, and actual distribution of residents within the area.

(c) "Population center distance" means the distance from the reactor to the nearest boundary of a densely populated center containing more than about 25,000 residents.

(d) "Power reactor" means a nuclear reactor of a type described in § 50.21 (b) or 50.22 of this chapter designed to produce electrical or heat energy.

(e) "Testing reactor" means a "testing facility" as defined in § 50.2 of this chapter

SITE EVALUATION FACTORS

§100.10 Factors to be considered when evaluating sites.

Factors considered in the evaluation of sites include those relating both to the proposed reactor design and the characteristics peculiar to the site. It is expected that reactors will reflect through their design, construction and operation an extremely low probability for accidents that could result in release of significant quantities of radioactive fission products. In addition, the site location and the engineered features included as safeguards against the hazardous consequences of an accident, should one occur, should insure a low risk of public exposure. In particular, the Commission will take the following factors into consideration in determining the acceptability of a site for a power or testing reactor:

(a) Characteristics of reactor design and proposed operation including:

(1) Intended use of the reactor including the proposed maximum power level and the nature and inventory of contained radioactive materials:

(2) The extent to which generally accepted engineering standards are applied to the design of the reactor:

having a significant bearing on the probability or consequences of accidental release of radioactive materials:

(4) The safety features that are to be engineered into the facility and those barriers that must be breached as a result of an accident before a release of radioactive material to the environment can occur.

(b) Population density and use characteristics of the site environs, including the exclusion area, low population zone, and population center distance.

(c) Physical characteristics of the site, including seismology, meterology, geology, and hydrology.

(1) Appendix A, "Seismic and Geologic Siting Criteria for Nuclear Power Plants," describes the nature of investigations required to obtain the geologic and seismic data necessary to determine site suitability and to provide reasonable assurance that a nuclear power plant can be constructed and operated at a proposed site without undue risk to the health and safety of the public. It describes procedures for determining the quantitative vibratory ground motion design basis at a site due to earthquakes and describes information needed to determine whether and to what extent a nuclear power plant need be designed to withstand the effects of surface faulting.

(2) Meteorological conditions at the site and in the surrounding area should be considered.

(3) Geological and hydrological characteristics of the proposed site may have a bearing on the consequences of an escape of radioactive material from the facility. Special precautions should be planned if a reactor is to be located at a site where a significant quantity of radioactive effluent might accidentally flow into nearby streams or rivers or might find ready access to underground water tables.

(d) Where unfavorable physical characteristics of the site exist, the proposed site may nevertheless be found to be acceptable if the design of the facility includes appropriate and adequate compensating engineering safeguards.

[27 FR 3509, Apr. 12, 1962, as amended at 38 FR 31281, Nov. 13, 1973]

§ 100.11 Determination of exclusion area, low population zone, and population center distance.

(a) As an aid in evaluating a proposed site, an applicant should assume a fission product release[1] from the core, the expected demonstrable leak rate from the containment and the meteorological conditions pertinent to his site to derive an exclusion area, a low population zone and population center distance. For the purpose of this analysis, which shall set forth the basis for the numerical values used, the applicant should determine the following:

(1) An exclusion area of such size that an individual located at any point on its boundary for two hours immediately following onset of the postulated fission product release would not receive a total radiation dose to the whole body in excess of 25 rem[2] or a total radiation dose in excess of 300 rem[3] to the thyroid from iodine exposure.

(2) A low population zone of such size that an individual located at any point on its outer boundary who is exposed to the radioactive cloud resulting

from the postulated fission product release (during the entire period of its passage) would not receive a total radiation dose to the whole body in excess of 25 rem or a total radiation dose in excess of 300 rem to the thyroid from iodine exposure.

(3) A population center distance of at least one and one-third times the distance from the reactor to the outer boundary of the low population zone. In applying this guide, the boundary of the population center shall be determined upon consideration of population distribution. Political boundaries are not controlling in the application of this guide. Where very large cities are involved, a greater distance may be necessary because of total integrated population dose consideration.

(b) For sites for multiple reactor facilities consideration should be given to the following:

(1) If the reactors are independent to the extent that an accident in one reactor would not initiate an accident in another, the size of the exclusion area, low population zone and population center distance shall be fulfilled with respect to each reactor individually. The envelopes of the plan overlay of the areas so calculated shall then be taken as their respective boundaries.

(2) If the reactors are interconnected to the extent that an accident in one reactor could affect the safety of operation of any other, the size of the exclution area, low population zone and population center distance shall be based upon the assumption that all interconnected reactors emit their postulated fission product releases simultaneously. This requirement may be reduced in relation to the degree of coupling between reactors, the probability of concomitant accidents and the probability that an individual would not be exposed to the radiation effects from simultaneous releases. The applicant would be expected to justify to the satisfaction of the Commission the basis for such a reduction in the source term.

(3) The applicant is expected to show that the simultaneous operation of multiple reactors at a site will not result in total radioactive effluent releases beyond the allowable limits of applicable regulations.

---

1. The fission product release assumed for these calculations should be based upon a major accident, hypothesized for purposes of site analysis or postulated from considerations of possible accidental events that would result in potential hazards not exceeded by those from any accident considered credible. Such accidents have generally been assumed to result in substantial meltdown of the core with subsequent release of appreciable quantities of fission products.

2. The whole body dose of 25 rem referred to above corresponds numerically to the once in a lifetime accidental or emergency dose for radiation workers which, according to NCRP recommendations may be disregarded in the determination of their radiation exposure status (see NBS Handbook 69 dated June 5, 1959). However, neither its use nor that of the 300 rem value for thyroid exposure as set forth in these site criteria guides are intended to imply that these numbers constitute acceptable limits for emergency doses to the public under accident conditions. Rather, this 25 rem whole body value and the 300 rem thyroid value have been set forth in these guides as reference values, which can be used in the evaluation of reactor sites with respect to potential reactor accidents of exceedingly low probability of occurrence and low risk of public exposure to radiation.

Note: For further guidance in developing the exclusion area, the low population zone, and the population center distance, reference is made to Technical Information Document

14844, dated March 23, 1962, which contains a procedural method and a sample calculation that result in distances roughly reflecting current siting practices of the Commission. The calculations described in Technical Information Document 14844 may be used as a point of departure for consideration of particular site requirements which may result from evaluation of the characteristics of a particular reactor, its purpose and method of operation.

Copies of Technical Information Document 14844 may be obtained from the Commission's Public Document Room, 1717 H Street NW., Washington, D.C., or by writing the Director of Nuclear Reactor Regulations, U.S. Nuclear Regulatory Commission, Washington, D.C. 20555.

[27 FR 3509, Apr. 12, 1962, as amended at 31 FR 4670, Mar. 19, 1966; 38 FR 1273, Jan. 11, 1973; 40 FR 8793, Mar. 3, 1975; 40 FR 26527 June 24, 1975]

Licensing Chronology

1972

February 1: Public Service Company of New Hampshire files with Site Evaluation Committee for a site certificate for Seabrook Units 1 and 2.

April: PSCO submits *Seabrook Nuclear Plant Condenser Water Study*, Seabrook Station Environmental Report, Construction Permit Stage.

June 19: Joint Hearings of the State of New Hampshire Public Utilities Commission and Site Evaluation Committee begin (end May 25, 1973).

1973

March 30: PSCO applies for an operating license for Seabrook Nuclear Station, Units 1 and 2, with the Atomic Energy Commission (AEC).

May: Initial application by PSCO for a construction permit is rejected by the AEC (for lack of sufficient information).

July: New application, with requested additional information, submitted by PSCO and accepted for docketing by AEC staff.

July 9: *Seabrook Station Environmental Report* issued, after previous submission (June 12), to AEC Director of Regulation. PSCO issues *Seabrook Station Preliminary Safety Analysis Report* (PSAR).

July 27: NHSEC approves PSCO site application for Seabrook (8–4 majority).

August: Notice of Atomic Safety and Licensing Board Hearing for Seabrook published in *Federal Register* (38 FR 21519).

August 14: Supplement to Environmental Report requested by NRC staff.

October 29: First Pre-Hearing Conference for ASLB Hearings held. (Docket Nos. 50–443, 50–444).

1974

January 29: Certificate of Site and Facility (RSA 162-F:8) granted to PSCO by NHPUC and SEC. New Hampshire Special Board and Water Resources Board, and New Hampshire

	Water Supply and Pollution Control Commission, grant applicant permission to install intake pipes and pump facilities from ocean to plant.
March 11:	Second ASLB Pre-Hearing Conference held.
April:	*Draft Environmental Statement* (DES) for Seabrook Nuclear Station, Units 1 and 2, submitted to AEC Directorate of Licensing.
May:	Third ASLB Pre-Hearing Conference held.
May 17:	LPB-74-36
	Licensing Board (ASLB) denies motion of NECNP and SAPL for certification of the issue of financial assistance to the Commission (AEC).
August 21:	First meeting of the Advisory Committee on Reactor Safeguards (ACRS). Second and final meeting held on August 22.
December:	*Final Environmental Statement* for Seabrook issued by AEC.
December 12:	Fourth ASLB Pre-Hearing Conference held.
1975	
March 13:	LBP-75-9
	Atomic Safety and Licensing Board compiles pleading and hearing schedule for Seabrook proceedings.
April 23:	*Society for the Protection of New Hampshire Forests, Audubon Society of New Hampshire* v. *Site Evaluation Committee* (115 NH 163, 337 A.2d 778). SAPL and SPNHF appeal SEC approval of PSCO siting application for Seabrook. New Hampshire Supreme Court orders the case remanded for the purpose of requiring that the SEC provide basic findings of fact on the existing record to support the ultimate conclusion it had reached. Later in 1975, SEC reissues a site approval report with amendments.
May 1:	LBP-75-28
	Pre-Hearing (ASLB) conference order No. 5 in part denies applicant's motion for summary disposition of the issue of evacuation of Hampton Beach (outside LPZ) and applicant's motion for referral of such a ruling to the Commission (NRC).
May 21:	ALAB-271 (see Appendix IV).
May 27:	Atomic Safety and Licensing Board Hearings begin in the matter of Public Service Company of New Hampshire et al. (Seabrook Nuclear Generating Stations, Units 1 and 2). Docket Nos. 50-443, 50-444. Subsequent hearing dates; 5/28 to 5/30, 6/3 to 6/6, 6/12, 6/13, 6/17 to 6/20, 6/23, 6/24, 6/30, 7/2, 7/3, 8/27 to 8/29, 9/3 to 9/5, 9/9 to 9/12, 9/17, 9/18, 9/24 to 9/26, 10/7 to 10/9, 10/14 to 10/17, 10/21 to 10/24, 10/28

	to 10/31, and 11/4 to 11/8 (54 days total).
May 29:	State of New Hampshire issues Section 401 Water quality certificate to applicant under Federal Water Pollution Control Act.
June:	EPA issues determination that once-through cooling is acceptable.
October 3:	LBP-75-61 ASLB denial of stay motion by several intervenors (SAPL, New Hampshire Audubon, Mrs. Weinhold), which would have precluded or delayed further NRC proceedings pending the outcome of EPA hearings concerned with similar issues (especially once-through cooling).
October 16:	ALAB-293 Appeal Board confirms ASLB conclusion that it was not legally precluded at the time from taking evidence on the cooling system issues which are within its domain, and that Appeal Board intervention is not warranted.
October 24:	SAPL and New Hampshire Audubon call for a mistrial of NRC hearings as Licensing Board Chairman Head is replaced by John M. Frysiak. Motion denied in LBP-76-4 (February 4, 1976).
1976	
February 24:	ASLB hearings reopened for certain seismic issues. Additional hearing date—February 27.
March 23:	EPA Hearings open, concerned with matters relating to intake and discharge (continue to April 2).
June 29:	Initial Decision by ASLB authorizing construction permit.
September 16:	Brief of Commonwealth of Massachusetts filed with Appeal Board in response to ASLB initial decision of June 29, 1976.
September 17:	Applicant files with Appeal Board initial brief in support of exception to the Licensing Board's initial decision. NRC staff files brief in support of its exception to the ASLB initial decision.
September 30:	ALAB-349 (see Appendix IV).
October 5:	CLI-76-15 (see Appendix IV). Commission stays effect of ALAB-349 (September 30, 1976).
October 6:	Petition for Review; *New England Coalition on Nuclear Pollution* v. *Nuclear Regulatory Commission and United States of America*; U.S.C.A., First Circuit, No. 76-1469.
November 5:	CLI-76-17 (see Appendix IV). Commission vacates suspension order of ALAB-349.
November 8:	ALAB-356 (see Appendix IV). Appeal board denies application for stay of construction at Seabrook site.
November 9:	NECNP response to NRC brief in support of exceptions to initial Licensing Board decision (filed with Appeal

	Board). EPA Regional Administrator reverses earlier decision and rules out once-through cooling for Seabrook.
November 12:	NRC staff brief brought before Appeal Board in response to the exceptions of all other parties to the initial decision.
November 17:	CLI-76-24 (see Appendix IV). Commission declines to review ALAB-356.
November 18:	Petition for Review; *NECNP, et al* v. *NRC, et al.*; U.S. C.A., First Circuit, No. 76-1525.
December:	Appeal Board orders reopening of ASLB hearings for discussion of siting and power plant cooling.
December 17:	Petition for review; *Audubon Society of New Hampshire* v. *NRC*, U.S.C.A., First Circuit, No. 76-1347. Court denies to review Appeal Board refusal to order construction stay.

1977

January	PSCO Board of Directors calls for a substantial scaling down of construction efforts at Seabrook.
January 21:	ALAB-366 (see Appendix IV). Appeal Board suspends the effectiveness of outstanding construction permits for the Seabrook facility.
January 24:	CLI-77-4 (see Appendix IV). Commission elects to review ALAB-366.
January 27:	ALAB-368 (see Appendix IV). Appeal Board identifies certain "troublesome" unresolved issues.
February 7:	CLI-77-5 (see Appendix IV). Commission denies applicant's motion for a further stay of ALAB-366.
February 17:	CLI-77-6 (see Appendix IV). Commission permits limited excavation work at Seabrook to continue.
March 31:	CLI-77-8 (see Appendix IV). Commission confirms ALAB-366 with modifications.
April 7:	ALAB-390 (see Appendix IV). Appeal Board denies that applicant need be concerned with emergency planning for area outside LPZ.
April 18:	ASLB Pre-Hearing Conference, re power plant cooling and alternate sites.
May 13:	Petition for Review; *NECNP* v. *NRC and U.S.A.*, U.S. C.A., First Circuit, No. 77-1219.
May 23:	First hearing date for reopened ASLB hearings, concerned with plant cooling and siting. Subsequent hearing dates on May 24, 25, and 27.
June 17:	EPA Administrator reverses Regional Administrator's earlier decision and reinstates the approval of once-through cooling for Seabrook.
June 29:	ALAB-416 (see Appendix IV). Appeal Board rules that construction permits will remain suspended, pending outcome of reopened ASLB hearings.

July 7:   Supplementary Initial Decision regarding Seabrook cooling and plant siting issued by Licensing Board (LBP-77-43).

July: NECNP files petition for Commission review of ALAB-422. Request is granted.

July 11:   Petition for Review; *NECNP, et al. v. NRC, et al.*; U.S. C.A., First Circuit No. 77-1306.

July 26:   ALAB-422 (see Appendix IV). Appeal Board affirms ASLB initial decision. ALAB-423 (see Appendix IV). Appeal Board grants applicant's motion for reinstatement of suspended construction permits.

July 28:   Petition for Review; *NECNP, et al. v. NRC, et al,*; U.S. C.A., First Circuit, No. 77-1342.

November 30:   Further Supplemental Initial Decision concluding that no southern New England sites obviously superior to Seabrook (LBP-77-65, 6 NRC 816).

1978

January 6:   Commission review and affirmation of ALAB-422, etc. (see Appendix IV).

January 11:   Petition for Review; *NECNP, et al. v. NRC, et al.*; U.S. C.A., First Circuit, No. 78-1013.

February 15:   Court of Appeals reverses June 29 decision of EPA Administrator, orders further hearings.

February 27:   Appeal Board decides to review ASLB Supplemental Initial Decisions.

May 1:   ALAB-471

                 Appeal Board finds ASLB Supplemental Initial Decisions inadequate, orders further hearings on alternate sites, but refuses to order a halt to construction.

June 26:   EPA remanded hearings before Administrator's "panel of experts" begin. NRC hears oral argument on review of ALAB-471.

June 30:   NRC orders construction stopped as of July 21, 1978.

July: EPA issues new decision reinstating Seabrook NPDES Permit.

July: NRC reinstates construction permit.

August: SAPL appeals EPA decision to Court of Appeals.

September: Licensing Board hearings on remanded alternate site issue.

September: Court of Appeals for the 1st Circuit upholds NRC permit, dismisses appeals by intervenors and by PSCO.

October: PSCO petitions U.S. Supreme Court to review Court of of Appeals decision on transmission line issue.

1979

January: Supreme Court refuses to review transmission line issue.

April: Court of Appeals rejects SAPL challenge to EPA action, upholds thermal discharge and intake permit.

September: Appeal Board Member Michael Farrar issues dissenting
                    opinion on seismic qualification issue, severely critical
                    of NRC's seismic approval of Seabrook.

III

Issues from Final Pre-Hearing Conference Order

1. Financial qualifications of applicant
2. Evacuation and emergency plans and provisions connected with the facilities
3. Seismology issues
4. CFR Part 100 issues, including adequacy of Low Population Zone (LPZ) and Population Center Distance (PDC)
5. Technical qualifications of applicant and contractors
6. Radiological issues
7. Decommissioning
8. Other miscellaneous health and safety issues
9. Need for power in New Hampshire and New England
10. Alternative energy sources
11. Transmission lines, including proposed and alternate routes
12. Aquatic impact, effects on marine ecology, turbidity
13. Cost-Benefit analysis
14. Miscellaneous environmental issues, including the effects of cooling towers
15. Alternative siting
16. Emergency Core Cooling System (ECCS) requirements and reliability
17. Aesthetics and archaeology
18. Use of public lands, access

Source: Transcript of hearings before NRC Atomic Safety and Licensing Board In the Matter of: Public Service Company of New Hampshire, et al. (Seabrook Nuclear Generating Stations Nos. 1 and 2); Docket Nos. 50–443, 50–444 at pp. 957–963 and at p. 973.

IV

Chronology of Appeals

ALAB-271: 1 NRC 478 (May 21, 1975)
Appeal Board denies applicant's petition for an order directing the Licensing Board to certify the issue of a construction permit applicant's obligation to devise an emergency evacuation plan for an area outside of the Low Population Zone (LPZ), finding that the applicant failed to make the requisite showing of exceptional circumstances.

ALAB-338: 4 NRC 10 (July 14, 1976)
Appeal Board denies application by intervenors New Hampshire Audubon and Seacoast Anti-Pollution League for a stay of construction at the Seabrook site, pending resolution of various appeals.

ALAB-349: 4 NRC 235 (September 30, 1976)
Appeal Board suspends outstanding construction permits for Seabrook Units 1 and 2 for reasons associated with the environmental effects of the uranium fuel cycle in the reactor licensing context. (Intervenors SAPL and New Hampshire Audubon)

CLI-76-15: 4 NRC 363 (October 5, 1976)
Commission Order staying the effect of ALAB-349, pending Commission review pursuant to 10 CFR 2.786.

CLI-76-17: 4 NRC 451 (November 5, 1976)
Commission rules that the construction-permit-suspension proceedings should be suspended and that construction at the Seabrook site may continue. Suspension order of ALAB-349 is thereby vacated.

ALAB-356: 4 NRC 525 (November 8, 1976)
Appeal Board denies application by SAPL and New Hampshire Audubon for stay of construction, pending resolution of the appeals. Review of ASLB Initial Decision is declined. ALAB-338 is confirmed and adhered to.

CLI-76-24: 4 NRC 522 (November 17, 1976)
Commission declines to review ALAB-356.

ALAB-366: 5 NRC 39 (January 21, 1977)
Appeal Board decision suspends the effectiveness of outstanding construction permits for the Seabrook facility (effective February 7, 1977), upon request by intervenors SAPL, New Hampshire

Audubon, and New England Coalition on Nuclear Pollution on the basis of a nonfinal EPA decision on the facility's cooling system.

CLI-77-5:   5 NRC 403 (February 7, 1977)
Commission denies PSCO motion for a further *pendite lite* stay of ALAB-366 and calls for further information from the applicant with respect to alternate sites. Work already in progress.

CLI-77-6:   5 NRC 407 (February 17, 1977)
Commission permits certain excavation work to continue on an interim basis at the Seabrook site, pending its review of ALAB-366.

CLI-77-8:   5 NRC 503 (March 31, 1977)
Commission rules for review of ALAB-366 and concludes that the construction permits which allow once-through cooling ought to be suspended, in light of EPA reversal of approval and the inadequacy of the record and Licensing Board findings. Commission affirms ALAB-366 with modifications, declaring that no benefit-cost analysis under NEPA could be struck.

ALAB-390:   5 NRC 733 (April 7, 1977)
Appeal Board rules that the applicant need not concern itself with emergency planning for areas outside of the facilities' LPZ. (Intervenors NECNP, Weinhold, and State of New Hampshire).

ALAB-422:   6 NRC 33 (July 26, 1977)
Board affirms on the merits the Licensing Board Initial Decision, which authorized the issuance of construction permits for Units 1 and 2 of the Seabrook facility.

ALAB-423:   6 NRC 81 (July 26, 1977)
Appeal Board grants applicant's motion to reinstate the previously suspended construction permits for Seabrook as of August 1, 1977.

CLI-77-14   5 NRC 1323 (1977)
Commission declines to review population center distance issue, but says it will address it in a rulemaking proceeding.

CLI-77-22   6 NRC 451 (September 15, 1977)
Commission grants NECNP petition for Commission review of ALAB-422.

CLI-77-25   6 NRC 455 (1977)
Commission denies PSCO's appeal of transmission line issue.

CLI-78-1   7 NRC 1 (January 6, 1978)
Commission reviews a number of major issues at the request of various intervenors. With respect to financial qualifications, the Commission reserves a decision, pending outcome of applicant's attempts to obtain rate increases by the NHPUC. In the matter of aquatic environmental impacts of the EPA once-through cooling approval, the Commission rules that there was no violation of NEPA (contrary to SAPL-Audubon claims), when PSCO moved coolant intakes offshore. Commission upholds ALAB-423.
SAPL v. *Castle* 572 F2d 872 (1st Cir. 1978)

ALAB-471: 7 NRC 477 (April 28, 1978)
Reversing Licensing Board on alternate sites.

CLI-78-14: 7 NRC 952 (June 30, 1978)
Suspension of license.

CLI-78-15: 8 NRC 1 (July 17, 1978)
Denial of motion to modify suspension.

ALAB-488: 8 NRC 187 (August 18, 1978)
Appeal Board continues with alternate site hearing unless ordered
by Commission to stop.

CLI-78-17 8 NRC 179 (August 9, 1978)
Reinstating permit.

ALAB-499 8 NRC 319 (September 11, 1978)
Decision not to look beyond original 19 sites.

PSCO v. *NRC* (T-lines) 582 F2d 77 (1st Cr. 1978)

NECNP v. *NRC* 582 F2d 87 (1st Cr. 1978)

ALAB-561 10 NRC (September 6, 1979)
Dissenting opinion of Michael Farrar, Member, Atomic Safety
and Licensing Appeal Board, on seismic issue.

V

Seabrook Case Statistics

Number of Years in Licensing: 6

Number of Hearing Days (NRC, EPA, and SEC)—Approximate: 110

Number of Pages of Transcript:	State (SEC)	5,800
	NRC	13,522
	EPA	2,000
	Total	21,322
Number of Exhibits:	State	123+
	NRC	80 (approximate)
	EPA	200 (approximate)
	Total	403

Applicant's Pre-Initial Decision Licensing Costs (including atty. fees) (est.): $15.4 million

Applicant's Total Costs as of March 1, 1978 (excluding construction costs) (est.): more than $30 million

Intervenors' Licensing Costs as of March 1, 1978 (est.): $170,000+

                                          NECNP $100,000

                                          SAPL   70,000

Direct Cost to the State of New Hampshire Attributable to Arrest, Temporary Incarceration and Prosecution of 1440 Demonstrators Who Occupied the Seabrook Construction Site in April 1977:

Precise totals are hard to come by, yet a number of figures are available. While incarcerated, the temporary inmates were costing the State of New Hampshire an estimated $50,000/day (*Concord Monitor*, May 4, 1977, p. 1). Estimates of total costs of the sit-in and subsequent incarceration and prosecution ranged from a low of $490,000 (*Concord Monitor*, May 13, 1977, p. 1) to a high of a million dollars (Attorney General of New Hampshire, David Souter, in the *Concord Monitor*, May 6, 1977, p. 1). PSCO contributed $74,604 to help defray the costs to the state.

VI
Determining "Reasonable Assurance"

The Seabrook case is unique in that it is the first instance of a serious intervenor challenge to the financial qualifications of an applicant seeking a construction permit for a nuclear facility. It is also a hard case, for although the principal applicant did not enjoy the best of financial health it was not clearly unqualified. The financial picture of the electric utility industry revealed in the pages of the Seabrook hearing transcript is not pretty, however; it reflects financial and regulatory ills that may be endemic to the industry as a whole.

The 2200mw Seabrook station would ultimately be owned by eleven utilities, whose financial responsibilities are set forth in a participation agreement entered into at the commencement of the project.[1] Of the eleven owners, four investor-owned utility companies agreed to own 90 percent of the facility [2] The ownership percentages originally proposed by the major participants follow:[3]

Public Service Company of New Hampshire	(PSCO)	50.0000
The United Illuminating Co.	(UI)	20.0000
The Connecticut Light and Power Co.		
(a subsidiary of Northeast Utilities)	(NU)	11.9776
New England Power Co.	(NEPCO)	8.9430

Under the participation agreement, PSCO is responsible as the "lead applicant" for obtaining regulatory approval for the two units of the facility. Costs are apportioned among the various owners in accordance with their ownership shares, and the ownership shares also determine electricity entitlements if and when the facility becomes operational. The dispute that developed over the financial qualifications of the applicant focused on PSCO, the leading and most heavily committed applicant.

As of the close of the NRC licensing hearings, PSCO's total corporate assets were about 480 million dollars.[4] Its share of the 1.2 billion dollar Seabrook plant estimated in 1972 would be about 600 million; its share of the 1.6 billion plant estimated in 1974 would be 800 million; its share of the 2.2 billion plant estimated in 1976 would 1.1 billion dollars; and its share of the 2.6 billion plant estimated in 1977 would be 1.3 billion dollars.[5] It is important to note the cost escalations because, though the licensing hearings spanned the years 1974-75, administrative appeals of various aspects of the licensing decision within the NRC were not concluded until 1978 and NRC did not render a final decision on the Seabrook financial qualifications issue until January 1978.

PSCO clearly could not finance its share of Seabrook over the eight-year construction period without borrowing most of the needed capital. Its average

189

retained earnings, for example, were in the neighborhood of 53 million dollars.[6] Hence, PSCO had to look to outside sources of capital—the large banks and the bond and stock markets.

Appendix C to the NRC's financial qualification regulations requires that applicants provide a proposed financing plan. It does not require, however, that the plan submitted be the one followed. A copy of the NRC's forms (from NRC staff's brief of October 7, 1977) required to be filled out pursuant to Appendix C is included as Appendix VII, below. It is significant that the information requested is required at the time the application is under review by the staff— relatively early in the licensing process. Updating such items as changes in cost is not required.[7] One element of the financing plan is the "sources of funds" sheet.[8] By this document the utility reveals how much of the capital required each year by the financing plan will be internally generated, how much by the sale of stock, how much by selling bonds, and so forth.

The sources of funds sheet submitted by PSCO is reproduced as Table 4. Although PSCO sponsored the document during the licensing hearings, it vehemently disclaimed any intention to finance its 50 percent share of Seabrook in the manner set forth in it.[9] PSCO's position was, simply, that the sources of funds sheet represented a "reasonable method"[10] of financing the plant. The staff of the NRC agreed with PSCO's contention that it did not have to produce and defend its actual financing scheme.

The distinction is not insignificant, because the sources of funds sheet submitted by PSCO contained certain assumptions that had become questionable, and which even PSCO's witnesses admitted were probably unsupportable.[11] The most glaring of these was the assumption that PSCO could market intermediate term bonds during 1976–83 at an interest cost of 8 percent. By successfully contending that it was not required to rely on the sources of funds sheet, PSCO could blunt attacks against it, arguing that such attacks would be academic exercises.[12]

Ordinarily, a utility like PSCO would secure its external financing primarily from the bond market. It would issue and sell five to ten year debentures to cover construction costs, which it would pay off, after the generating facility became operational, with proceeds from the sale of long-term first mortgage bonds.[13] To the extent that the sources of funds sheet reveals at least preliminary thinking of PSCO's management (though PSCO disclaimed it), it is probably representative of the kind of financing PSCO intended to rely upon.[14] The reason interim financing was contemplated is that under PSCO's bond indenture, construction work in progress was not permitted to be used as bondable property to support the sale of long-term mortgage bonds.[15] Thus, since PSCO could not market long-term bonds to pay for construction in advance, its construction financing had to be based on unsecured debentures and adequate amounts of stock sales, with the hope that stock equity would over the long haul displace the debt.[16]

The amount of external funding required by PSCO was extremely large in comparison with the averages of the utility industry.[17] Hence, critical to the company's financing of the Seabrook project was its ability to attract capital. The company had experienced several bad years. Its earnings per share of

Table 4

Applicant: *PUBLIC SERVICE COMPANY OF NEW HAMPSHIRE*   Nuclear Plant: *SEABROOK NUCLEAR STATION*

Sources of Funds for System-Wide Construction Expenditures During Period of Construction of Subject Nuclear Power Plant (See Note)

(Thousands of Dollars)

	Construction Years of Subject Nuclear Power Plant							
Security Issues and Other Funds	1975	1976	1977	1978	1979	1980	1981	1982
Common Stock	$ 5,000	$17,000	$ 31,000	$ 49,000	$ 49,000	$ 30,000	$23,000	$13,000
Preferred Stock	15,000	13,000	19,000	27,000	27,000	20,000	17,000	—
Long Term Debt	20,000	45,000	65,000	94,000	94,000	70,000	60,000	32,000
Notes Payable	(26,550)	(22,800)	(13,075)	27,165	60,101	17,312	(38,498)	(28,700)
Total	$13,450	$52,200	$101,925	$197,165	$230,101	$137,312	$61,502	$16,300
Internal Funds								
Net Income	$24,000	$26,920	$ 32,700	$ 41,640	$ 52,500	$ 62,180	$69,960	$776,040
Less: Preferred Dividends	4,000	5,120	6,400	8,240	10,400	12,280	13,760	14,440
Common Dividends	10,000	14,200	17,100	21,700	27,400	32,400	36,500	40,000
Retained Earnings	10,000	7,600	9,200	11,700	14,700	17,500	19,700	21,000
Deferred Taxes	1,900	3,300	6,000	11,340	19,100	24,057	13,300	14,500
Investment Tax Credit	3,500	1,000	950	1,900	2,000	12,700	1,200	12,700
Depreciation	16,000	16,800	17,700	18,900	20,200	23,600	33,200	37,900
Allowance for Funds	(4,200)	(7,400)	(13,300)	(25,200)	(42,400)	(53,500)	(29,500)	(32,200)
Sinking Fund & Working Capital	9,800	(2,600)	(2,800)	(2,800)	(2,800)	(2,800)	(2,800)	(2,800)
Total	$37,000	$18,700	$ 17,750	$ 15,840	$ 10,800	$ 21,557	$35,100	$51,700
TOTAL FUNDS	$50,450	$70,900	$119,675	$213,005	$240,901	$158,869	$96,602	$68,000
Construction Expenditures								
Nuclear Power Plants	$27,798	$44,470	$ 81,286	$165,580	$192,824	$109,119	$43,152	$13,000
Other	22,652	26,430	38,389	47,425	48,077	49,750	53,450	55,000
Total	$50,450	$70,900	$119,675	$213,005	$240,901	$158,869	$96,602	$68,000
Subject Nuclear Plant	$22,813	$34,313	$ 70,500	$154,255	$170,751	$108,269	$43,152	$13,000

Note: The information shown on this sheet is not a forecast of what will actually occur. It is a projection based on anticipated construction expenditures and capital requirements and on certain assumptions, including assumptions as to the cost of additional capital and as to the adequacy of revenues during the period.

common stock had been declining steadily, as had the market value of its common stock. At the time PSCO's financial status was reviewed by the staff of the Nuclear Regulatory Commission, and at the time of the licensing hearings, its financial picture was not rosy:

1. Between 1972 and 1973 the company began to experience sagging earnings. Its earnings per share of common stock dropped dramatically between 1972 and 1973, from 2.52 to 2.22.[18] According to the testimony of an NRC staff witness, private utilities ordinarily generate about one third of their construction cash requirements internally, and PSCO's earnings in 1973 and 1974 did not permit it to raise this much cash for the Seabrook project.[19]

2. The "earnings coverage ratio"[20] (the ratio of the company's earnings to its fixed charges) had decreased dramatically since 1970. Although this ratio had been near 4 historically, by December 1974 it had been reduced to 1.83.[21] Ordinarily, the financial rating services, Moody's and Standard and Poor's, will wave a caution flag to investors when a company's coverage ratio falls much below 3.[22] In addition, the indenture agreements under which PSCO's long-term mortgage bonds are held contain limits to the amount of new capital sales, based on earnings coverage figures.[23] A coverage ratio of 2.16, PSCO's ratio as of October 31, 1975, is only slightly over the minimum requirement to issue new debt.[24]

3. For two years PSCO had been unable to market its common stock at prices at or above book value. The book value of the stock was about 21 dollars per share between 1973 and 1975. The market price had bottomed out at 12 dollars per share in 1974, and at the time of the NRC hearings it was selling for about 16 dollars.[25] In fact, the market value of PSCO's stock as a percentage of book value had steadily declined from a high of 170 percent in 1968 to 51 percent in 1974.[26]

4. PSCO's bond rating had been reduced by the two financial rating services from A to BB and Baa. This had direct significance for the marketing of the company's bonds. Moody's defines Baa bonds as:

> "Bonds which are rated Baa are considered as medium grade obligations, i.e., they are neither highly protected nor poorly secured. Interest payment and principal security appear adequate for the present, but certain protective elements may be lacking or may be characteristically unreliable over any great length of time. Such bonds lack outstanding investment characteristics and in fact have speculative characteristics as well."

These bonds are the lowest rated that are considered qualified for commercial investment.

As a result of the downgrading of its securities PSCO had to pay between 9 and 12.75 percent on bonds issued in 1974.[27] Restoration of the bond rating to "A" was considered a high corporate priority by PSCO's management.[28]

5. PSCO's total energy sales, which had grown at a compound rate of 9.1 percent from 1960 through 1970, decreased considerably after the 1973 energy crisis. Total sales during 1974 increased by only 0.4 percent.[29] Thus the validity of the company's earlier projections of a solid 8 percent annual growth in sales, hence its real earnings projections, were placed in doubt.

The loss of its favorable bond rating had disturbed PSCO's management. In 1974 it argued before the New Hampshire Public Utilities Commission that it was vital to obtain a 14 percent return on shareholder's equity so that its bond rating could be reestablished.[30] The company's largest previous capital-raising project had involved only 85 million dollars,[31] and it was about to undertake a massive capital-raising effort, by most standards,[32] in a market that was increasingly wary of utility debt offerings. If, as suggested by an economist retained by NECNP to oppose PSCO, when utility bond ratings fall below A, "available buyers shrink to a point where the ability to market large issues becomes doubtful,"[33] PSCO, because of its small size and poor earnings position, was treading on shaky ground if it could not succeed in having its bond rating restored. Because of PSCO's small size and the massive nature of the Seabrook undertaking, its reliance on the market to raise such large amounts of capital was unusual.[34]

Early in 1975 the state Public Utilities Commission authorized the 14 percent rate of return requested by PSCO. Both PSCO's management and the NRC staff assumed that this rate action would have a positive impact on the company's earnings, and would precipitate restoration of the "A" bond rating by the end of 1975.[35] In addition, PSCO's financial vice-president testified in the licensing hearings that as a result of the rate action, the company's stock would be selling at or above book value shortly after the end of that year.[36]

Though generally agreeing with PSCO's predictions about its future earnings, the NRC staff cautioned its endorsement of PSCO by stating that "it is necessarily implicit in these findings that there be rational regulatory policies and relatively stable capital market conditions."[37]

It became apparent during the licensing hearings held during May and June of 1975 that neither at that time nor in the foreseeable future would the "capital market conditions" affecting utilities in general and PSCO in particular be stable. This uncertainty was admitted by PSCO's financial vice-president, Robert Harrison, in testimony before the NRC licensing board:

> Q. (Mr. Roisman): So . . . What you are saying is to some extent you are the victim of the marketplace. You can't postpone for two years like someone might wait to buy an air conditioner until prices went down—you can't afford to do that except in a relatively narrow band?
> A. (Witness Harrison): Within a relatively narrow band. The definitional problems of relatively narrow bands, several months we might be able to defer.
> Q. You have a judgment as to what you think the interest rate will be in the fall for the bonds you are thinking of issuing at this time?
> A. No, I do not, because I will recall to you that I just indicated that in March of '74 we sold bonds at 9 percent and in October of '74 we sold them at 12-3/4, and that is a 3-3/4 difference. We are looking at a market of 11 percent. Another change of 3-3/4 downward would get us to 7-3/4, and that is too precipitous a movement in this time span we are looking at, so I don't have any judgment as to the interest rates.

> Q. You think it is typical of the bond market today?
> A. I think quite possibly it could be.
> Q. How long do you think that is going to last?
> A. I have no judgment as to that.[38]

Indeed, PSCO's partners in the Seabrook venture could not agree on the future market for their securities. Their estimates of the interest cost of bonds ranged from Northeast Utilities' pessimistic 13 percent to PSCO's unrealistically optimistic 8 percent,[39] which led one economist to point out that of the applicant utilities, those in good financial condition tended to be pessimistic about the future, while those like PSCO in financial straits tended to be bullish.[40]

Two financial experts were produced by NECNP to support its claim that PSCO was not financially qualified to build Seabrook. Those witnesses testified that PSCO would have difficulty raising its needed cash in the financial market, and that if it could raise the money at all, it would be at a very high cost to PSCO.[41]

They argued that PSCO's size and its earnings potential were important factors that set it apart from other utilities in an industry that was already generally depressed. For example, of the earnings claimed by PSCO over the period of construction in the scenario presented in the "sources of funds" sheet, the largest component in the last half of the construction period was an allowance for funds used during construction (AFDC).[42] Rather than representing cash, which would be available to the company or its investors, AFDC is an accounting device that treats interest costs on money borrowed for construction as if it were income.[43] Real earnings, over three of the construction years, would be less than the company's annual depreciation charges.[44] Although the "rule of thumb" in the investment community is that AFDC should not exceed about 10 percent of a company's earnings,[45] on the basis of PSCO's own optimistic market assumptions the range of AFDC as a percentage of earnings over the six-year construction period was from 17.5 percent to 86 percent.[46] The quality of PSCO's earnings was so low that, in the opinion of the intervenor experts, informed investors might not buy PSCO's bonds.[47] One of these experts, Professor James Nelson of Amherst College, testified that unless the market value equaled or exceeded book value, PSCO could not market the large amounts of stock contemplated by it without seriously eroding the value of the outstanding stock.[48]

Table 6 sets forth the growth rates in PSCO's net income necessary to sustain construction of the Seabrook facility on the timetable assumed to be viable at the time of the licensing hearings. With a deferred construction schedule or an upward revision in prices, each of the amounts listed in Table 6 would, of course, have to be adjusted upward. PSCO was estimating an annual growth rate in prime sales of about 8 percent per year.[49] The experience of the 1973–74 dip in demand puts that assumption in some doubt. Even if the assumption as to growth in prime sales held true, PSCO's earnings growth would not be equivalent to it, but in all probability would be lower, because of rapidly increasing costs, unless it received substantial rate increases.[50]

It was apparent by the end of the licensing hearings that PSCO would require frequent and substantial rate increases in order to build the Seabrook plant. The amount of revenue needed to be raised in this manner would depend on the amount of money the company could raise in the market place,[51] and that amount was by no means agreed upon by the experts. If PSCO's predictions were correct, and if the plant were financed as outlined in the sources of funds

Table 5

GROWTH RATES IN NET INCOME BEFORE INTEREST NECESSARY TO SUSTAIN CONSTRUCTION OF SEABROOK NUCLEAR POWER PLANT[a]

Required Income Before Interest at Various Interest Rates
(000 Omitted)

Cost of Borrowed Money	1975	1976	1977	1978	1979	1980	1981	1982
8.0% Interest[b]	$41,000	$46,520	$56,700	$72,000	$ 90,380	$106,620	$119,600	$129,360
9.0% "	41,175	47,160	58,050	74,375	93,965	111,260	125,075	135,380
10.0% "	41,350	47,800	59,400	76,750	97,550	115,900	130,550	141,400
10.5% "	41,438	48,120	61,075	78,938	100,342	119,220	134,288	145,410

Annual Growth Rates Necessary to Sustain Above Income

	1975	1976	1977	1978	1979	1980	1981	1982
8.0% Interest[b]	18.8%	13.5%	21.9%	27.0%	25.5%	18.0%	12.2%	8.2%
9.0% "	19.3	14.5	23.1	28.1	26.3	18.4	12.4	8.2
10.0% "	19.8	15.6	24.3	29.2	27.1	18.8	12.6	8.3
10.5% "	20.0	16.1	26.9	29.2	27.1	18.8	12.6	8.3

[a] Data: Public Service Co. of New Hampshire Sources of Funds sheet dated January 27, 1975

[b] Interest rates and preferred dividend rates assumed to be equal.

sheet submitted to the NRC staff, the company would be asking the rate-payers to pay about 4 percent more money for electricity each year of the construction period. If the cost of the plant or the cost of PSCO's borrowed money increased, it would have to ask for more—possibly as much as 6 percent to 10 percent. If the NECNP's predictions proved true and commercial investors balked at PSCO's bonds, the company would be compelled either to abandon the project or to ask the state to bail it out by permitting it to charge its customers in advance for the cost of building the plant—causing them to shoulder massive increases in the cost of electricity in order to generate cash to build a plant that would not produce electricity for a number of years, and thus from which many of the rate-payers (such as those who die or move to another state) would derive no benefit.[52] Such an approach to construction financing, termed "inclusion of construction work in progress" (CWIP) in the rate base, is controversial, and is discussed in some detail above, pages 119–123, and herein.

The "regulatory climate" had become the critical factor in PSCO's financial qualifications equation. On numerous occasions during their testimony, PSCO's witnesses stated their belief that the state Public Utilities Commission would provide needed rate increases[53] and pointed to the February 1975 NHPUC decision in which the company had been permitted to earn a 14 percent rate of return on common stock equity as proof that the state Commission was responsive to its needs.[54]

The portion of the NRC licensing hearings that was devoted to PSCO's financial qualifications was conducted during May and June of 1975, but the licensing hearings dragged on well into the winter of 1976. Before the termination of the hearings, PSCO suffered additional bad news. Late in the fall it became known that two of its partners, Northeast Utilities and United Illuminating Company, owners of about 32 percent of the Seabrook project, were attempting to withdraw.[55] In addition, PSCO's hoped-for financial rebound following its February 1975 rate increase did not materialize. Its bonds had not been restored to "A" rating by the financial rating services; and its stock, though stronger than before the 1975 rate increase, was still selling at less than its book value. The Company's earnings, however, continued to drop. The prospectus issued for an October 1976 stock offering shows that net income for 1975 (12 months ending July 31, 1976) declined over the previous year, with a resultant drop in earnings available for common stock by about a million dollars, from $17,204,000 to $16,205,000.

In February 1976 PSCO's management was telling a subtly but very different story to the Federal Power Commission. In testimony filed before the FPC in support of PSCO's attempt to obtain an increase in its wholesale rates, PSCO vice-president Robert Harrison testified:

The Indenture under which Public Service Company of New Hampshire issues its mortgage bonds precludes the mortgaging of property for which all necessary permits have not been received. As a result the long-term debt portion of the financing of the Seabrook nuclear station will have to be done through the issuance of debentures. *Since debentures normally are rated one notch*

*lower than the mortgage bonds of the same company the proposed deben-
tures, absent an improvement in the rating will be rated Ba/BB. A Ba/BB
rating security is considered speculative in character and presents a serious
marketing and interest cost problem* [emphasis added].[56]

A financial consultant to PSCO was similarly pessimistic. He told the FPC
that the company was in real danger of being unable to market its common
stock at any price, and that it faced a substantial dilution of its shareholder's
equity if it sold the amount of stock it needed to finance the plant at a price
much below book value.[57] This testimony is surprisingly similar to that submitted earlier to the NRC by one of NECNP's witnesses, Professor Charles
Nelson of Amherst College. For example, the PSCO consultant, Zvi Benderly,
argued that investors would be likely to regard PSCO's stock as somewhat more
risky than in the past, a proposition put forward by Nelson and originally
disputed by PSCO.[58] Benderly also acknowledged that the unusually large
AFDC component in PSCO's earnings would discourage investors, a point made
by Nelson.[59]

PSCO's arguments to the FPC seem to be inconsistent with what it told
the NRC. Harrison, for example, had told the NRC in May 1975 that he anticipated rapid restoration of the company's debt rating,[50] and another PSCO
witness, Sanford Ege, had told the NRC that he had had discussions with persons
in the rating companies, and based on those discussions it was reasonable to
conclude that PSCO's "A" rating would soon be restored.[61] He also had told
the NRC that the company would have no difficulty raising funds even if its
BAA rating were retained.[62] The difference between the NRC testimony and
that presented to the FPC is in the opinions expressed by experts rather than
in facts upon which perjury might be alleged; nevertheless, it becomes apparent
that the utility was either varying its story to fit the needs of different regulatory bodies, or that circumstances had in fact changed.

In either case, the intervenors felt that the NRC record should have been
reopened and PSCO ordered to explain the discrepancy. They also sought
additional evidence with respect to the apparent withdrawal of two of PSCO's
major co-owners, Northeast Utilities and United Illuminating. Intervenor SAPL
filed a motion to this effect, but it was denied by the licensing board.[63]

Several months later the board ruled that PSCO was financially qualified to
constuct the Seabrook facility. Its initial decision read as if the intervenor's
testimony and PSCO's recent difficulties did not exist. The licensing board's
findings of fact simply pointed to PSCO's sources of funds sheet and acknowledged that some rate increases would be required, but concluded that PSCO had
recently (in 1975) been granted an increase.[64] Its reasoning was simple:

In the Board's view the preponderance of the expert testimony in this case
is that the necessary funds will be forthcoming from the market although
the cost of money will be higher than originally projected by PSCO.[65]

The Appeal Board's Version

The licensing board's decision was, on the whole, poorly reasoned. It did not evaluate the arguments of NECNP's experts, as it was required to do as an adjudicatory board. NRC's appeal board acknowledged that the licensing board "fell short" of its "responsibilities," and that it failed in its obligation to support its decision and to explain why it rejected the evidence and the arguments of the intervenors.[66] Nevertheless, the appeal board upheld the licensing board's decision—by rewriting it, concluding that all of the evidence about PSCO's inability to market its securities was not critical to the inquiry into the company's burden of showing that it has "reasonable assurance" of raising the necessary capital. What was important in the eyes of the appeal board was, simply, the "regulatory climate"—that is, the willingness of the New Hampshire Public Utilities Commission to grant the company rate increases. As to this, the appeal board reasoned:

> the applicants here are public utilities which are regulated by state regulatory bodies. Those bodies have considered and approved the Seabrook facility. The New Hampshire Public Utilities Commission (PUC) has issued a "certificate of Site and Facility" for the plant. PUC Docket No. D-SF6205 Commission Report and Order No. 11,267, January 29, 1974. In doing so, it found, *inter alia*, that uncontradicted evidence "showed such a significantly lower cost from a nuclear plant than from a similarly-sized fossil plant as to eliminate even considering a fossil plant unless the nuclear plant was beyond any possibility of becoming a reality" . . . *Given these considerations, it is scarcely likely that the PUC would stand in the way of the establishment of those rates necessary to enable Public Service to fulfill the obligations imposed upon it by its nuclear facility licenses* [emphasis added].[67]

In short, the appeal board assumed that the PUC had locked itself into future rate relief for PSCO as a result of action it took approving Seabrook under the state's electric utility siting law, and that fact alone was sufficient to establish PSCO's financial qualifications. Unfortunately, the matter is somewhat more complex than the appeal board's statement implies.

A close analysis of the circumstances under which the PUC decision was made reveals that it is of little or no significance to, and clearly does not mandate, later rate decisions. The statute under which the decision was made, NH RSA 162-F, requires the PUC to make the following findings based on an evidentiary record:

> that the construction of the facility:
> a) Will not unduly interfere with the orderly development of the region with due consideration having been given to the views of municipal and regional planning commissions and municipal legislative bodies;
> b) Is required to meet the present and future demand for electric power;
> c) Will not adversely affect system stability and reliability and economic factors; and
> d) Will not have an unreasonable adverse effect on aesthetics, historic sites, air and water quality, the natural environment, and the public health and safety.[68]

The statute clearly does not require the PUC to approve the utility's finances.

The weakness of the appeal board's justification is even more apparent in the light of some additional facts concerning the state "climate" that were known to it at the time the decision was made. Among the other reasons advanced by SAPL in its motion to reopen the record was that early in 1976, PSCO vice-president Harrison had testified before a state legislative committee that enactment of a pending bill which would have prohibited outright the inclusion of CWIP in the rate base would prevent PSCO from constructing "any base-load additions to generating capacity including the Seabrook plant."[69] CWIP had traditionally not been permitted in utility rate bases by the PUC, and since PSCO had told the licensing board in 1975 that it could finance Seabrook without CWIP,[70] it was unreasonable for the appeal board to assume that the company would have told the PUC a less optimistic story in 1974, before it had lost its "A" bond rating. The Harrison testimony was clear evidence that things had changed so that whatever had led the PUC to its conclusion in 1974 was not necessarily true in 1976. In any event, it was folly for the appeal board to assume, as it must have assumed, that the PUC's "approval" of the Seabrook plant for the limited purposes set forth in the New Hampshire law would necessarily force it later to change one of the fundamental premises of utility-rate regulation by including CWIP in the rate base. The appeal board seems to have recognized this problem, but skirted it by stating essentially that unless there was a statutory bar to including CWIP in the rate base, it was not important to it that PSCO might now be faced with having to ask the PUC to include it.[71]

The NHPUC decision was finally issued in 1974, before PSCO's demand curve slackened. Moreover, it was based on a record devoid of any evidence whatever on alternative means of meeting the demand, such as with coal. Neither of these facts was addressed by the appeal board, which chose to cast its conclusion in general terms.[72]

In defense of the board it can be said that it did not rely solely on the 1974 NHPUC decision in support of its ultimate conclusion. It also referenced the 1975 PUC decision allowing PSCO its 14 percent rate of return[73] and made a legal argument to the effect that the PUC would have to allow rate increases sufficient to permit a rate of return high enough not to be confiscatory.[74] The board equated this with "reasonable rate relief," arguing that the PUC would have to allow PSCO to raise its rates, whether it wanted to or not.[75]

PSCO's lawyers, in a brief filed in opposition to NECNP's appeal of the decision, characterized the appeal board's reasoning in the following manner:

> The dissent[76] suggests that under the majority's view "the financial qualifications inquiry is virtually meaningless" . . . This is not so. What the inquiry must be in the case of a regulated electric utility is into the regulatory climate in which it operates. For example, if it appeared that company X needed a rate increase to build a facility and that the rate regulators had refused a certificate for or otherwise formally indicated an unwillingness to allow it in the rate base when completed, financial qualifications would be in doubt.[77]

Another way of stating this argument is that if the state PUC had not formally said "no" prior to the NRC proceedings, then any utility-applicant must be found financially qualified, regardless of its actual financial condition.

The Commission's Version

The appeal board's ruling created a new financial qualifications standard. The NRC staff had been proceeding under the assumption that an applicant's actual financial condition and its ability to raise capital in the market were the relevant issues under the regulation.[78] In the one other case in which the financial health of an applicant was an issue, a licensing board did not rely on the "regulatory climate" standard. In 1974 the NRC was conducting licensing hearings with respect to Unit 3 of the Millstone Nuclear Power Station when it was learned that one of the owners, Central Vermont Public Service Corporation (CVPSC) was in financial difficulty. CVPSC's bonds had been delisted by the rating services, and were not marketable. It was the owner of only 3.694 percent of the Millstone Unit, and the licensing board found it "marginally" qualified.[79] Subsequently, CVPSC was required to sell its small interest to other participants. While a lag in rate relief was cited as partly responsible for CVPSC's plight, it was not shown that the Vermont Public Service Board (Vermont's PUC) had or would refuse to give the company needed rate increases.[80] Arguably, under the appeal board's rule set down in *Seabrook*, CVPSC would have been in no real difficulty, and no issue would have arisen in the *Millstone* proceeding.

PSCO's earnings did not improve, but rather steadily declined in the 2½ years following the 1975 rate increase. By mid-1977, its management appears to have concluded that the company could not raise the money to build the Seabrook plant through the normal money market. It asked the New Hampshire Public Utilities Commission to permit it to increase its base rates by 26 percent and to allow CWIP in the rate base. During the same time period, the company's lawyers were defending the appeal board's decision—then on appeal to the NRC Commissioners—arguing that PSCO could raise the needed funds. They never mentioned the new rate petition.[81]

The case finally presented to the PUC was markedly different from the one that had been presented to the NRC licensing board. On October 12 and 13, 1977 PSCO vice-president Harrison told the PUC that the company's earnings per share had declined 18 percent in the eight months between year-end 1976 and August 31, 1977, from $2.54 per share to $2.08 per share.[82] The company had never been able to earn the authorized 14 percent rate of return, and in fact its situation was worse than before the 1975 rate increase.[83] In addition, the company's bond ratings had not been restored, and it was unable to market its medium term debentures, which had been rated by Moody's and Standard and Poor's as "not of investment quality."[84] Its bankers, moreover, had informed PSCO that since its securities might be further downrated, they would not provide the company with lines of credit necessary to provide cash for the Seabrook plant.[85] The banks, PSCO said, simply would not extend credit to it over the financing period of the Seabrook project, so long as it had a BA/BB rating.[86] Without access to the revolving bank credit that PSCO "desperately" needed, the company was forced to increase its internal generation of cash substantially, and the only way it could achieve that goal was through inclusion of CWIP in its rate base, and with yearly rate increases of a magnitude never before sought.[87] Only then, PSCO argued, would rerating the company's first mortgage bonds even be possible, and only then would it be possible to finance the construction program—to "go from the state of questionable perhaps to one of relative assurance."[88] Thus, while PSCO was urging the NRC that the licensing board correctly found there was "reasonable assurance" that it could raise the money to build Seabrook, it was at the same time telling the state PUC that the assurance was "questionable."

PSCO, which two years earlier had confidently told the NRC that it could market debentures at 8 percent, that it expected to see its bond ratings shortly restored to "A," and that it would have no trouble raising needed funds in the market, was now on its knees asking the state to bail it out of a financial crisis. It was, according to another of its financial consultants in "severe financial distress," "teeter[ing] precariously on the brink of financial disaster."[89] Among the factors the witness felt were contributing to PSCO's financial distress were its small size in relation to its burden in constructing its share of Seabrook,[90] it's continuing poor coverage ratio, the fact that "87% of the electric utilities [listed in Solomon Brothers index] have ratings higher than Public Service Company of New Hampshire," and that it is only one of twelve utilities with a straight Baa/BBB rating.[91]

PSCO was out of credit. It had commenced construction of Seabrook in August 1976 immediately upon the licensing board decision; and except for a period of several months during which its permit was suspended,[92] it had worked steadily on the project, pouring millions of dollars into it each month. Without credit, cash or any reasonable likelihood of being able to raise the $159,000,000 needed to continue the project in 1977 and $143,000,000 needed in 1978,[93] PSCO found itself in the almost absurd position of having to argue to the NRC that it was now financially qualified to build Seabrook because it was broke and "on the brink of financial disaster."[94] Because it was in such bad shape, the company argued, the state PUC would have to allow it the requested rate increase, and would have to allow CWIP in the rate base, and since those things were sure to happen, the company's cash position would improve, its bond ratings would be restored, and all would be well again. PSCO's lawyers also began to argue that the NRC should not even bother looking into its qualifications, because, they urged, "the statute [Atomic Energy Act] permits the Commission to decide that there is not need for any inquiry at all with respect to financial qualifications." They argued, in an effort to neutralize the impact of appeal board member Farrar's devastating dissenting opinion, that section 182 (a) of the Atomic Energy Act itself contains no 'requirement' that an applicant be financially qualified.[95] They protested loudly that there were no safety factors involved in a company's financial health, since construction of the plant was so closely regulated by the NRC staff.[96]

This turn of events caused the lawyer representing intervenor NECNP to characterize the state of affairs as a "Mad Hatter's tea party, where regulations mean whatever the Applicant wants them to mean and one proves something by proving what it is not."[97] The staff of the NRC found itself in somewhat of a dilemma. It had supported PSCO throughout the proceedings, but on the basis that PSCO would be able to raise construction capital in the market, by means of the scheme set out in the source of funds sheet, and consistent with the staff's normal approach to the financial qualifications issue.[98] PSCO had pulled the rug out from under the staff's position by shifting from the fund-raising method relied on by the staff, to one involving remortgaging all its assets and relying entirely on the hope of advance rate-payer financing in the form of CWIP, a method which it had, as least passively, disavowed during the licensing proceedings.

Faced with having to defend its previous position and being at the same time apparently unable to bring itself to the point of agreeing with NECNP and SAPL, the staff's legal position collapsed in confusion. It argued weakly to the Commission that its initial judgment about PSCO's ability to raise capital was correct (a position that even PSCO had essentially abandoned by this time), and urged that PSCO's new position was wrong. PSCO, the staff argued, "ignores among other things, the importance of prudent financial planning, evidence of which is essential to a finding of financial qualifications."[99]

The staff tried unsuccessfully to reconcile its position with the decision of the appeal board majority. It argued that the appeal board's decision was not as limited as PSCO's, but its argument was unconvincing and without conviction. It was reduced to a feeble attempt to keep the recent PSCO state and FPC testimony out of the record, as if to preserve a fictitious picture of PSCO's financial condition.[100]

In one sense it is the imprecision of the Atomic Energy Act and the vagueness of Part 50 regulations that allowed the Seabrook situation to arise. Yet in another sense the NRC staff must bear a certain measure of the responsibility for its failure over the years to establish a meaningful set of standards upon which to base a reasoned judgment as to an applicant's ability to raise necessary funds. In still another sense, in defense of the NRC it was generally assumed until 1973 that any major electric utility would, almost by definition, be able to raise enough money to construct a generating plant. After all, from the beginning of the civilian reactor program until about 1972, electric utilites were experiencing rapid growth and generally decreasing or stabilizing operating costs. (Indeed, PSCO during the 50's and 60's ordinarily went to the PUC for rate *decreases*). Generating stations were small, and the capital costs relatively low. One cannot condemn the NRC too harshly for failing to perceive what would happen to the utility industry during the 1970's.

Nevertheless, it is clear that, at least for PSCO, something went wrong. PSCO had committed itself to the Seabrook project in 1970 or 1971, at a time when the AEC had estimated nuclear plant capital costs to be about $134 to $150 per kilowatt of nuclear capacity. The AEC estimates proved to be 50 to 280 percent too low by 1973,[101] and by 1976, the year the construction permit was issued, the costs had escalated to $1,200 per kilowatt. In addition, PSCO, like other utilities, had experienced rapidly increasing operating costs after 1971 and sagging sales after 1973. And PSCO, a small utility when compared with most others committeted to an 1100 mw nuclear plant, took on an inordinately large undertaking in its Seabrook commitment. It could not, by 1978, finance its share of the Seabrook plant in the manner in which private corporations are supposed to finance capital assets, and it is far from clear that it ever had that capacity.

The Commissioners of the NRC finally issued their decision on NECNP's appeal of the financial qualifications issue on January 6, 1978, nearly a year and a half after tne construction permit was issued, and construction begun at the Seabrook site. Except for its lengthy apology for taking so long, and a tacit admission that perhaps construction should not have been permitted to proceed while the appeals were pending, the decision did little to improve the NRC'S regulatory stature.

The appeal board decision was affirmed by the NRC, but the way the Commissioners arrived at that result requires close examination. They admitted that the present regulation was vague,[102] that in enacting it the Atomic Energy Commission had in fact stated that financial qualifications were of importance to its safety responsibilities. They rejected PSCO's argument that its status as a regulated public utility should be sufficient to qualify it without further inquiry. Then, in the next breath, they said that in the absence of "facts" in the record of the AEC's rule-making, or "evidence" in the Seabrook record that a shortage of capital would result in a compromise of safety, either by utilities in general or by PSCO in particular,[103] PSCO was in fact financially qualified.

The decision purported to establish a new standard, in that it defined "reasonable assurance" to mean "that the applicant must have a reasonable financing plan in light of relevant circumstances."[104] This new standard the Commissioners further defined in relation to what they saw as the difference between the majority and dissenting opinions of the appeal board:

> The division between the majority and dissent focused in part on the concept of "difficulty." The majority asserted concern should center on "whether the funds can be obtained and not the price of or difficulty of obtaining them" 6 NRC at 79. The dissent countered that difficulty in raising funds was precisely the circumstance in which corner-cutting was likely to occur. 6 NRC at 108.
>
> Both majority and dissent presumably would agree that at a certain point, an applicant could face so much difficulty in obtaining funds that the likelihood of its being able to finance the plant would fall below the level of "reasonable assurance." They appear to differ on what is "reasonable"; the majority would establish a low threshold . . . while the dissent urges an exacting standard. As we have indicated, we believe that the correct approach falls between the majority and the dissent. Anticipated difficulties in raising funds are relevant to the reasonable assurance determination, but a showing of some potential difficulty would not necessarily preclude that determination, all other relevant factors being taken into account.[105]

It appears that the Commissioners could not quite bring themselves to the outright abandonment of the rule, as the appeal board majority had so forthrightly proposed, and yet they were, like the appeal board, unable to find an applicant unqualified if their agency had previously licensed it. They acknowledged that PSCO was having a hard time raising the money it needed but decided that it was not having a hard enough time to be unqualified. They did not say just how hard, short of absolute inability, it would have to get before they would conclude that the "assurance" was no longer "reasonable." They told the staff to go back and propose a new rule for that.

It may be that a withdrawal or reduction of PSCO's bond ratings would be the sort of difficulty the Commissioners would consider fatal to the company's position.[106] We do not know, of course, since the opinion leaves the standard as vague as before. Moreover, it is hard to see how PSCO is in materially better shape financially than the example cited by the NRC. The withdrawal of the bond rating, it appears, would not make the company's securities any less marketable than they were at the time it went before the PUC to ask for CWIP to be included in its rate base—for at that time the company testified that it could not market them at all.

Of course, if the Commissioners had wanted to, they could have pointed to PSCO's October testimony before the state PUC as evidence that the company's position had deteriorated to the point that "difficulty" had nearly become "inability." They could have decided that a utility that had to rely on rate-payer relief was not qualified. They did neither, confining themselves in the first case to the "record" before them (which did not include the subject testimony, although the Commissioners had been made aware of it in the oral argument by SAPL's lawyers); they simply avoided the second.

Implicit in the opinion are repeated hints that the Commission is not convinced that anything short of bankruptcy will create potential safety problems. For example, it states that "recent experience does not suggest that a utility short of funds will cut corners on safety."[107] There is no explanation provided for this statement, and no data or examples to support it. There is also a lengthy discussion of the staff's monitoring and inspection capability, with a self-serving conclusion that it has the ability to bring construction "to a halt when deficient practices indicated a safety problem."[108] The reasonableness of these statements and the conclusion implicit in their presence in the decision is discussed above, pages 126–129; but it is important to realize that by making them, the NRC can influence (if not unalterably prejudice) its future rule-making proceedings.

In a sense the NRC, though it directed its staff to rethink the financial qualifications rule, had already made a new rule in the Seabrook decision. By abandoning safety as the basis of the existing rule and by finding PSCO qualified, it was implicitly accepting PSCO's argument, even though the opinion explicitly rejected it. The prevailing standard became the "reasonableness" of the regulatory climate. That amounts to nothing less than amending the regulation without going through the rule-making procedures required by the Federal Administrative Procedure Act (5 U.S.C. Sec. 501 et seq.).

The questions that arise from the Seabrook case are many, and they are not easy to answer. Is PSCO's plight a bellwether, foreshadowing the end of privately financed nuclear generating capacity?[109] Is it reasonable for a private utility to expect the state to authorize it to charge its rate-payers higher rates to raise capital that it is itself unable to raise in the financial market? What are the long-range implications of such a practice to the consumers and to the utility? And what of the NRC's role in determining the financial qualifications of applicant utilities? If it now has no standards by which to judge utilities, should it develop them? And, if so, what should these standards be?

VII

Sample of "Request for Additional Financial Information"

(as used by NRC staff)

1. Provide the most recent cost estimates for each unit grouped as follows: (a) total nuclear production plant costs; (b) transmission, distribution, and general plant costs; and (c) nuclear fuel inventory cost for the first core. The cost estimates should be in dollars escalated through the year of construction completion. Also, complete the attached schedule entitled, "Plant Capital Investment Summary," for each unit using the most recent cost estimates. Indicate the estimated site labor requirements express as "man-hours/kWe." Indicate the average site labor pay rate in dollars per hour (including fringe benefits) effective at month and year of NSSS purchase. Indicate the estimated month and year of construction start for each unit and the earliest and latest estimated dates for completion of construction of each unit.

2. Provide copies of the joint ownership agreement (contract) among participants. The Staff will later require copies of the agreement after it is executed. The executed agreement must necessarily be in substantial conformity with the agreement previously provided.

   Provide a detailed explanation of the provisions governing progress payment to be made to the project manager by each additional participant for its share of all costs of design and construction of the subject facility. This may be accomplished by reference to pertinent portions of the joint ownership agreement.

3. Provide the following information for each investor-owned applicant:

   a. Complete the attached schedule entitled, "Sources of Funds for System-Wide Construction Expenditures During Period of Construction of Subject Nuclear Power Plant," through the year of earliest estimated completion of the final unit. Indicate the assumptions upon which the "Sources of Funds" statement is based. These assumptions include, but are not necessarily limited to: (a) rate of return on average common stock equity; (b) preferred stock dividend rate; (c) long-term and short-term debt interest rates; (d) market/book ratio with respect to the projected common stock offerings; (e) common stock dividend payout ratio; (f) target capital structure; (g) resultant SEC and indenture interest coverages over the period of construction; and (h) annual growth rate in kWh sales and price per kWh. Provide a brief explanation of the basis for each assumption.

b. Provide copies of the 1977 1st, 2nd, and 3rd quarters (and 4th quarter, when available) income and retained earnings statements and balance sheet. Provide the same statements for the most recent 12-month period. Also, provide copies of similar statements for the corresponding periods ended in the previous year.

c. Provide copies of the 1975 and 1976 Annual Reports to Stockholders, copies of the prospectus for the Company's most recent security issue and copies of the most recent SEC Form 10-K. Provide copies of the preliminary prospectus for any pending security issue. Continue to submit copies of the Annual Report for each year thereafter as required by 10 CFR 50.71 (b).

d. Provide copies of the most recent Officer's Certificate or Net Earnings Certificate prepared in conjunction with the issuance of mortgage bonds or debentures and showing interest coverage calculations using the tests set forth in the applicable indenture. Explain bondable property addition provisions as they relate to restrictions on the issuance of new long-term debt. Provide copies of the portions of the indenture relating to interest coverage tests of alternative earnings tests and bondable property additions. Provide calculations of net earnings and interest coverage for the most recent 12-month period using the definitions of net earnings and annual interest requirements (on debt presently outstanding) using the most restrictive test set forth in the mortgage bond indenture. Assuming a range of interest rates considered realistic by the utility, state the additional amount of first mortgage bonds which could be issued under the most restrictive test based on net earnings as defined by indenture for the most recent 12-month period.

e. If the corporate charter contains a preferred stock coverage requirement, provide copies of that portion of the charter. Assuming a range of dividend yields considered realistic by the utility, state the additional amount of preferred stock that could be issued by applying the most restrictive test for preferred dividend coverage for the most recent 12-month period.

f. Provide a detailed explanation of all other restrictions or constraints on the issuance of short and long-term debt, preferred stock, preference stock and common stock. Short-term debt should include bank lines of credit and commercial paper, if any. Indicate compensating balance requirements for bank loans.

g. Describe the nature and amount of the company's most recent rate relief action and the anticipated effect on revenues. Provide copies of the rate order and opinion. In addition, indicate the nature and amount of any pending rate relief action(s). Use the attached form to provide this information. Provide copies of the submitted, financially-related testimony of the staff and company in the most recent rate relief action or pending rate relief request.

Describe aspects of the company's regulatory environment including, but not necessarily limited to, the following: prescribed treatment of allowance for funds used during construction and of construction work in progress (indicate percentage and amount included in rate base); form of rate base (original cost, fair value, other); accounting for deferred income taxes and investment tax credits; and fuel adjustment clauses in effect or proposed.

h. Provide a list of generating units, transmission and distribution facilities and general plant projects to be constructed during the period of construction of the subject nuclear power plant, showing the type of facility, net capacity of each generating unit, the dollar amounts to be expended for each facility during each of the years involved, and in-service date of each facility.

i. Complete the attached form entitled, "Financial Statistics" for the most recent 12-month period and for the years ended December 31, 1976 and December 31, 1975.

4. The following information is required from each cooperative applicant:

a. Indicate the percentage ownership in the facility and any difference between this and the cooperative's percentage entitlement to the electrical capacity and output of the units. Explain the reason for the difference, if any.

b. Provide a detailed statment of the projected sources of funds and respective dollar amounts for each cooperative participant's total contribution to the subject project. Include a detailed explanation of the assumptions upon which the projected sources of funds are based.

c. Indicate the amounts of the respective dollar payments to be made to the project manager by each cooperative system participant upon execution of the ownership agreement. Provide estimates of the total additional payments to be made by each such participant subsequent to the execution of the agreement and through completion of the units.

d. If financing is to be provided through REA guaranteed sources, the applicants must provide copies of favorable letters of intent from REA regarding the proposed REA loans. These must be provided prior to issuance of the construction permits. Indicate whether the REA has provided loans to the applicants in the past.

e. If membership cooperatives are involved, explain the contractual arrangements between the cooperative and its members that will provide funds for interest payments on the loan(s) and its eventual retirement. Provide representative copies of such contracts.

f. Provide copies of excerpts from state statutes on which the cooperatives are relying as authority to incur debt and to take other actions necessary to acquire partial ownership of the subject facility.

g. Describe the rate-setting authority and rate covenants of the cooperatives and how that authority will be used to ensure the satisfaction of financial obligations in relation to the design and construction of the subject facility.

h. Describe the nature and amount of each cooperative's most recent rate relief action(s) and its anticipated effect on net margins. Provide copies of the rate order(s). In addition, indicate the nature and amount of any pending rate relief action(s).

i. Provide copies of the latest annual and interim financial statements. Also provide copies of similar statement for the corresponding periods ended in the previous year. Continue to submit copies of the annual financial statement each year as required by 10 CFR 50.71 (b).

j. Provide a list of generating units, transmission and distribution facilities and general plant projects to be constructed during the period of construction of the subject nuclear power plant, showing the type of facility, net capacity of each generating unit, the dollar amounts to be expended for each facility during each of the years involved, and in-service date of each facility.

PLANT CAPITAL INVESTMENT
SUMMARY

BASIC DATA

   Name of plant   _____ Cost basis: at *start of construction*
   Net capacity   ____ MW(e)   _____
   Reactor type   _____ _____
   Location   _____ *Type of cooling*
                                         Run of river _____

Design and construction period   Natural draft cooling
   Month, year NSSS order   towers _____
      placed _____   Mechanical draft cooling
   Month, year of commercial   towers _____
      operation_____   Other (describe)_____
   Length of workweek_____ hours
   Interest rate, interest
      during construction _____ simple? or compound?

COST SUMMARY

Account Number	*Account Title*	*Total Cost* (thousand dollars)
DIRECT COSTS		
20	Land and land rights	$ _____
	PHYSICAL PLANT	
21	Structures and site facilities	_____
22	Reactor plant equipment	_____
23	Turbine plant equipment	_____
24	Electric plant equipment	_____
25	Misc. plant equipment	_____
	Subtotal	$ _____
	Spare parts allowance	_____
	Contingency allowance	_____
	Subtotal	$ _____
INDIRECT COSTS		
91	Construction facilities, equip't, and services	$ _____
92	Engineering and const. mg't. services	_____
93	Other costs	_____
94	Interest during construction	_____
	Subtotal	$ _____
	Start of construction cost	$ _____
	*Escalation during construction (___ % yr.)	_____
	Total plant capital investment ($ ___ /KW)	$ _____

*Indicate separate escalation rates for site labor, site materials, and for purchased equipment, if applicable.

Applicant: _____   Nuclear Plant: _____

**Sources of Funds for System-Wide Construction Expenditures During Period
of Construction of Subject Nuclear Power Plant**
(millions of dollars)

	Construction Years of Subject Nuclear Power Plant									
	19__	19__	19__	19__	19__	19__	19__	19__	19__	19__
Security issues and other funds										
Common stock	$	$	$	$	$	$	$	$	$	$
Preferred stock										
Long-term debt										
Less: Refundings										
Notes payable										
Contributions from parent-net										
Other funds										
Total										
Internal funds										
Net income										
Less:										
preferred dividends										
common dividends										
Retained earnings										
Deferred taxes										
Invest. tax cred.-deferred										
Depreciation and amort.										
Net Working Capital Changes										
Less: AFDC										
Total										
TOTAL FUNDS	$	$	$	$	$	$	$	$	$	$
Construction expenditures *										
Nuclear power plants	$	$	$	$	$	$	$	$	$	$
Other										
Total const. exp's.	$	$	$	$	$	$	$	$	$	$
Subject nuclear plant	$	$	$	$	$	$	$	$	$	$

*Exclusive of AFDC (allowance for funding used during construction)

ATTACHMENT FOR ITEM NO. _____

RATE DEVELOPMENTS

	Electric	Gas	Steam

Granted

Annual amount requested—test year basis (000's)
Date requested
Annual amount granted—test year basis (000's)
Percent increase
Effective date
Rate of return on rate base authorized
Rate of return on common equity authorized

Revenue Effect (000's)

Amount received in year granted
Amount received in subsequent year

Pending Requests

Amount (000's)
Percent increase
Date filed
Date by which decision must be issued
Rate of return on rate base requested
Rate of return on common equity requested

ATTACHMENT FOR ITEM NO. _____
FINANCIAL STATISTICS

12 months ended

	1976	1975
	(dollars in millions)	

Earnings available to common equity
Average common equity
   Rate of return on average common equity

Times total interest earned before FIT:
   Gross income (incl. AFDC) + current and
   deferred FIT ÷ total interest charges +
   amortization of debt discount and expense

Times long-term interest earned before FIT:
   Gross income (incl. AFDC) + current and
   deferred FIT ÷ long-term interest charges
   + amortization of debt discount and
   expense

Bond ratings (end of period)
   Standard and Poor's
   Moody's

Times interest and preferred dividends earned
after FIT:
   Gross income (incl. AFDC) ÷ total interest
   charges + amortization of debt discount
   and expense + preferred dividends

AFUDC
Net income after preferred dividends
   %

Market price of common
Book value of common
   Market-book ratio (end of period)*

Earnings avail. for common less AFDC +
   depreciation and amortization, deferred
   taxes, and invest. tax credit adjust.-
   deferred
Common dividends
   Ratio

Short-term debt
   Bank loans
   Commercial paper

*If subsidiary company, use parent's data.

	12 months ended	
	1976	1975
	(dollars in millions)	

Capitalization (*Amount* & *Percent*)
   Long-term debt
   Preferred stock
   Common equity

Notes

Introduction

1. See, e.g., Haggett and Surrey, Opposition to Nuclear Power: A Review of International Experience, 4 *Energy Policy* 286 (1976), and Taylor, The Struggle against Nuclear Power in Europe, 7 *Ecologist* 216 (1977). (Both published in Great Britain.)

2. Haggett and Surrey at 289 (discussing a demonstration by farmers concerned with the impact of cooling tower-generated fog on their crop production).

3. According to the European press, in most examples.

4. This demonstration involved two reactor sites and a proposed lead sulfate factory.

5. Taylor at 219. This decision was reversed by the Bavarian Administrative Court on appeal, apparently on the grounds that there was no legal basis for issuing an injunction for the reason given by the lower court.

6. *Washington Post,* November 13, 1978, p. A-20.

7. Haggett and Surrey at 306.

8. Id.

9. See, generally, Frank Dawson, *Nuclear Power, Development and Management,* Seattle, University of Washington Press (1976), Chapter 6.

10. Id., 191–192.

11. Muntzing, L. M., Siting and Environment: towards an effective nuclear siting policy, 4 *Energy Policy* 3 at 8 (1976).

12. Dawson's book (note 9 above) is an excellent history of the AEC, and should be read by anyone with more than a passing interest in the subject.

13. This statement is not intended to imply *political* power. That is quite another matter and not within my scope here. The "power" referred to is the breadth of the regulatory authority delegated to the agency by Congress; it is considerable.

1. The Beginnings

1. The condensers, which serve to cool steam from the turbine until it condenses to liquid water before being returned to the steam generators, use cold water as the cooling medium. "Once through" cooling systems take water from the ocean, or a river or lake, circulate it through the condensers, and

return it to its source, significantly warmer after having absorbed the heat from the steam pipes in the condenser. An alternative mechanism involves the use of a semiclosed system employing cooling towers. Under that system the same water is continuously recirculated through the condensers, and the heat it takes on is removed from it by evaporation in the cooling tower. The first method requires the use of massive amounts of water, and the discharge of heat, considered a pollutant, to cooler water bodies. The second is expensive to operate and requires the construction of huge cooling towers, as high as 700 feet.

2. These are discussed in detail in Chapter 7.

3. N.H. Rev. Stat. Ann. §162–F:8.

4. Siting laws are discussed in greater detail in Chapter 2. For a full discussion of these concepts, see F. Bosselman, D. Fevrer, and C. Sieman, *The Permit Explosion,* ULI Management and Control of Growth Series, Urban Land Institute, Washington, D.C. (1976).

5. N.H. Rev. Stat. Ann. §162–F:9.

6. This combination of roles proved somewhat difficult when imposed upon a single lawyer.

7. During the early stages of development of the law, the drafters of the legislation debated whether to make it a professional body rather than a collection of state officials. As with a similar suggestion to fund a full-time staff, the decision was made not to do so, since it was unlikely that the legislature, in a state perennially short of money, would agree to any appropriation.

8. The law did permit the committee to engage a consultant and charge the cost back to the permit applicant in connection with a specific application. No such authority existed, however, with respect to the committee's rule-making responsibilities, under the law as originally enacted.

9. PSCO also retained the large and prestigious Boston law firm of Ropes and Gray, which remained behind the scenes in the state proceedings. When the licensing proceedings escalated to the federal level, PCSO's local lawyers dropped out, and the Boston firm took over.

10. Berlin, Roisman and Kessler had had previous experience in nuclear licensing cases, and one of the firm's partners, Anthony Z. Roisman, had become well known in antinuclear circles for his representation of the Calvert Cliffs Coordinating Committee in a successful lawsuit against the Atomic Energy Commission in which the United States Court of Appeals (D.C. cir.) overturned a nuclear power plant construction license after finding that the AEC's regulations violated the National Environmental Policy Act of 1969. *See Calvert Cliffs v AEC*, 449 F2d 1109 (1972). The firm ceased to represent SAPL after the state hearings terminated, but remained in the Seabrook battle representing another and larger citizen group, the New England Coalition on Nuclear Pollution (NECNP), which joined the fray at the AEC level.

11. Robert Backus has more than once stated that the Seabrook case changed his life. He entered the case reluctantly as a public interest gesture of the prestigious law firm of which he was a junior partner. His law practice, largely oriented toward commercial and defense litigation, had no public interest or environmental leanings heretofore. He knew little about the issues surrounding the nuclear debate, nor of environmental law. As his participation in the Seabrook

case continued, however, he became increasingly interested in its issues and increasingly vocal about his developing views on nuclear power. His relationship with the law firm deteriorated at a similar pace. Finally, in 1976, Backus and three other young lawyers formed their own firm, and he began to devote a substantial amount of his time to public interest cases.

12. None of the safety issues raised in the later federal proceedings were given a hearing at the state level, primarily as a result of the doctrine of *Northern States Power* v *Minnesota*, 3 ERC 1041 F 2nd 1143 (8th Cir.) (1972), which holds that states are not permitted to regulate the radiation-related aspects of nuclear power plants. Though the intervenors (particularly Counsel for the Public) argued that *Northern States Power* could be distinguished from a siting case, the state siting committee simply avoided the issue.

13. Which would cost more, the tunnels or the ditch, is a debatable point, and there is at least some evidence to suggest that PSCO's real motivation behind the change was economic. It became apparent that the marsh, which is underlain with peat and soft clay, provided little support for the huge pipes PSCO proposed for carrying water to and from the plant. Both the peat and the clay are almost jelly-like in their consistency, and compact greatly under a solid, heavy object. In order to avoid near-total structural instability, PSCO probably would have had to stand the pipes literally at the end of long pilings, potentially a very costly venture.

14. Hearing Record before the Site Evaluation Committee, Statement of Franklin Hollis, post June 19, 1972, p. 40.

15. This dispute was resolved by the EPA. The basic arguments made at the state hearings were refined and elaborate models constructed by PSCO and the EPA in an effort to determine just how closed or open the system was, and to predict the impacts of the cooling water system. By the end of 1978 there was still no agreement on these matters among PCSO, government, and intervenor scientists, and EPA's administrator decided the case.

16. This decision was later overturned by the New Hampshire Supreme Court in *Society for the Protection of N.H. Forests et al. v Site Evaluation Committee*, 115 NH 163, 337 A2d 778 (1975). In its opinion the Court stated that the committee had violated fundamental principles of due process of law in its failure to make findings of fact based on the record.

17. See, e.g., *Manchester Union Leader*, editorial, "Nuclear Power Witchhunt," by William Loeb, March 24, 1976.

18. The federal law and the role of the Environmental Protection Agency in the Seabrook case are discussed in Chapter 7.

19. Thomson ultimately succeeded in 1975 in replacing a majority of the Fish and Game commissioners with his own appointees; they wasted no time in beginning an effort to remove Corson from office. The Director went on the offensive, however, and sued the Governor and his commission, successfully contending that they had no authority to remove him at will. See *Corson* v *Thomson et al.*, 116 NH 344, 358 A2d 866 (NH Supreme Court 1976).

20. Rudman's meeting invoked the wrath of environmental groups, who charged that the attorney general violated the state's open meeting law by getting the water pollution agency to agree to the terms of the permit out of

the public view. See *Society for the Protection of N. H. Forests et al.* v *Water Supply and Pollution Control Commission,* 115 NH 192, 337 A2d 788 (NH Supreme Court 1975).

21. *Society for the Protection of N. H. Forests et al.* v *Site Evaluation Committee,* 115 NH 163, 337 A2d 778 (NH Supreme Court 1975).

2. Regulatory Issues

1. For a compilation and analysis of these laws, see *Power Plant Siting in the United States,* Southern Interstate Nuclear Board, 1974; and *Issues in Power Plant Siting,* Federal Energy Administration Office of Siting (1976). See also, M. Baram, *Environmental Law and the Siting of Facilities,* Ballinger, 1977; Energy Facility Siting, Congressional Research Service, Library of Congress (4/10/75); Berlin, Gill, and Yarrington, Power Plant Siting: An Overview of Legislation and Litigation, *Environment Reporter,* No. 8 (1973).

2. These are the subject of extensive discussion in Chapter 3.

3. See Baram, *Environmental Law and the Siting of Facilities,* at 35–39, where this process is schematized.

4. Testimony of Eliot Priest before the New Hampshire Bulk Power Site Evaluation Committee, June 1972.

5. New York's siting law allows the state siting agency to override local controls and other state agency's permitting requirements, providing true *one stop* licensing. New York Public Service Law, § 140 et seq. New Hampshire is typical of those states whose siting law is in addition to, rather than supplanting, other state and local regulatory controls. N. H. Rev. Stat. Ann. Chapter 162-F. Maryland presents a third variant—a state siting law that requires the state itself to select and acquire power plant sites—taking the utilities out of the planning process altogether. Article 66c, Anno. Code Md. § 763–768. Ch. 31 (1971). The Maryland approach is discussed in the text below.

6. See, e.g., Bosselman, et al., *The Permit Explosion,* Urban Land Institute (1977); Baram, *Environmental Law and the Siting of Facilities,* Ballinger (1977); and Development and the Environment: Legal Reforms to Facilitate Industrial Site Selection, Final Report of Special Committee on Environmental Law, American Bar Association (1978).

7. Power plant siting legislation was submitted to Congress by the Carter administration in March 1978. See H. R. 11704, S. 2775.

8. E. g., NH RSA 162-F:8 (supp).

9. E. g., New York Siting Law, Article 8, NY State Public Service Law (Laws of 1972, Chapter 385).

10. 42 U. S. C. 4321 et seq. It applies only to major *federal* actions.

11. Similar problems with the use of the National Environmental Policy Act are dealt with in Chapter 7.

12. R. Keeney and K. Nair, Nuclear Siting Using Decision Analysis, 5 *Energy Policy* 223 (September 1977). For a fuller description of the methodology used, see Nair et al., An Approach to Siting Nuclear Power Plants: The Relevance of Earthquakes, Faults, and Decision Analysis, IAEA-SM 188/18 (1975), pub. in

Proceedings of the Symposium on Siting of Nuclear Facilities, Vienna 1974, (IAEA Vienna 1975).

13. WASH—1400, Reactor Safety Study (NUREG—75/014), U. S. Nuclear Regulatory Commission (1975).

14. See, e. g., *The Risks of Nuclear Power Reactors: A Review of the NRC Reactor Safety Study*, Union of Concerned Scientists, Cambridge, Mass. (1977); American Physical Society, *Review of Modern Physics*, 47, Supplement 1, Summer 1975

15. Joel Yellin, The Nuclear Regulatory Commission's Reactor Safety Study, 7 *Bell Journal of Economics* 324 (1976).

16. Shortly after NEPA became effective, the AEC ruled in the *Midland* case that, for NEPA purposes, doses received by offsite members of the public must be calculated using "realistic" rather than "conservative ' assumptions. This meant that in deriving a value for potential human deaths or injuries resulting from a hypothetical accident, one must not assume a "worst case" scenario but rather (for example) that the plant's safety systems work as designed and that releases of radiation are kept within design limits. This ensures that in the NEPA calculations the cost attributed to human exposure to radiation will be a very low number. Since that number is lumped with all the other costs and benefits attributed to the site, it is obviously not a significant factor in an overall comparison of the site with alternatives required by NEPA.

17. *Northern States Power Co.* v *Minnesota* 447 F2d 1143, 3 ERC 1041 (8th cir. 1971) determined that the Atomic Energy Act of 1954 had given *exclusive* authority to regulate radiation hazards to the AEC.

18. The bills were not enacted into law.

19. H. R. 11704, S. 2775, 95th Congress, 2d sess. See Improving Regulatory Effectiveness in Federal/State Siting Actions, NUREG 0195 (May 1977).

20. The AEC's track record on this score is not encouraging. For a depressing account of its selection of Weston, Illinois, as the site of a research facility, see Lowi and Ginsberg, *Poliscide*, Macmillan, 1976.

21. *Public Service Company of New Hampshire* v *Nuclear Regulatory Commission*, Brief before the United States Court of Appeals for the First Circuit.

22. See, e. g., *Natural Resources Defense Council* v *Nuclear Regulatory Commission*, 547 F2d 633, 9 ERC 1149 (DC Cir. 1976); *Conservation Society of Southern Vermont* v *Secretary of Transportation*, 508 F2d 927, 7 ERC 1236 (2d Cir. 1974); *Warm Springs Dam Task Force* v *Gribble*, 378 F. Supp. 240, 6 ERC 1737 (N.D. Cal. 1974).

3. Siting and Public Risk

1. WASH-1400, NUREG, 75/014 (US NRC 1975).

2. Compare, e.g., WASH-1400 (US NRC 1975) with Union of Concerned Scientists, *The Reactor Safety Study*, Cambridge, Massachusetts (1977). See also *Nuclear Power: Issues and Choices*, Ford Foundation Study (1977), pp. 213–242. Much of the methodology employed in WASH-1400 was repudiated by the NRC late in 1978.

3. Compare WASH-1250, The Safety of Nuclear Power Reactors and Related Facilities (U. S. Atomic Energy Commission, 1974), with John W. Goffman

and Arthur Tamplin, *Poisoned Power* (Rodale Press, 1971). And see, generally, *Nuclear Power: Issues and Choices* (above), pp. 159-196.

4. That is a principal argument of the NRC's Reactor Safety Study.

5. The AEC's WASH-1250, The Safety of Nuclear Power Reactors and Related Facilities, contains such admissions, although, like the RSS, it relies on low probabilities of occurrence as a basis for concluding that the risk is minimal.

6. The term "residents" had been defined administratively to include transients, although the NRC weights transients to discount their significance to reflect occupancy times. See Seabrook Nuclear Power Station, ALAB-422, 6 NRC 33. The regulation also requires that the PCD be measured to the nearest concentration of people, regardless of political boundaries.

7. These limits, set forth in 10 CFR Section 100.11, apply to an individual standing on the outer boundary of the LPZ throughout the entire passage of the radioactive cloud assumed to occur as a result of a "class 8" design-basis accident. Anyone *inside* the boundary is assumed to need evacuation.

8. Frank Dawson, *Nuclear Power: Development and Management of a Technology*, University of Washington Press (1976) at p. 77.

9. 27 FR 3509(1962).

10. See Clifford Beck, Engineering Out the Distance Factor, 5 *Atomic Energy Law Journal* 4 (1963) at p. 245.

11. 7 *Bell Journal of Economics* 1 (1975) at 317.

12. Id.

13. See *Virginia Electric Power Co.* (North Anna 1 and 2), ALAB-324 NRCI 76/4 Slip. Op. at 16.

14. Congressional Record at H3330 Vol. 123 No. 65 (4/20/77).

15. At p. 72.

16. The NRC Appeal Board ruled in *Seabrook* that as a matter of law, evacuation could not be required under the NRC regulations outside of the LPZ. Testimony by a state police official introduced into the licensing hearings raised significant questions about the state's ability to move people out of the beach area quickly, because of limited transportation corridors.

17. As of 1979. Congress, in 1980, mandated certain changes.

18. For examples of this debate, see *Proceedings of the Symposium on the Containment and Siting of Nuclear Power Plants*, Vienna (1967) at 735 (IAEC 1967); National Academy of Sciences, National Research Council, *The Effects on Populations of Exposure to Low Levels of Ionizing Radiation*, Washington (1972); Goffman and Tamplin, *Poisoned Power* (1971).

19. It was not until the late 1960's and early 1970's that the Commission, prodded by public criticism of its activities, attempted to evaluate these matters. The result was the widely publicized emergency-core cooling-system tests and later ECC's hearings, and the so-called Rasmussen study of risks, each of which has been the target of substantial criticism both within and without the government. See, e. g., Sierra Club–Union of Concerned Scientists, *Preliminary Review of the AEC Reactor Safety Study* (Cambridge, Mass., 1974); Nader and Abbotts, *The Menace of Atomic Energy*, Norton (1977) 94-125; R. von Hippel, Looking Back on the Rasmussen Report, *Bulletin of Atomic Scientists*, February 1977

at p. 47; USEPA Statement 520/3-76-009, Reactor Safety Study (WASH 1400): A Review of the Final Report (Washington, June 1976).

20. For an evaluation based on the latter assumption, see H. Bresser and W. Schwarzer, "Siting of Nuclear Power Plants in Metropolitan Areas: Estimation of Population Doses Due to Accidental Release of Fission Products," reprinted in *Proceedings of the Symposium on the Containment and Siting of Nuclear Power Plants* (1967, International Atomic Energy Agency, Vienna).

21. For example, initially the Commission simply failed to promulgate routine radiation emission standards other than those grossly aimed at public health that are found in Part 20 of the Commission's regulations. As evidence mounted that there is a tendency of certain fission by-products to have more deleterious effects at lower levels than previously assumed, the Commission in 1970 ducked the issue by enacting a new but vague standard: that emissions be "as low as practical." What is "practical" is, of course, dictated by the economics of the industry, not by medical necessity. After nearly five years of protracted "generic" rule-making hearings, the Commission quantified the "as low as practical" standard by issuing Appendix I, which contains numerical guidelines for routine emissions that are far more stringent than Part 20 limits. The Commission has never adequately dealt with the even more complex problem of setting limits responsive to the accumulation and concentration of fission products in organisms that are part of the human food chain. For a thorough discussion of this matter, see David Rittenhouse Inglis, *Nuclear Energy: Its Physics and Its Social Challenge,* Addison-Wesley (1973), pp. 130–145; and R. Nader and J. Abbotts, *The Menace of Atomic Energy* (Norton, 1977), pp. 75–81.

22. See A. Hammond, W. Metz, and T. Maugh, *Energy and the Future,* Washington, Am. Assoc. for the Advancement of Science (1973).

23. W. K. David and J. E. Robb, Nuclear Plant Siting in the United States of America, in *Symposium on the Containment and Siting of Nuclear Power Plants* IAEA, Vienna, (1967), p. 8.

24. Id., p. 10.

25. Bresser and Schwarzer, "Siting of Nuclear Power Plants in Metropolitan Areas" (above, n. 20).

26. Southern California Edison Co. (San Onofre Units 2 and 3), ALAB-268, 1 NRC 383 (1975).

27. *Porter County Chapter, Isaac Walton League v AEC,* U.S. Ct. App. 515 F2d 513, 7ERC 1721 (7th Cir. 1975).

28. See ALAB-268, 1 NRC 383, 404-405.

29. By the time the Seabrook proceeding came along, both the NRC staff and the utility applicant disregarded even the "early years" requirement, and produced population and land use data for transients valid only to 1980, *prior* to intial reactor operation. If it were not for the citizen group intervenors, the record would have been totally devoid of relevant predictive demographic data. See ALAB-422 p. 20, 6 NRC 33 at 46 (1977).

30. A related issue is the extent to which radiation safety problems are factored into the Commission's alternate site analysis undertaken pursuant to NEPA. This issue is discussed in Chapter 7.

31. The in-service date of Unit 2 is based on PSCO statements made during the spring of 1977.

32. New England Coalition on Nuclear Pollution Hearing Exhibit 12, Transcript at 4864.

33. Wilber Smith and Associates, Roadway Network Evaluation, PSCO Hearing Exhibit App. No. 8 at 51.

34. Transcript, pp. 3631-33.

35. AEC Final Environmental Statement for Seabrook Units 1 and 2, Table 2.1 at p. 2-11 (1974).

36. This is the text of the rule as amended by the NRC on June 24, 1975.

37. See Figure 4, above p. 53.

38. NECNP Requests for Findings of Fact and Rulings of Law submitted to the Atomic Safety and Licensing Board, at pp. 51-53.

39. Southern California Edison Co. (San Onofre Units 2 and 3), ALAB-268, 1 NRC 383 at 404 (1975).

40. PSCO Requests for Findings of Fact and Rulings of Law submitted to the Atomic Safety and Licensing Board, at pp. 52-56.

41. NECNP Brief in Reply to Applicants and Staff's Opposition to Exceptions (11/26/76) at 23, and NECNP Brief in Support of Exceptions (9/17/76) at 28-29.

42. ASLB, Hearing Transcript 4486.

43. ASLB Hearing Transcript 4403 at 11.

44. According to Grimes. See his Testimony, Transcript 4495.

45. ALAB-422 at 20, 6 NRC 33, 46 (7/26/77).

46. Id.

47. Id. at 30, 31 (ALAB pages).

48. Id. at 29, note 13, and at 28. The Appeal Board cites as authority for the latter proposition 27 Fed. Reg. 3509 (1962), which I have discussed above, p. 45.

49. 27 Fed. Reg. 3509 (1962), quoted in more detail above.

50. See WASH-1250, The Safety of Nuclear Power Reactors and Related Facilities, Table 5-2 at 5-10.

51. PSCO Exhibit No. 8: Wilber Smith and Associates, Roadway Network and Evaluation Study, at 57.

52. ASLB Hearing Transcript at 3631.

53. Id.

54. Interestingly, the Appeal Board did not list as an issue how far into the plant's operating life population projections should be made.

55. Public Service Company of New Hampshire (Seabrook Station Units 1 and 2), ALAB-422 at 32, 6 NCR 33 at 48-49 (1977).

56. Id.

57. Id., at 33, 6 NRC 33 at 49 (1977).

58. Id., at 34, 6 NRC 33at 49 (1977).

59. Id., at 35, 6 NRC 33 at 50 (1977).

60. See note 2 to 10 CFR 100, Appendix I.

61. "Report of the Working Party on the Experimental Manipulation of the Genetic Composition of Microorganisms," Cmnd 5880 (London, Stationery Office, 1975).

62. Letter, December 10, 1974, from William Stratton, Chairman of the ACRS to Chairman, Atomic Energy Commission.

63. 10 CFR §100.3 (b); Southern California Edison Co. (San Onofre Nuclear Generating Station, Units 2 and 3) ALAB-268, 1 NRC 383, 404-405 (1975).

64. Transcript of Argument before Joint Appeal Boards, In the Matter of New England Power Company, et al., and Public Service Company of New Hampshire, et al., Docket Nos. STN-50-568, 569 and 50-443, 444, pp. 115-116 (February 1977).

65. See pp. 50-59.

66. Midland is another case in which a nuclear facility is sited close to a population center—in that case portions of the City of Midland, Michigan.

67. ALAB-390, 5 NRC 733 (April 7, 1977).

68. Id., Part II.

69. Id., note 1. Unstated, but undoubtedly a related concern, is the status of several of the previously licensed sites if the rule were changed to require looking at those people beyond the LPZ. Midland, for example, is a reactor located virtually inside of the industrial and commercial suburbs of a city. See Final Environmental Statement, Consumer's Power Company (Midland Plant Units 1 and 2), p. II-2 (1972).

70. ALAB-390 at 24, 5 NRC 733 (1977).

71. Id.

72. 10 CFR 100.10(b).

73. William Lowrence, *Of Acceptable Risk: Science and the Determination of Safety*, William Kaufman, Inc. (1976) at p. 76.

74. Id., at 110.

75. See *Buckley* v *Valeo*, 424 U.S. 1, 44 LW 4127 (1976); *First National Bank of Boston* v *Bellotti*, 435 U.S. 765, No. 76-1172 (April 26, 1978).

76. Lowrence, *Of Acceptable Risk*, 82-85.

77. See, e.g., Hearing Record, H.R. 8631, 94th Congress 149 to 196 (1975).

78. In a memorandum dated November 7, 1973, the NRC's Assistant Director for Site Safety applied this guide to the Seabrook site and concluded that the site would not qualify, urging that an expanded search for alternate sites be undertaken. The memorandum stated: "We have concluded that the weighted population for 1980 exceeds 400 persons/sq. mile . . . (The average population density of New Hampshire was 82 persons/sq. mile.) Since a major fraction (about 80%) of the land area of the state would not exceed 400 persons/sq. mile, we recommend that an intensive . . . study . . . identify suitable alternate sites or definitely demonstrate that the lower population sites should not be selected because of significant environmental, economic or other disadvantages when compared to Seabrook." The population density limit became 500 persons/sq. mile when the draft regulation guide was adopted. See Reg. Guide 4.7 (Revision 1, November 1975).

79. *Washington Post*, "10 Nuclear Power Plants Rated 'Below Average' in Safety," Sunday, November 26, 1978. Interestingly, of the 10 plants given a below average rating, seven are located close to urban centers, with high nearby population density.

80. In late May of 1979, following the Three Mile Island accident, SAPL petitioned the NRC to reopen the Seabrook site suitability issue and to reconsider

its refusal to require an evacuation plan for the beach area. That motion was pending without action at the time this was written.

4. The Licensing Procedure: How It Works

1. See 42 USC 5814 and 42 USC 5841.

2. By far the most comprehensive historical analysis of the AEC is Frank Dawson, *Nuclear Power: Development and Management of a Technology,* Seattle, University of Washington Press, (1976). In addition, for those interested in other views of this agency's activities from 1946 to 1976, the Rand Corporation issued a series of four reports under the sponsorship of the National Science Foundation, titled and numbered as follows:

Perry, et al., Development and Commercialization of the Light Water Reactor, 1946–1976, R-2180-NSF (Rand Corp., 1977).

Rolph, Regulation of Nuclear Power: The Case of the Light Water Reactor, R-2104-NSF (Rand Corp., 1977).

Allen, Nuclear Reactors for Generating Electricity: U.S. Development from 1946–1963, R-2116-NSF (Rand Corp., 1977).

Gandara, Electric Utility Decisionmaking and the Nuclear Option, R-2148-NSF (Rand Corp., 1977).

3. Two lengthy, rather theoretical discussions of this process are Jacks, The Public and the Peaceful Atom: Participation in AEC Regulatory Proceedings, 52 *Texas L. Rev.* 466 (1974); and Murphy, Atomic Safety and Licensing Boards: An Experiment in Administrative Decisionmaking on Safety Questions, 33 *Law & Contemp. Problems* 566 (1968).

4. Atomic Energy Act, 42 USC § 2239(a).

5. Id.; also 10 CFR Pt. 2, App. A.

6. See, generally, 10 CFR Part 51.

7. NUREG 75/071, Policy Issues Raised by Intervenor Requests for Financial Assistance in NRC Proceedings, page G-1 (1975).

8. 10 CFR 51.22 and 51.26. While the regulation permits the Licensing Board to modify the EIS as a result of revelations in the hearing, the basic document is a staff product.

9. 10 CFR 2.104.

10. A Licensing Board, consisting of three members, is appointed by the NRC at the time an application is docketed. The Board is composed of individuals who are either fulltime NRC employees for that purpose, or part-time consultants, usually drawn from academic institutions or from the national laboratories.

11. The RESAR, as it is termed, is actually produced by the reactor vendor and is the generic report for the reactor type chosen by the applicant.

12. A literal reading of 10 CFR Section 2.714 would seem to compel an intervenor to have all of its contentions together at this stage and be ready to defend them against an applicant's motion for summary judgment. The requirement, however, was softened by the NRC's Appeal Board.

13. 10 CFR § 2.743.

14. See, e.g., discussion in Boasberg et al., Policy Issues Raised by Intervenor

Requests for Financial Assistance in NRC Proceedings, USNRC, NUREG 75/071 at 114-115.

15. Vermont Yankee Nuclear Power Corporation, ALAB-124, 6 AEC 358 at 365.

16. 10 CFR 2.756.

17. See also Ebbin and Kasper, *Citizen Groups and the Nuclear Power Controversy*, M.I.T. Press (1974) at 210; and Jacks (above, note 3).

18. 10 CFR 2.762.

19. See, e. g., *Virginia Petroleum Jobbers Assn.* v. *FPC*, 259 F2d 921, 925 (DC Cir. 1958).

20. The Court was considering actions taken by the NRC and the EPA.

21. *Audubon Society of New Hampshire* v. *United States*, Memo Opinion (unpublished) (1st Cir. 1976).

22. Affidavit of Thomas Sherry, filed with the Appeal Board on March 4,1978.

5. The Licensing Procedure: Seabrook

1. See First Prehearing Conference Order, dated October 29, 1973, Dockets 50-443, 50-444, USAEC.

2. See Appendix II.

3. One of the financial experts, though nominally an NECNP witness, was actually produced by the State Attorney General. The Attorney General had no appropriation for hiring expert witnesses, and could not convince the governor, who by this time was vocally opposed to continued state presence in the hearings, to authorize the use of state funds for that purpose. The attorney General did, however, have statutory authority to call on the University of New Hampshire for assistance in environmental litigation, and was able thereby to secure limited expert testimony.

4. Ironically, NECNP's case was prophetic. It argued essentially (a) that in the long run energy conservation and solar power could be substituted for what they saw as the true energy demand to be met by Seabrook and (b) that in the short and intermediate term, coal was at least as inexpensive, and probably less expensive, than nuclear power. Current economic thinking appears to validate this position. See, e.g., Charles Komanoff, "Doing without Nuclear Power," *New York Review of Books*, Vol. 26, No. 8, May 17, 1979.

5. It is interesting in this regard to compare the Seabrook hearing transcript with the Vermont Yankee operating license transcript, compiled five years earlier. In *Seabrook* the issues are discernible and cogent. *Vermont Yankee* by comparison seems confused and aimless. The two cases are particularly useful to compare in that the principal lawyers and parties in both are the same. The more complete and better organized Seabrook record illustrates, I think, two factors—the maturing of nuclear intervenors and a corresponding commitment on their part to invest substantial economic resources in their cause. It also reflects an increased understanding of the process on the part of the intervenor lawyers.

6. The NRC has two categories of ASLB members: fulltime and part-time.

The fulltime members are usually NRC or National Atomic Laboratory employees who have generally been longtime members of the nuclear establishment, or lawyers who are licensed administrative law judges. The part-time members are drawn from outside the NRC for their expertise in relevant subject areas.

7. Had the board adopted this position, construction on the plant would not have begun when it did, and the NRC would not have been subject to the criticism, reflected in another part of this book, that it permitted the plant to gain an advantage by sinking massive amounts of capital into construction while important licensing decisions were pending.

8. Personal communication to me by Robert Backus, attorney for the Seacoast Anti-Pollution League.

9. Personal communication to me by Ellyn Weiss, attorney for the Commonwealth of Massachusetts.

10. SAPL did ultimately raise the issue on appeal, only to have it rejected by the court, which found no requirement in the Federal Administrative Procedure Act for such initial licensing as that undertaken by the NRC.

11. The Board ordered PSCO to go around the swamp rather than through it, adopting the NRC staff's recommended position.

12. Alan S. Rosenthal in *Atomic Energy Licensing and Regulation*, Philadelphia, Pa., American Law Institute (1977) at p. 9.

13. Under the rule the NRC retains discretion to accept or not accept a tendered appeal. If it refuses to take the appeal, the appealing party goes immediately to court, as before. See 10 CFR 2.786, 42 Fed. Reg. 22129 (1977).

14. SPNHF's sole issue before the NRC was the route of the transmission lines. It had argued for an even greater avoidance of the Great Cedar Swamp than the NRC staff had proposed, and was not enamored of the obvious compromise made by the ASLB. It decided, nevertheless, to remain content with its modest gains. PSCO, however, appealed the transmission line action, contending that the ASLB lacked the authority to order a change in the route of the line. PSCO did not prevail before the NRC, and took its case to the Court of Appeals, where it also lost, and finally to the United States Supreme Court, which refused to hear its appeal.

15. The Seabrook site was a particularly poor one for natural draft cooling towers. PSCO later concluded that even with cooling towers, long, expensive bedrock tunnels would have to be constructed to carry "makeup" and "blowdown" water. Moreover, towers 600–900 feet high on the flat coastal plain would be such an intrusion on the landscape that the chairman at the ASLB later admitted that their impact would be "gross."

16. The intervenors had asked the board to do this a year earlier, and it had rejected the request.

17. Initial Decision at 90 et seq. See also ASLB's order attached thereto.

18. 259 F2d 921, 925 (DC Cir. 1958).

19. The NRC itself has utilized a similar standard, but only in situations where the stay (or suspension of a license) follows a court determination that there is a defect in the agency action. See ALAB 458, *In the Matter of Consumers Power Co.* (Midland Plants, Units 1 and 2) February 14, 1978; slip

opinion at pp. 5 and 6.

20. Public Service Company of New Hampshire, Case No. 76-7, 10 ERC 1267 (1977).

21. See ALAB-366, 5 NRC 39 (1977) and LBP 77-43, 6 NRC 134.

22. *Seacoast Anti-Pollution League* v. *Costle*, 572 F2d 872 (1st Cir. 1978).

23. See below, Chapter 7, for a discussion of this issue.

24. CLI 78-14, 7 NRC 952 (June 30, 1978).

25 CLI 17-78, 8 NRC 179 (August 9, 1978). SAPL's appeal of the administrator's decision later was upheld by the Court of Appeals.

26. Subsequent to the Seabrook dispute, the NRC decided to study its "immediate effectiveness rule," and has convened a task force to analyze the issue and make recommendations.

27. One notable exception was a $15,000 donation from the San Francisco-based Stern Foundation, which funded NECNP's court appeal of the NRC's final decision upholding the ASLB. The antinuclear movement is not totally without its benefactors.

6. Financing: Who Bears the Cost?

1. 42 USC § 2232 (a).

2. 42 USC § 2133 (b).

3. *In Re Power Reactor Development Co.*, 1 AEC 128, 136 (1959).

4. 10 CFR 50.33 (f).

5. *In the Matter of Public Service Company of New Hampshire*, Seabrook Station Units 1 and 2, ALAB 422 at 97, note 52.

6. At 167–168 (Dissenting opinion).

7. Fuel cycle costs, the other component the regulations require an applicant to predict, should, except for inflation, be relatively easy to develop, since the government itself plays a significant role in the fuel cycle cost, such as the enrichment cost, and closely regulates others.

8. PSCO Sources of Funds Sheet for System-Wide Construction Expenditures during period of construction for Seabrook Nuclear Station.

9. See Bureau of National Affairs, Energy Users Report (November 22, 1977) at 12.

10. The interaction between the regulatory programs of the Environmental Protection Agency and the Nuclear Regulatory Commission is an important subject that is dealt with in Chapter 7.

11. The case for deliberate understatement is purely circumstantial, although it could be argued that PSCO was forced to reveal the real costs to the state Public Utilities Commission when it sought a rate increase in 1977. Since it was forced to ask that construction work in progress (CWIP) be added to the rate base, in order to make that argument it had to reveal the full cost of the project. In any event, I do not choose to pursue the question here.

12. PSCO convinced the EPA in 1975 that it was not a "new source," hence not subject to the requirements of section 306 of the Federal Water Pollution Control Act. Section 306 defines a "new source" as one whose construction has "commenced" prior to EPA's issuance of proposed standards affecting it.

Construction is "commenced," under the section, when contracts are entered into. EPA's new source regulations for steam electric generating stations were proposed in 1974, and PSCO paraded before EPA a long string of contracts with vendors, entered into prior to that time, for components as large as a turbine and major portions of the reactor vessel.

13. Affidavit of David J. Lessels, SAPL Exhibit 10 before ASLB, Direct Testimony on Need for Power, attached to SAPL-Audubon Motion to Reopen Record as to Financial Qualifications (March 1976). Interestingly, intervenor SAPL-Audubon tried to have Lessels' study introduced into the NRC hearing record, and asked the Licensing Board to subpoena him to testify. The Board chairman refused to do so, ruling that Lessels was not qualified to present financial testimony, since his academic degree was in law and not economics or finance, ignoring the fact that Lessels had worked for a number of years in the utility finance field.

14. *Concord Monitor,* "Lessels Says PUC Bars Electric Rate Challenge," December 16, 1975, p. 1.

15. *Concord Monitor,* "Thomson Nuclear Policy Adoped by Council 4-0," March 4, 1976, p. 1.

16. It is a well known fact that the capital cost to construct a fossil fuel generating station is less than that required for a nuclear station. The NRC staff admitted this. See Seabrook Final Environmental Statement at p. 9-3. At the present time coal facilities are not subjected to the lengthy, federal licensing proceedings required for nuclear plants.

17. Testimony of Trawicki before the NHPUC, pp. 13-17.

18. If electricity could be beamed to consumers like radio, television, and microwaves, a competitive situation might be possible.

19. This assumption does not hold, of course, for those determined enough, clever enough, and wealthy enough to build a structure that is heated by wood or the sun and is lighted by a water power generator or a wind generator and storage batteries, or for an industry such as pulp and paper, which is able to generate its own electricity as a by-product of an industrial production process.

20. NHRSA 387:7.

21. See *FPC v Hope Natural Gas Company,* 320 U. S. 591 (1944).

22. See, Bonbright, *Principles of Public Utility Rates,* Columbia Univ. Press (1961).

23. PSCO Vice President Harrison testified that the savings would amount to $800,000,000 over the thirty-year life of the Seabrook plant (October 12, 1977). Testimony before the NHPUC at 112-113.

24. If PSCO were a cooperative, these problems would not be present. A consumer-owned or publicly owned utility places both the risks and the benefits on the rate-payer—a vastly more equitable situation than exists when an investor-owned utility injects CWIP into its rate base.

25. As of the date this was written, the Connecticut PUC had refused to permit the inclusion of CWIP in the rate base of Connecticut Utilities.

26. See, generally, E. Berlin, C. Ciccheti, and W. Gillen, *Perspective on Power: The Regulation and Pricing of Electricity,* Cambridge, Massachusetts, Ballinger (1975). It is not as price elastic as other, less necessary commodities, however.

27. Applicant (PSCO's) Direct Testimony before the Atomic Safety and Licensing Board, No. 23.

28. This is, of course, not a problem for a very large utility financing a more or less continuing construction program. It is the magnitude of the project, its "lumpiness," as Professor Nelson described it, that is a major component of the problem. See Direct Testimony of James Nelson before the Atomic Safety and Licensing Board at 42–43.

29. The NRC Commissioners permitted the intervenors' lawyers to introduce portions of the PUC transcript at the oral argument of NECNP's appeal of the financial qualifications portion of the Appeal Board's decision in ALAB-422. The final blow of the staff's apparent attempt at preserving its fictitious version of the record raised speculation in the press–for the first time since the licensing began in 1972-that the Seabrook project might be doomed financially. See 222 BNA Energy Users Report 19 (1977).

30. In contrast to the New Hampshire pattern, the Massachusetts Siting Council decided to hold hearings on the proposed Montague facility, proposed by Northeast Utilities, coterminously with the NRC licensing proceedings.

31. See, generally, Dawson, *Nuclear Power: The Development and Management of a Technology*, chapters 4 and 5.

32. Brief of NECNP before the Atomic Safety and Licensing Board at p. 52.

33. Brief of Applicants before the Nuclear Regulatory Commission at 23.

34. This is difficult to do in a licensing proceeding, however, since it necessarily involves an attack on the adequacy of the NRC's regulations—something the commission prohibits in licensing proceedings.

35. NECNP did refer, in its brief to the appeal board, to testimony by three former General Electric Company engineers who had resigned their positions over disputes about the safety of nuclear reactors, and in particular boiling-water reactors. However, that reference was by a simple footnote to testimony given to the Joint Committee on Atomic Energy, without any explanation of its relevance to the issue.

36. See Testimony of William Anders, former Chairman of the NRC, before the Joint Committee on Atomic Energy, March 2, 1976 (Hearings on Investigation of Charges Relating to Nuclear Reactor Safety, Vol. 1 at 267).

37. See, generally, Hearings on Investigation of Charges Relating to Nuclear Reactor Safety, JCAE, Vol. 2 at 1758 et seq. See also Testimony of William Anders before Committee on Government Operations, February 5, 1975—Hearing Record at 51, 54, 153, and 224–225.

38. Id. See also Testimony of Donald Knuth, Senate Committee on Government Operations Hearing Record at 60–61.

39. See 10 CFR Part 55.

40. Union of Concerned Scientists, *The Risks of Nuclear Power Reactors*, at 188.

41. Testimony of Robert Pollard, former NRC employee, before the Joint Committee on Atomic Energy, February 23, 1976 (Hearing Record at 133–134).

42. This practice has been criticized. See Testimony of Dale Bridenbaugh, Gregory Minor, and Richard Hubbard before JCAE, February 18, 1976 (Hearing Record at 562 et seq.).

43. Id. at 549–550.

44. Union of Concerned Scientists, *The Risks of Nuclear Power Reactors*, pp. 54–55.

45. The "defense in depth" approach has been explained by former NRC Chairman Anders to mean the following: "This approach assumes that all defects will not be eliminated and that people will err and material will fail our best efforts to the contrary. Also we assume that nature will treat nuclear facilities in extremely harsh ways. Defense in depth responds to these conservative—some say unrealistic—assumptions by requiring that nuclear facilities be designed to: first, provide a large margin of safety for possible human error as well as for defects in materials and equipment and for acts of nature; second, provide backup systems that will compensate automatically for essential equipment or human error that might occur in correcting any potential unsafe condition; and third, provide equipment to limit the public consequences of even highly unlikely accidents." . . . "fourth, to establish standards to minimize the possible occurrence of human error, equipment and materials failures, including the highest standards of financial and managerial qualification for holders of licenses." Testimony Before JCEAC March 2, 1976.

46. IE Bulletin No. 74–10B, January 24, 1975.

47. It was estimated by the NRC that the incremental cost to the three owners of Millstone 1, a 690 Mw BWR shutdown for pipe-crack inspection in 1974 and 1975, was on the order of $200,000 per day. Joint Hearings on NRC Action Requiring Safety Inspections Which Resulted in Shutdown of Certain Nuclear Power Plants, at pp. 58-59. The Millstone plant supplied about one seventh of the energy on the owner's system.

48. I am here thinking of action similar to that initiated with respect to the pipe cracks. Though there was no imminent threat to public safety if the reactors continue to operate (it turned out), the prudent cause was for the NRC to do what it did. Despite anticipated NRC protests to the contrary, in a system heavily enough dependent on BWR's to cause power-supply problems if a shutdown occurred, it is questionable whether the agency would have been so quick to act.

7. The Power Plant and the Environment

1. *New Hampshire* v *Atomic Energy Commission*, 406 F2d 170 (1st Cir. 1969) Cert. den. 395 U. S. 962 (1969).

2. The National Environmental Policy Act of 1969, 42 USC §4321 et seq. (effective January 1, 1970).

3. NEPA, §102 (2) (C).

4. NEPA, §102 (2) (E).

5. 33 U.S.C. §§1311 (b) (1) (A) and 1311 (b) (1) (B); 33 U.S.C. §1342.

6. *Calvert Cliffs Coordinating Committee* v *AEC*, 499 F2d 1109, (D. C. Cir. 1971), 2 ERC 1779.

7. 35 Federal Register 18469 (12/4/70) (10 CFR Part 50, Appendix D).

8. *Calvert Cliffs* (note 6, above).

9. 10 CFR Part 50, App. D at 249 (1971).

10. Id.

11. *Calvert Cliffs Coordinating Committee* v *AEC*, 449 F2d 1109 at 1119 (D.C. Cir. 1971).

12. Id at 1117.

13. Id at 1124.

14. Id at 1117 (note 11, above).

15. *Committee for Nuclear Responsibility* v *Seaborg*, 463 F2d 796 (D.C. Cir. November 2, 1971). The agency had previously sought to avoid compliance with NEPA altogether, by arguing that congressional authorization of funds for the nuclear test nullified NEPA's requirements with respect to it. This argument was rejected in an earlier decision. *Committee for Nuclear Responsibility* v *Seaborg*, 463 F2d 783 (D.C. Cir. October 5, 1971).

16. Id at 797.

17. Id at 798.

18. Ibid.

19. See *Committee for Nuclear Responsibility* v *Schlesinger, et al*, 404 US 917 (November 6, 1971) (Douglas, Brennan, and Marshall, JJ., dissenting).

20. *Scientists' Institute for Public Information* v *AEC*, 481 F2d 1079, 5 ERC 1418 (D.C. Cir. 1973).

21. Brief of AEC to Court of Appeals at 12.

22. Id at 34.

23. 481 F2d at 1097, 5 ERC at 1429.

24. Id at 1098 and 1430.

25. *Natural Resources Defense Council* v *Nuclear Regulatory Commission*, 539 F2d 824, 8 ERC 2065 (2d Cir. 1976), cert. granted 429 US 1312 (1977), dismissed as moot 430 US 944 (1978).

26. *Natural Resources Defense Council* v *Nuclear Regulatory Commission*, 547 F2d 633, 9 ERC 1149 (D. C. Cir. 1976), reversed and remanded sub nom. *Vermont Yankee Nuclear Power Corp.* v *NRDC*, 435 US 519, 11 ERC 1439 (U. S. Supreme Court 1978).

27. *Aeschliman* v *NRC*, 547 F2d 622, 9 ERC 1289 (D.C. Cir. 1976), reversed sub nom. *Consumers Power Company* v *Nelson Aeschliman, et al.*, 435 US 519, 11 ERC 1439 (U. S. Supreme Court 1978).

28. 10 CFR 2.802.

29. See Administrative Procedure Act, 5 U.S.C. §553, and *SEC* v. *Chenery Corp.*, 332 US 194, 203 (U. S. Supreme Court 1947).

30. An excellent discussion of the ECCS hearings and opposing industry and intervenor viewpoints is contained in *Citizen Participation In Energy-Related Decisionmaking*, Workshop Proceedings, MITRE Corporation-National Academy of Public Administration (1977).

31. GESMO is an acronym for the NRC's Generic Environmental Statement on Mixed Oxide Fuel.

32. 539 F2d at 832, 8 ERC at 2069.

33. 40 Fed. Reg. at 53061.

34. *Calvert Cliffs Coordinating Committee* v *AEC*, 449 F2d 1109 at 1122.

35. 40 Fed. Reg. at 53062.

36. 539 F2d 824 at 843, 8 ERC 2065 at 2078. The second circuit's decision was taken on appeal by the Supreme Court but dismissed as moot prior to decision, because newly elected President Carter had taken actions that resulted in a termination of the GESMO proceedings and (at least temporary) abandonment of the mixed-oxide fuel program.

37. In Re Consumers Power Company; RAI-74-1-19 at 32 (1974).

38. Id. The NRC's attitude may have been prompted by its institutional dislike of energy alternatives to nuclear power. At a symposium at Dartmouth College held in February 1978, Marcus Rowden, an NRC commissioner during the *Midland* review, stated that it was his view that energy conservation and alternatives to nuclear plants were state issues, not federal issues. Such reasoning flies in the face of NEPA, and may account for the NRC's recalcitrance in this regard.

39. 547 F2d 622 at 628; 9 ERC 1289 at 1293.

40. See RAI 74-1-19 at 32, note 7.

41. *Aeschliman* v *NRC*, 547 F2d 622 at 628, note 13; 9 ERC 1289 at 1293, note 13.

42. *Vermont Yankee Nuclear Power Corporation* v *NRC*, 435 US 519 at 550-551, 11 ERC 1439 at 1451 (1978). (The Aeschliman case was consolidated with *Vermont Yankee* on appeal, hence the change in name.)

43. Id; 435 US at 552-554; 11 ERC at 1452.

44. Id.

45. Id.

46. 435 US at 554; 11 ERC at 1452.

47. The reference is to a report of the Advisory Committee on Reactor Safeguards (ACRS), an independent group of scientists established by the Congress who are required to comment on the safety of specific nuclear projects.

48. 435 US at 557-558; 11 ERC at 1454.

49. 10 CFR §51.22 and 51.26.

50. 10 CFR §51.52 (b) (3).

51. The source of this information is a conversation between the author and Robert Geckler, NRC Environmental Project Manager for the Seabrook proceeding.

52. Id.

53. § 102 (2) (E).

54. PSCO used this argument with respect to sites located in the State of Maine.

55. See PSCO testimony on alternate sites, post Transcript p. 10286.

56. Transcript 13262.

57. The staff environmental project director.

58. The Oak Ridge Seabrook project director.

59. Transcript 13263.

60. Transcript post 4403, pp. 2-3, Tr. 4411-12, 4414-15.

61. Transcript 10301-10303, 4401.

62. See Transcript 10346-10350 and 10361.

63. See Transcript 10352-10358. Intervenor NECNP argued that it was

reasonable to apply a cost factor of $1,000 per man-rem; multiplying it by the product of (1) the number of rems assumed by 10 CFR Part 100 to be received at the Low Population Zone boundary in the event of a design basis loss of coolant accident after two hours, and (2) the number of people located at about that distance from the reactor, NECNP calculated that the Seabrook site should receive a $99,000,000 penalty over the more sparsely populated Moore Pond site under such an analysis. Although one might quarrel with NECNP's numbers, it is clear that some sort of quantification of the relative risk is possible. The NRC failed even to approach this level of sophistication in its own alternate site analysis.

64. Transcript post 10286.

65. FES pp. 9-4 through 9-10; ALAB-366 at 40, 5 NRC 39 at 65.

66. Initial Decision, 3 NRC 857 at 907-911.

67. See ALAB-366, 5 NRC 39, affirmed by the NRC, CLI-77-8, 5 NRC 503 (1977).

68. ALAB-471 at p. 74, 7 NRC 477 (1978).

69. Id. See also ALAB-423, 6 NRC at 119-121 (dissenting opinion).

70. ALAB-471 at p. 77, 7 NRC 477 (1978).

71. 5 NRC at 503 at 539 et seq. (1977).

72. 5 NRC 503 at 526.

73. See ALAB-471 at p. 4, note 2, 7 NRC 477 (1978).

74. 5 NRC 503 at 531.

75. See also *Power Reactor Co.* v *Electricians*, 367 US 396 at 415 (1961).

76. Transcript 13294.

77. ALAB-471, slip opinion at 32, 7 NRC 477 (1978).

78. Id.

79. CLI 78-15, 8 NRC 1 (1978).

80. ALAB-488, 8 NRC 187 (1978).

81. The Court's opinion is reported at 582 F2d 87 (1st Cir. 1978).

82. As this chapter is being written, the NRC had not completed its review, and the further, final appeal to the Court had not occurred.

83. Slip opinion at p. 13.

84. Id.

85. Id.

86. Id at 15, Citing *Aeschliman* v *NRC*, 547 F2d 622 at 632, note 20 (D. C. Cir. 1976), *Porter County Chapter of the Isaak Walton League* v *AEC*, 533 F2d 1011 at 1017, note 10 (7th Cir. 1976) and *Union of Concerned Scientists* v *AEC*, 499 F2d 1069 at 1084, note 37, (D.C Cir. 1974). A review of each of these citations reveals only limited support for the Court's conclusion. In each case the footnoted statement was not a firm holding of the Court but an apparently gratuitous statement based on facts peculiar to the case. None of those cases involved the enormous expenditure which occurred in the Seabrook project.

87. Id., pp. 14-15.

88. In the case of the Seabrook plant, the intake tunnels descend vertically to a depth in excess of 200 feet below sea level. The pressures at this depth were sufficient to kill many organisms.

89. In the mid-1970's, millions of alewife herring were killed at the intake of the GINNA nuclear power station on Lake Ontario. See *Final Environmental Impact Statement, GINNA Nuclear Power Station Unit 1*, U. S. Nuclear Regulatory Commission, 1975.

90. 33 U.S.C. 1201 et seq.

91. 33 U.S.C. 1311 (b) (1) (A) and 33 U.S.C. 1311 (b) (2) (A).

92. Id.

93. 33 U.S.C. 1316 (a) (1).

94. 33 U.S.C. 1326 (a).

95. 33 U.S.C. 1326 (b).

96. 33 U.S.C. 1342.

97. The term "interested" is used in the context of court decisions that define a legal interest for purposes of having standing to challenge an agency decision. See, e. g., *SCRAP* v *United States*, 414 U. S. 1035 (1973).

98. EPA has subsequently changed its rules to permit the ALJ to make a recommendation in such cases.

99. To do so would have taken a "number of years . . . perhaps a decade," according to Dr. Ernest Salo, a member of the NRC's Licensing Board, who, in a dissenting opinion to the Initial Decision approving Seabrook, concluded that its impact on the aquatic ecosystem would be "unacceptable." Initial Decision, 3 NRC 857 (ASLB 1976) (Dissenting Opinion, note 40).

100. Id. Dr. Salo pointed out that PSCO's studies on the distribution and abundance of clam larvae were among the weakest it produced, and he disagreed with this conclusion.

101. Though the Seabrook plant was not yet under construction at the time the permit was issued, EPA ruled that it was not a "new" source, as a result of the broad language of Section 306 (a) (1), which exempts from "new source" requirements facilities for which contracts had been entered into. PSCO had ordered a turbine and several other components having long fabrication times, even though it had not yet received a construction permit from the NRC. From the standpoint of Section 316 (a), however, it made little difference, since EPA was at the time requiring cooling towers for both "new" and "existing" sources.

102. 5 U.S.C. 501 et seq.

103. See, e.g., *Wall Street Journal*, 2/24/78 and Id., "Review and Outlook," 2/1/77.

104. See "Political Battle over Seabrook," *New Hampshire Times*, March 2,1977.

8. The Public Perception of Civil Disobedience

1. See "At Montague Farm, a 1960's activism in the 1970's," *Boston Globe*, February 17, 1976.

2. M. Harris, "From Manchester to the Sea: a Nonviolent March against Nuclear Energy," *New Hampshire Times*, April 14, 1976. Led by a longtime social activist named Arthur Harvey, the Guild is described as a "curious organization of fruit harvesters and apple tree pruners" who "live a spartan existence based upon Ghandian principles of nonviolence," and whose "structure is modeled after the medieval crafts guilds." Id. p. 12.

3. See "Our Backyard Nuke: Is It Worth It?" Danvers, Massachusetts, *Week-ly*, March 10, 1976. See also "Clams Gird for N-Protest at Seabrook," *Boston Globe*, April 29, 1977.

4. "N.H. Nuclear Power Protest . . . ," *New Hampshire Times*, August 24, 1976.

5. "Police, Military Set for N.H. N-Protest," *Boston Globe*, April 28, 1977.

6. *Boston Globe*, April 30, 1977.

7. *New York Times*, May 1, 1977, p. 26.

8. For example, the Alliance published a tract called, *"It's a Fact": Understanding the Seabrook Nuclear Power Plant*, in which the following statement occurred: "This cooling system has not yet been approved by the Environmental Protection Agency. If they reject it and call for cooling towers instead, the plant cannot be built because of that added expense. The one dissenting vote of the NRC's licensing board was from Ernest Salo, a marine biologist who was concerned with the potential harm to clams and lobsters and thermal pollution. Clam, lobster and fish larvae would be killed when caught on the intake tunnel's screen. The heated water would force some types of fish to leave the area (a rich fishing bank), but would attract other species. When nukes are shut down, fish attracted to the warmer waters die of cold shock from the temperature change. Kills of hundreds of thousands of fish due to cold shock have been reported at other coastal nuclear plants. The fishing industries of Maine, New Hampshire and Mass. are thus threatened. The plant would also destroy salt marshes which are invaluable breeding and nesting areas for fish and birds."

It was clearly not accurate for the Alliance to state that Seabrook with cooling towers "cannot be built because of that added expense." PSCO repeatedly stated that the plant would be built with or without cooling towers, and no one ever made a serious argument that cooling towers would be too expensive. Similarly, clam, lobster, and fish *larvae* would not be "caught on the intake tunnel's screen." Although they would be killed, they would pass through the plant. Only large organisms would be impinged on the trash screens. The statement that the "heated water would force some types of fish to leave the area" is insupportable. This was never seriously contended by the intervenors, and the evidence did not indicate that such would be the case. There was also no evidence that, at Seabrook, fish (if any) would be attracted to the discharge plume in number sufficient to cause significant mortality due to reverse thermal shock in the event of a shutdown. Finally, the construction plan involved little destruction of saltmarsh, contrary to the assertion made by the Alliance. There are potentially serious aquatic problems associated with the cooling system, but they are far more subtle than the overstatements made by the Alliance. Statements like these damaged its credibility as a serious opponent of nuclear power.

9. Id.

10. "Arrests End N-Site Protest," *Boston Globe*, May 2, 1977, p. 1. "Hundreds Wait in Busses All Night for Arraignment in Atom Protest," *New York Times*, May 3, 1977.

11. See *Boston Globe*, May 4, 1977; *New York Times*, May 4, 1977; *Boston*

Globe, May 10, 12, 13, 1977. Some of the sentences later imposed were relatively severe, and actually exceeded general recommendations made by then Attorney General David Souter. Souter had been attorney general during the 1977 demonstrations, which cost the state well over a million dollars. He had not expected the mass arrests and refusal of bail, and had recommended rapid processing of the trespass charges and minimal sentences. He viewed the demonstrations as similar in character to the anti-Vietnam War protests during 1968 and 1969 at large colleges and universities in the East, and thought that the demonstrators should be treated in the same manner as students arrested during those years for occupying college administration buildings. He was privately shocked at the harshness of some of the sentences imposed on the 1977 demonstrators by the state superior court.

12. See Ronald Dworkin, *Taking Rights Seriously*, Cambridge, Harvard University Press (1977).

13. Id.

14. They also, in 1976 and 1977, violated a court injunction, premised on the laws against trespass.

15. That the activity was licensed by the NRC would not affect this argument. It would regard the construction permit as a license to kill, which is arguably beyond the government's authority.

16. The NECNP was particularly rancorous after the NRC suspended the Seabrook construction permit in June 1978 as a result of a motion it filed following a February court decision nullifying EPA's approval of the project. The NRC announced its decision to a group of Clamshell Alliance protestors who had congregated outside the hearing chambers, and the press erroneously reported the decision as a result of the demonstrations.

17. See NUREG-0203, Improving Regulatory Effectiveness in Federal/State Siting Actions: State and Local Planning Procedures Dealing with Social and Economic Impacts from Nuclear Power Plants, U. S. N.R.C. January 1977. See also Improving Regulatory Effectiveness in Federal/State Siting Practices, 42 Fed. Register, 31846 (June 23, 1977) and S. 2775, 95th Congress, 2nd session.

18. *Washington Post,* January 20, 1979, p. 1. See also NUREG CR-0400, Report of the Risk Assessment Review Group, U. S. N.R.C., 1979.

Appendix VI

1. Applicant's Exhibit No. 6, Hearing before Atomic Safety and Licensing Board: New England Power Pool Agreement (1971).

2. *Public Service Company of New Hampshire* (Seabrook Station, Units 1 and 2), ALAB-422 at 84, 6 NRC 33 (1977).

3. These percentages are as of the issuance of ALAB-422. As of the spring of 1977, two of these owners, United Illuminating Company and Northeast Utilities, had attempted to back out of the project because they had determined that their electric systems would not need the power produced by the facility. Under the participation agreement, these facilities could withdraw from the

project only if they found purchasers for their respective shares. No purchaser had yet been found as of the date of writing this note.

4. Public Service Company of New Hampshire, Annual Report 1976, p. 12 (May 12, 1977).

5. Numbers approximate. See also, U. S. Nuclear Regulatory Commission, Supplement No. 3 to Safety Evaluation Report In the Matter of Public Service Company of New Hampshire, Seabrook Station, Units 1 and 2 (March 14, 1975).

6. PSCO Annual Report, p. 11 (May 1977). See Transcript of Hearing before ASLB, pp. 1319-1320.

7. In a contested case, however, it can be assured that an astute intervenor will produce new, unfavorable evidence and that the applicant will produce new, favorable evidence.

8. See sheet titled "Sources of Funds for System-Wide Construction Expenditures during Period of Construction of Subject Nuclear Power Plant," Appendix, VII, at p. A 211.

9. Transcript of Hearing before Atomic Safety and Licensing Board at 1276.

10. Id.

11. Id at 1234.

12. See Transcript at 1279-1280. It became clear that the sources of funds sheet used by the staff was insufficient to provide adequate data for an assessment of the capability of an applicant to raise the funds it said it needed. PSCO Vice President Harrison testified that if one changed the assumptions, such as the interest rate at which bonds would have been sold, nothing else on the sheet would change, since things like the number of shares of stock the company would have to market could change, and such variables are not accounted for in the staff's sheet.

13. Testimony of Robert J. Harrison, PSCO Vice President, before the New Hampshire Public Utilities Commission, p. 129 (October 11, 1977).

14. Transcript of Hearing before Atomic Safety and Licensing Board at 1256, 1266, 1336, 1354, 1539.

15. Testimony of Sanford Ege, Transcript 1320-1321.

16. Id at 1550.

17. Id at 1534.

18. Annual Report, Public Service Company of New Hampshire, 1975.

19. Transcript post 1225 at p. D-11. PSNH could genrate only about 10 percent of its needed capital internally. Testimony of James R. Nelson, NECNP Exhibit No. 1 at p. 29.

20. This is also called "interest coverage ratio" by some analysts. The "interest coverage ratio" as utilized by financial analysts is derived by dividing a company's net operating income by interest being paid by the company on its obligations. Testimony of James Horrigan, Transcript at 2362.

21. Transcript at 1811.

22. Testimony of James Horrigan, Transcript at 2364.

23. Testimony of T. E. Jackson, consultant to NRC staff, Transcript Post 1225, p. D-10.

24. Id.

25. Testimony of Robert Harrison, Transcript at 1259, 1265.

26. Id at 1293.

27. Id at 1318.

28. Id at 1580. Upon receipt of an order by the New Hampshire Public Utilities Commission authorizing a whopping 14 percent rate of return on common stock equity, PSCO's management became convinced that restoration of bond ratings was likely before the end of 1975. Testimony of T. E. Jackson, Transcript Post 1225, pp. D-10 to D-11, and at 2038; cf. Testimony of Robert Harrison, Transcript at 1673. As is discussed below this prediction was overly optimistic.

29. Testimony of Robert Harrison, Transcript at 1298.

30. See note 50, and testimony quoted at Transcript 1347.

31. Testimony of Robert Harrison, Transcript at 1558.

32. Testimony of Professor James Nelson, Transcript at 1811.

33. Id at 1827.

34. See Testimony of Sanford Ege, Transcript at 1533-1534.

35. Testimony of T. E. Jackson, Transcript Post 1225, pp. D-10 to D-11, and at 2038. See also Testimony of Robert Harrison, Transcript at 1673. A similar situation arose with respect to the proposed Sundesert Nuclear Station in California, the principal (50 percent) owner of which is the San Diego Gas and Electric Company. In November 1977 a subcommittee of the California State Energy Commission recommended that SDG and E reduce its ownership to 33 1/3 percent in order to avoid too great a financial strain. See Bureau of National Affairs *Energy Users Report* at 27 (December 1, 1977).

36. Transcript at 1577-1579. Neither prediction was borne out as of the late fall of 1977.

37. Supplement No. 3 to the Safety Evaluation Report by the Office of Nuclear Regulation, USNRC. In the Matter of Public Service Company of New Hampshire, Seabrook Station, Units 1 and 2 at 20-4 (March 4, 1975).

38. Transcript at 1244-1245. In addition, a financial officer for United Illuminating Company, the second largest owner of the Seabrook project, characterized the market as "frightened," and "highly selective with regard to utility common stocks," Transcript at 1414.

39. This curiosity is discussed by Professor Nelson in NECNP Exhibit 1, pp. 33-38.

40. Transcript at 2303.

41. Statement of James R. Nelson, Charles Merrill Professor of Economics, Amherst College, NECNP Exhibit 1; Statement of James O. Horrigan, Professor of Business Administration, University of New Hampshire, NECNP Exhibit 2.

42. See also Transcript at 2372. The following table lists the AFDC component of earnings—based on the sources of funds sheet submitted by PSCO—which contained financing assumptions most favorable to it:

Year 1:	17.5%
Year 2:	27.5%
Year 3:	40.7%
Year 4:	60.5%

Year 5: 80.8%
Year 6: 86.0%

Source: Transcript at 1991.

43. PSCO's Vice President, Robert Harrison, explained the reason for the accounting in this way: "AFDC . . . . is increasing . . . the value of the plant, and you depreciate a higher amount because of the fact that AFDC is included in the cost . . . ," Transcript at 1718.

44. NECNP Exhibit 1 and 30.

45. This fact was acknowledged by PSCO's financial vice president, Robert Harrison, in response to an inquiry from a member of the licensing board. See Transcript at 1723. To this extent he did not disagree with NECNP witness Nelson, who testified that the "quality of earnings" starts to erode if AFDC exceeds 10 percent of earnings. Transcript at 2279.

46. See below, note 54.

47. Transcript at 2259–2263, 2267–2273, 2366.

48. Transcript at 2273. See also Testimony of Robert Harrison, Transcript at 1572.

49. Transcript at 1749.

50. PSCO's 1976 Annual Report seems to bear this out. The company's annual growth rate in prime sales, computed by using the least squares method, was 4.5 percent from 1971 to 1976. Its earnings, however, grew only 2.8 percent in the same period. During 1976 the company's earnings per share dropped 10 percent from the 1975 level, while its prime sales for the same period increased 8.5 percent. PSCO Annual Report, pp. 1 and 6.

51. PSCO's position with respect to rate increases was odd. PSCO Vice President Harrison initially testified that the company "had no plans to apply for rate relief . . . ," Transcript at 1359. However, when pressed on cross-examination with respect to the numbers in the sources of funds sheet, he admitted to the need for annual rate increases of from 3.8 to 5.1 percent, under the assumption that bonds and stock could be marketed as proposed. Transcript at 1588.

52. Construction work in progress—or CWIP, in industry parlance—is discussed in more detail on pp. 118–125, *supra*.

53. See, e. g., Testimony of Sanford Ege at 1543. Testimony of Robert Harrison, id.

54. Id. The revenue expected to be produced by the 1975 decision was about 17 million dollars.

55. UI's withdrawal from PSCO's first attempt to build a nuclear plant forced PSCO to abandon the project in 1969.

56. Testimony of Robert J. Harrison before the Federal Power Commission, February 9, 1976, *IN RE* Application of Public Service Company of New Hampshire.

57. Testimony of Zvi Benderly before the Federal Power Commission, February 9, 1976, *IN RE* Application of Public Service Company of New Hampshire.

58. Benderly FPC Testimony at p. 10 and Nelson Testimony, NECNP Exhibit 1, pp. 13–14, 32–33.

59. Id at 11 and Transcript at 2259-2260.

60. Transcript at 1673-1675.

61. Transcript at 1581-1590.

62. Transcript at 1700.

63. The inconsistencies bothered the NRC's appeal board, however. Though sustaining the licensing board's denial of SAPL's motion, the appeal board noted that "we are not insensitive to the vice inherent in different stories being told to different legislative or regulatory bodies. At least in the absence of changed circumstances or other substantial cause, such a practice is worthy of condemnation even if, as seems to be the case here, perjury is not involved." ALAB-422 at 102, note 53. How all of the assumptions implicit in this note could be made without reopening the record and taking evidence to ascertain the facts is puzzling. It is at least arguable, e. g., that conditions *had* changed, and that PSCO's plight was worse than assumed by PSCO at the time it presented its case to the licensing board. If this was the case, there is no excuse for the licensing board to deprive the record of the facts.

64. See LBP-76-26, 867-868.

65. Id at 917.

66. ALAB-422 at 90, 6 NRC 33 (July 22, 1977).

67. Id at 92.

68. NHRSA 162-F:8.

69. ALAB-422 at 100, 6 NRC 33 (1977).

70. Harrison had mentioned CWIP in his testimony before the licensing board, but only as a regulatory change that would make financing Seabrook easier. Applicant's Direct Testimony No. 1, p. 6, Post Transcript at 1177, and Transcript at 1750. See also Supplement 3 to Seabrook Safety Evaluation Report at D-15.

71. ALAB-422 at 101, 6 NRC 33 (1977).

72. It apparently did not trouble the appeal board that the licensing board had found PSCO financially qualified on an assumption that it could raise its funds from the market. The appeal board, under the NRC's rules, has the authority to "fix up" a faulty licensing board decision. Here the appeal board shifted the very basis on which the financial qualifications decision was made, from one premised on an assumption that the market would be responsive to PSCO to one premised on a very different assumption: that the state PUC would permit the rate-payers to finance the facility in the event that the market failed to respond.

73. ALAB-422 at 94, 6 NRC 33 (1977).

74. Id at 92-93.

75. References to "reasonable rate relief" have become commonplace in the NRC's literature. See, e. g., *Duke Power Co.* (William B. McGuire Nuclear Station, Units 1 and 2), LBP 73-7, 6 AEC 92 at 114 (1973); *Virginia Electric Power Company* (North Anna Power Station, Units 3 and 4), LBP 74-56, 8 AEC 126, 147 (1974), and *Union Electric Co.* (Callaway Plant, Units 1 and 2), LBP 76-15, 3 NRC 445, 465 (1976).

76. Board member Farrar dissented, creating a 2-1 split decision.

77. Brief of applicants before the Nuclear Regulatory Commission, *In the*

Matter of Public Service Company of New Hampshire, et al., Docket Nos. 50–443 and 50–444 (10/7/77), at. p. 12 (footnote 9).

78. See Appendix VII.

79. Northeast Nuclear Energy Company (Millstone Nuclear Power Station, Unit 3), LBP–74–58, RAI–74–7 (1974) at pp. 193–196.

80. PSCO, too, suffered from "rate regulatory lag." It took two years and a trip to the state Supreme Court before PSCO received its 1975 rate increase. See *Public Service Company of New Hampshire* v *State*, 113 NH 497, 311 A2d 513 (1973).

81. See brief of *Applicants on Review of Decisions of the Atomic Safety and Licensing Appeal Board*, Docket Nos. 50–443, 50–444 (10/7/77), pp. 10–25. Testimony filed by PSCO in the rate proceeding during October of 1977 was revealed by intervenors, SAPL/Audubon, during an oral argument before the Commission on November 3, 1977. Since different lawyers represented PSCO before the NRC and the PUC (a Boston firm in the former and a Concord, New Hampshire, firm in the latter case), it is altogether probable that the right hand did not know what the left hand was doing—that is, it is entirely possible that PSCO's management did not tell the company's NRC counsel about the rate request. During oral argument, PSCO's lawyers argued strenuously that the state PUC would ultimately allow CWIP in the rate base.

82. Testimony of Robert J. Harrison, Petition for an Increase in Rates, NHPUC Docket No. DR 77–49, Vol. 1 and 24–25 (October 12, 1977).

83. Id.

84. Id at 130.

85. Vol. 2 at 82–83 (October 13, 1977).

86. Id.

87. Id at 84, Vol. 1 at 33.

88. Vol. 1 at 80–81.

89. See Testimony of Trawicki before the New Hampshire Public Utilities Commission at 6–20.

90. Id at 14.

91. Id.

92. The suspension was ordered by the NRC after the Regional Administrator of the U. S. Environmental Protection Agency decided to refuse to issue a § 316 (a) and (b) permit for the plant's once-through condenser cooling water system. The suspension was in effect for about five months, and the construction permit was reinstated when the Administrator of EPA reversed the RA's determination. This transaction is discussed in detail above, in Chapter 7.

93. Testimony of Robert Harrison before the NHPUC at 25 (October 12, 1977).

94. See below, note 101.

95. Brief of Applicants before the Nuclear Regulatory Commission at 10 (October 7, 1977). Section 182 (a) is quoted in its relevant part in the opening paragraph of the chapter and is cited to the United States Code in note 1.

96. Id at 23–24.

97. NECNP Request for Permission to File Late Response to SAPL/Audubon's Motion to Reopen Record, November 11, 1977, at p. 6.

98. See Appendix VII for the staff's line of inquiry to applicants with respect to their financial qualifications and also Table 4, p. 195.

99. NRC Staff Response to the Briefs of All Other Parties on Review of ALAB-422 and ALAB-423 at 3, note 5 (October 17, 1977).

100. Id at pp. 4 to 6.

101. D. F. Ford, "Nuclear Power: Some Basic Economic Issues," Testimony before the House Committee on Interior and Insular Affairs Subcommittee on Energy and the Environment, Cambridge, Massachusetts (April, 28, 1975).

102. NRC slip opinion—*In the Matter of Public Service Company of New Hampshire* (Seabrook Station) (January 6, 1978) at 11 (7 NRC 1, 11).

103. Id at 24.

104. Id at 23.

105. Id at 28-29.

106. In a footnote to the opinion there appears the following statement: "*In Northeast Nuclear Energy Company* (Millstone 3) the Licensing Board found that a 3.964 percent participant possessed only 'marginal' financial qualifications; its earnings had plummeted, and Moody's Investors Service had withdrawn its ratings of all of the utility's outstanding first mortgage bonds. 8 AEC 187 (1974). Despite the weakness of this participant, the Licensing Board found that the applicant possessed the necessary financial qualifications. The Appeal Board endorsed the Licensing Board's findings, and observed that *if the participant had owned a substantially larger share of the facility, such as the 40% interest of another participant, the applicant's financial qualifications would have been 'doubtful.'*" (8) (emphasis added)

107. Id at 24.

108. Id at 26.

109. In 1977 two other utilities were frustrated by financial problems in their efforts to construct nuclear facilities. San Diego Gas and Electric Company faced a potential order from a state agency to reduce its ownership of a proposed nuclear plant by 20 percent (see note 35, above). And in November 1977 the Connecticut Public Utilities Commission refused to grant rate increases requested by Northeast Utilities (another of the Seabrook partners) to enable it to build a nuclear plant at Montague, Massachusetts.

Index

DATE DUE

15 '81	
DEC 2 8 1994